THE ESSENTIALS OF
CONFIDENT
COMMUNICATION

UNLOCK REAL-WORLD SKILLS TO
SPEAK WITH CONFIDENCE, COMMAND THE ROOM
AND TURN SMALL TALK INTO MEANINGFUL MEMORABLE MOMENTS
ON STAGE AND IN EVERYDAY LIFE

PROFESSIONAL SKZ PUBLISHING

CONTENTS

THE ESSENTIALS OF HOW TO TALK TO ANYONE

The Fast Track Guide to Start Conversations, Decode Body Language, Speak with Confidence, and Build Real, Lasting Connections

PROFESSIONAL SKZ PUBLISHING

Contents

— · —

WHY THIS BOOK, WHY NOW

A few years ago, a young professional, let's call her Emily, so as not to embarrass her fully, walked into a networking event clutching a lukewarm coffee and a pocket full of hopes (aka business cards). Her goal? Make meaningful connections and give out her cards.

Her reality? A room full of strangers, surface-level conversations, and the quiet thrum of self-doubt. She hovered at the edge of the room, waiting for the "right moment" to speak up. It never came. She gave out zero business cards that night.

If you've ever felt that, awkward, unsure, wishing you had a roadmap to guide you through social landmines, you're not alone.

This book is the guide I wish Emily had in her hands that day.

Whether you're navigating your first big job, trying to meet new people in a new city, or just tired of feeling invisible in everyday conversations, this book is here to help. Not with gimmicks or one-size-fits-all scripts, but with real, flexible tools you can actually use. Tools rooted in psychology, empathy, and experience.

What You'll Find Inside This isn't your typical communication book. It doesn't try to turn you into someone you're not. Instead, it helps you build confidence by understanding who you are, how others operate, and how to narrow that gap authentically.

You'll learn:

- How to read a room and know when to speak up

- How to move from small talk to something real

- How to listen in a way that makes people feel deeply understood

- How to handle tense conversations with grace

- How to adapt your communication style across cultures, teams, and situations

- And how to build long-term relationships, not just one-time wins

Along the way, you'll find relatable stories, simple frameworks (like DISC and body language cues), and interactive prompts designed to help you practice, not just read.

Who This Is For This book is for young professionals, introverts, and anyone on a path of personal growth. If you've ever walked away from a conversation wishing it had gone differently, this book is for you. If you've ever struggled to speak up in meetings, connect on dates, or just *feel heard*, this is for you.

Why I Wrote This Like you, I've stood in rooms where I felt out of place. I've fumbled introductions, stayed silent when I had something to say, and walked away wishing I'd shown up more fully. That's why I've spent years studying the art and science of communication, because I knew there had to be a better way. I knew I could be better and more outgoing... at least when I had to be or wanted to be.

Now, I want to pass that better way on to you.

This book isn't about perfection. It's about *progress*. It's about showing up one conversation at a time with more clarity, curiosity, and confidence.

By the end, you'll not only have learned how to communicate more effectively, but you'll have practiced it. You'll have seen it in action. And you'll know how to apply it to your real life.

So if you're ready to stop overthinking every interaction and start building real, meaningful connections, let's begin.

Welcome to the first conversation that could change everything.

– Jared Johnson at Professional Skills Publishing

Me!   Me Leading a Workshop!

A New Way to Practice: Voice ChatGPT

This book isn't just about reading, it's about doing. And for the first time, thanks to a powerful new tool called **Voice ChatGPT**, you now have a way to actually *practice* your communication skills in a safe, low-pressure environment.

So, what is Voice ChatGPT? It's an interactive voice-based feature that allows you to speak naturally to an AI-powered coach, just like having a conversation with a real person. You can say a sentence out loud and hear how it sounds. You can practice phrasing difficult questions, trying out multiple ways to say the same thing until one feels right. You can even rehearse entire social situations, like introducing yourself or responding with empathy in a tense moment.

What makes this such a breakthrough is that tools like this didn't exist for most of us until now. Practicing social skills used to mean trying them out with another person, often with a fear of messing up. But with Voice ChatGPT, you can rehearse in private. It's like having a patient, always-available speaking partner who's never going to judge, interrupt, or make you feel awkward.

If you're shy, introverted, or just someone who learns best through *doing*, this tool gives you a way to build real-world confidence from the comfort of your own space. You don't need to be tech-savvy to use it, just tap an app on your phone and start talking. You'll find **voice practice prompts** throughout this book to help you get started. Say them once, say them ten times, tweak your tone, adjust your phrasing, however you want to show up; this gives you space to figure it out.

Because communication isn't just about what you know, it's about what you can *say out loud* when it matters. Voice ChatGPT helps you bridge the gap between knowing and doing, one conversation at a time.

If you haven't downloaded the ChatGPT app yet, consider this your prompt to do so!

Quick Peek: What's Coming in Each Chapter

- **Chapter 1:** Understanding <u>DISC</u> helps you recognize the unique ways people communicate so you can adapt with empathy, not effort. It's not about changing who you are; it's about meeting others where they are to build stronger, more meaningful connections.

- **Chapter 2**: <u>Small talk</u> is more than filler; it's a connection starter. With a curious mindset, a few go-to conversation starters, and a willingness to practice, you can turn even the simplest exchange into something meaningful.

- **Chapter 3**: <u>Active listening</u> and empathy are the keys to real connection. When you focus on understanding others, you stop overthinking and start building trust, confidence, and meaningful conversations.

- **Chapter 4:** When your <u>body language</u>, facial expressions, and tone align with your words, your message becomes more powerful and your connections more authentic. This chapter shows you how to communicate with your whole presence, not just your voice.

- **Chapter 5:** <u>Confidence</u> isn't about eliminating fear but showing up anyway. This chapter gives you real tools to move through social anxiety, reframe rejection, and speak up with calm clarity, one authentic interaction at a time.

- **Chapter 6**: <u>Storytelling</u> transforms everyday moments into meaningful connections. When shared with authenticity, structure, and heart, your personal stories can inspire, engage, and leave a lasting impression, no matter the setting.

- **Chapter 7:** Learn how to <u>navigate conflict</u>, handle criticism with curiosity, and speak up assertively, turning tough conversations into opportunities for connection, growth, and trust.

- **Chapter 8:** <u>Cross-cultural</u> communication isn't about perfection but curiosity, empathy, and respect. When you stay open and adapt with intention, you turn cultural differences into opportunities for connection.

- **Chapter 9:** <u>Mindful communication</u> begins with presence, not performance. Listening with intention, breathing through anxiety, and pausing before you speak create space for more honest, respectful, and connected conversations.

- **Chapter 10**: <u>Genuine connection</u> isn't built on small talk; it's built on trust, vulnerability, and showing up consistently. When you lead with curiosity, honesty, and care, conversations deepen and relationships grow.

- **Chapter 11**: <u>Real-life conversations</u> are where your communication skills come to life. By stepping into everyday scenarios with intention and awareness, you're not just practicing; you're becoming the kind of communicator who creates trust, connection, and lasting impact.

Build the Life You Came For

I've read my fair share of self-help books. Many were packed with great advice, yet I often closed them feeling overwhelmed, unsure where to start, or what to actually *do*. That's exactly what I want to fix with this section.

At the end of every chapter, you'll find **a clear, doable action**, something simple and specific you can try this week. If you do nothing else from each chapter, do this. It's your next best step toward real progress.

Each item will be a simple 'Yes, I Did It' or 'No, I Didn't Do It' type of exercise. So, there are no excuses for not understanding or knowing what to do next.

With that, Let's Go!

Pro Tip: Want to Learn Faster and Stay Focused? Try This

Here's a trick I wish someone had told me years ago: if you listen to the audiobook *while* reading the physical book or ebook, something weirdly amazing happens: you learn faster and remember more.

Your brain stores the info in more places at once. Pretty cool, right?

Personally, I started doing this because I kept zoning out. I'd read a paragraph and realize I hadn't absorbed any of it. But when I played the audiobook alongside my reading, I stayed more focused, and I actually enjoyed the experience more.

If you're like me, someone who wants to get the most out of a book but occasionally needs a little help staying locked in, I made the audiobook version for you.

And don't worry, this isn't some sales pitch. I've priced the audiobook as low as the platform allows. This is just a tip I've found incredibly useful, and I wanted to pass it along in case it helps you too.

I figured I'd put this "pro tip" early on. This way, you'd have a chance to do it if you found the opening chapter valuable enough to earn your attention.

One more trick: try to finish a chapter in one sitting. Stopping mid-way can leave you feeling stuck, but finishing gives your brain a little "win" and builds momentum for the next one.

So if you're ready to try it out, grab the audiobook, press play, and let's keep going together.

— • —

STAY IN THE LOOP

& LET'S KEEP THE CONVERSATION GOING!

Want a few extra tools in your back pocket? Join my email list to get occasional tips, conversation hacks, best practices, and real-world updates to help you keep leveling up your communication game.

You'll also be the first to hear about new resources, free downloads, and behind-the-scenes insights from me, the author. Whether you're looking to sharpen your skills or stay connected with what's next, I'd love to keep in touch.

Scan the QR code or visit:

https://epsbonus.professionalskillspublishing.com/talktoanyone

to sign up in less than 30 seconds.

No spam. Just real, helpful stuff when you want it.

Talk soon,

Jared

Chapter One

— • —

The Secret to Getting Along With (Almost) Everyone

Personality Styles

Have you ever noticed how some people can walk into a room and instantly connect with everyone there? I grew up envying those people because I was not one of them.

It's as if they possess a magical ability to make others feel at ease, understood, and valued. Other people seemed to gravitate to them.

It always seemed that when I started talking with someone, they were more interested in looking over my shoulder to see who else was in the room, who else was more important, and who else was more engaging for them to move on to.

But here's the truth: engaging others is not some mystical talent. It's a skill, a skill that can be learned and honed, and it starts with understanding the very foundations of how we communicate.

You might wonder what makes an interaction successful or why sometimes conversations just flow naturally while at other times they feel stilted and awkward. At the heart of it lies your own communication style. It's your unique way of expressing thoughts, emotions, and ideas, shaped by countless experiences and influences - basically, your past.

Identifying your style is core to this book because it affects how you interact with others and, just as importantly, how they interact with you.

Communication Styles & Different Personalities

Identifying your natural communication style is like looking in a mirror. It will reflect who you are; not just your words but the nuances of your expressions (do you have a resting bitchface), gestures (do your arms resemble windmills when you talk), and tone (are you boring people to death).

Some people communicate directly, preferring clear and straightforward exchanges (and are considered aggressive, assertive types). Others might lean towards an indirect approach, wrapping their messages in nuance and subtlety (and come off as flaky or passive).

You might find yourself more detail-oriented, focusing on specifics and facts (too in the weeds), or perhaps you gravitate toward the big picture (lost in the clouds), painting broad strokes with your conversations. Recognizing these tendencies is the first step in understanding how you come across to others.

I'm sure you've been at a bustling party, trying to mingle. You will notice one person is the life of the party, engaging everyone with animated stories, while another stands quietly by the snack table, observing the scene. These two individuals represent a spectrum of personality types, each bringing unique communication styles. Understanding these differences can drastically improve your interactions.

Recognizing these traits can help you choose words and tones that align with their preferences, creating more engaging and effective communication. Adapting your communication style to complement different personalities isn't about changing who you are; it's about creating a connection that acknowledges and respects those differences.

Why? Because without other people, you are just talking to yourself!

Understanding People Quickly with DISC

I love the DISC personality structure because it is a simple, four-type personality model that helps you understand yourself and others **quickly!**

Unlike more complex systems that require hours of tests and long reports, DISC gives you fast, useful insights into how people behave, communicate, and make decisions. Best of all, it's practical and can be **done live with the other person**. Without asking them to take a test.

Once you know how someone leans on the DISC scale, you can adjust your approach to make the conversation smoother, more natural, more effective, and **more engaging!**

The Four DISC Types

Here's the quick breakdown of the four DISC types:

- **D = Dominance** Fast-paced, direct, goal-oriented. They value results and don't have time for fluff.

- **I = Influence** Outgoing, optimistic, people-focused. They love stories, energy, and connection.

- **S = Steadiness** Calm, loyal, thoughtful. They like predictability and hate conflict.

- **C = Conscientiousness** Detail-oriented, analytical, careful. They care about doing things the right way.

Most people are a mix of two, with one or two traits standing out more than others. You can often spot someone's DISC style just by observing how they respond in everyday situations.

Finding Your DISC

What is your DISC style? The easiest way is to take one of the many free online DISC personality tests. While many of these sites have upsells, we don't need that for our work here.

I don't have any affiliation with this group, but I've tried out their online DISC test, and it works great without requiring you to provide a lot of personal information.

https://discpersonalitytesting.com/free-disc-test/

If you prefer, we can also try a mini-DISC snapshot test. Here's a super simple way to figure out your DISC style. Answer these two questions:

1. **When you're talking to others, are you more:**

   A. Fast-paced and assertive

   B. Slower-paced and thoughtful

2. **Are you more focused on:**

   A. Tasks and results

   B. People and relationships

Now, combine your answers into your likely DISC Style:

- 1A + 2A = Dominance (D)

- 1A + 2B = Influence (I)

- 1B + 2B = Steadiness (S)

- 1B + 2A = Conscientiousness (C)

A Closer Look at Each DISC Style

Now that you've had a taste of the four DISC styles, let's dig a little deeper. Think of this as your personal decoder ring for human behavior. The more you understand each style, the better you'll connect, adapt, and communicate in a way that actually lands.

D – Dominance

Driven. Decisive. Direct.

People with a dominant style are goal-getters. They're assertive, results-focused, and they move fast. D's love challenges, **don't mind confrontation**, and are wired to lead. Efficiency matters to them - a lot. **Conversations with D's are often short, to the point**, and geared toward *what's the outcome?*

How they think:

- "What's the bottom line?"

- "Let's move. What's next?"

- "Tell me what I need to know - not the whole backstory."

How they communicate:

- Fast-paced, confident, and **blunt** (non-Ds mistake this as aggressive or anger, it is not. It is just how a D communicates, don't take it personally)

- Results-driven, often using action verbs

- Comfortable giving direction and making quick decisions

What motivates them:

- Winning, achievement, getting things done

- Having control over outcomes

- Big challenges or high-stakes situations

I – Influence

Enthusiastic. Expressive. Inspiring.

I's are the talkers, the storytellers, and the **life of the party** (or at least the most chatty person at the coffee shop). They thrive on connection and **bring energy**

into the room. They're optimistic and spontaneous, which makes them a joy to be around, but they are sometimes not the most detail-oriented. They are the **trendsetters** and often the most stylishly dressed – frequently a good way to spot an 'I' is their clothing.

How they think:

- "Who's here? Let's connect!"

- "This could be fun!"

- "Let's wing it and see what happens."

How they communicate:

- Warm, animated, and friendly

- Tends to speak in stories or big-picture ideas

- May go off-topic, but they're great at making people feel included

What motivates them:

- Social recognition, fun, and freedom

- Opportunities to inspire or influence others

- A sense of belonging

S – Steadiness

Supportive. Stable. Sincere.

S-style individuals are **calm, dependable, and loyal**. They're your steady, reliable presence - the kind of people who value harmony and **avoid rocking the boat**. They're also **great listeners**. S's don't love sudden change, but they'll go the distance for people they care about.

How they think:

- "Is everyone okay?"

- "Let's keep things comfortable."

- "We don't need to rush into anything."

How they communicate:

- Soft-spoken, thoughtful, and kind

- Prefers to listen before responding

- Often uses calming, affirming language

What motivates them:

- Stability and routine

- Strong relationships

- Feeling safe and respected

C – Conscientiousness

Careful. Correct. Analytical.

C's are the quality-control experts of the personality world. They value **precision, logic**, and structure. These are your thinkers - the ones who want to get it right the first time. They **may not say much at first**, but it's usually well thought out when they speak.

How they think:

- "What's the data say?"

- "Let's analyze before acting."

- "I want to make sure this is accurate."

How they communicate:

- Precise, structured, often formal

- Favors logic over emotion

- Tends **to ask clarifying questions** or challenge vague claims

What motivates them:

- Accuracy and excellence

- Being seen as competent

- Clear rules, expectations, and procedures

How to Spot a DISC Style in Conversation

While no one walks around wearing a name tag that says "Hi, I'm a C!", there are signs to look for in how people behave, speak, and react. Here's what to listen and look for:

If they... they might be a...

- Talk fast, get to the point, skip small talk = **D – Dominance**

- Use animated language, smile a lot, share stories = **I - Influence**

- Ask about how people are doing, take their time, avoid conflict = **S - Steadiness**

- Ask questions about data, definitions, or systems = **C - Conscientiousness**

Quick Tips:

- **Watch pace:**

  ○ Fast-paced = D or I

- ○ Slower-paced = S or C

- **Watch focus**:

  - ○ Task-focused = D or C.

  - ○ People-focused = I or S

- **Notice questions**:

  - ○ D's ask "what?"

  - ○ I's ask "who?"

  - ○ S's ask "how?"

  - ○ C's ask "why?"

Most importantly, don't get caught up in trying to label someone too fast. Use this tool as a *guide*, not a box. People are dynamic. DISC helps you tune in, not typecast.

Reflection Activity: Who Have You Talked To?

Understanding DISC is one thing - *seeing it in your own life* is where it really clicks. This quick reflection activity helps you spot the different DISC styles in people you've already interacted with and consider how those conversations went.

Take a few minutes to think back on recent conversations, at work, with friends, or even in a coffee shop line. Grab a pen or jot your answers in the notes app on your phone.

1. Think of a "D" Style Person You Know:

- Who is someone you know that's direct, fast-moving, or task-focused?

- How do they usually speak or make decisions?

- What's worked well when talking to them? What hasn't?

My D-style contact: _____

Best way I've connected with them: _____

What I'll try next time: _____

2. Think of an "I" Style Person You Know:

- Who's the life of the party or loves to talk things out?

- What energizes them in a conversation?

- How do you usually respond to their energy?

My I-style contact: _____

Best way I've connected with them: _____

What I'll try next time: _____

3. Think of an "S" Style Person You Know:

- Who's loyal, calm, and prefers to avoid conflict?

- What helps them feel safe and heard?

- How do they react to pressure or change?

My S-style contact: _____

Best way I've connected with them: _____

What I'll try next time: _____

4. Think of a "C" Style Person You Know:

- Who's detail-focused, asks a lot of questions, or needs time to think?

- What kind of communication do they prefer?

- How can you respect their process?

My C-style contact: _____

Best way I've connected with them: _____

What I'll try next time: _____

Final Reflection:

Now look across your answers. Where do you naturally connect? Which style challenges you the most? What's one small adjustment you could make to become a more adaptable communicator starting this week?

Recognizing and Adapting

Once you understand your DISC style, we can move to flexibility in communication. Being flexible involves more than just adapting your words; it requires a shift in perspective.

It also allows me to introduce a cutting-edge tool that will help even the shyest of people practice and gain personal insights. In the past, we often introduced role-playing scenarios where you engage with different personality types. This required another person. Not anymore!

Feedback exercises can greatly enhance your communication skills. In the past, and honestly, you can still do this, you were required to invite a trusted friend or colleague to observe your interactions and provide honest feedback on your conversations.

I hated this! This was not me, and I never, not once, invited a friend to help me with this... to my own detriment. However, with today's technology, we don't have to do that anymore. We can have AI do it with us.

Today's generative AI models (like ChatGPT) now offer **voice modes.**

AI Natural Voice Mode

One of the most powerful tools available to you as a reader and a communicator-in-training is the voice conversation feature in ChatGPT. This tool allows you to have natural, back-and-forth spoken conversations with the AI, much like chatting with a coach or role-play partner.

It's designed to sound and respond like a real person, which makes it an ideal space to practice the skills you're learning in this book, starting conversations, adjusting your tone, building confidence, or even working through tricky social scenarios (all of which come later in this book).

You can use it to simulate a networking event, rehearse small talk, or explore how different DISC personalities might respond in real time.

To access it, download the ChatGPT mobile app. *While other AI models may have this feature, I've only used ChatGPT, and that's where my expertise is. So, in teaching you, I want to make sure I only recommend and work with you on the tool I'm an expert in.* Open the ChatGPT mobile app, tap the icon that looks like four vertical lines, and start speaking. One note, OpenAI, the parent company of ChatGPT, may change the icon in the future, so click each one and find the one you need.

There's no script, pressure, or judgment, just a flexible, supportive way to get more reps in. Think of it as your personal communication coach where you can test ideas, ask questions, or practice being more present and clear in your conversations.

We will use this **powerful** training tool throughout this book. Let's try it out in this first quick exercise.

ChatGPT Voice Prompt: DISC Styles Practice
Open the app and speak into it!

"Hello! I'm practicing how to recognize different personality styles using the DISC model. I'd like you to be my personal communication coach. Let's do an exercise where you speak to me in the tone and style of one DISC type at a time, Dominance, Influence, Steadiness, and Conscientiousness. For each one, carry on a short, natural conversation with me (just 3 to 5 sentences), staying fully in character. After each example, stop and let me guess which DISC style you were using. Then tell me if I got it right, give me a bit of feedback, and move on to the next style. Let's go through all four."

What happens next? ChatGPT will start talking to you, role-playing the scenario just like a friend or coach would. Talk back, ask questions, and repeat the exercise as many times as you need. It won't judge you. It won't get frustrated with you. It won't put you down for asking a dumb question. Your goal is to get comfortable using Voice Mode and to confidently identify the DISC personality type being portrayed.

Chapter Wrap: Why Understanding People Changes Everything

Understanding DISC isn't about putting people in boxes - it's about opening doors. The more you recognize and respect different communication styles, the easier it becomes to build genuine connections. Whether chatting with a high-energy Influencer or navigating a detail-focused Conscientious type, this framework gives you a practical, people-first lens to guide your conversations.

And as you grow in your ability to adapt your style, you'll find that communication gets easier, not because people change, but because you've learned to meet them where they are. Keep practicing. Keep observing. And remember, the goal isn't perfection - it's connection.

Understanding and adapting to different personalities enriches communication skills and relationships. People feel valued when their individuality is recognized and respected, leading to deeper connections and more effective collaborations.

Despite best efforts, personality clashes can still occur. Not everyone is going to like you even if you've done nothing wrong or to them. Conflict resolution strategies become essential tools in these situations and we will work on those later in this book.

For now, practice with the voice AI model. Listen to people at work, at school, in the coffee shop, or at the store. Based on what and how they talk, can you assign them a style?

Build the Life You Came For

What should you do next?

- **Self-Assessment Time**
  Take a free online DISC assessment. Which quadrant do you most resonate with? What are your strengths and blind spots in conversations?

- **Observe & Assign DISC Types in the Wild**
  Choose 5 people that you know or spend a day people-watching, at work, at the gym, in line at the coffee shop. Based on speech, energy, and behavior, assign a DISC style to these 5 different people. Just guess. The goal is to sharpen your awareness.

CHAPTER TWO

—·—

TALK WITHOUT THE CRINGE: YOUR GUIDE TO NATURAL, NOT FORCED, SMALL TALK

The Fear of Starting a Conversation

U nderstanding where conversation anxiety comes from is key to overcoming it. Many people feel anxious, nervous, and even panicked when starting a conversation with someone they don't know. **"Why would they want to talk to me?"** is screaming in their heads. How do I know this? It was, and at times still is, me.

This anxiety stems from past experiences, societal expectations, or personal insecurities (yep, this last one is mine all the way). Psychologically, it's often linked to the fear of being evaluated negatively, of being judged. These feelings can paralyze anyone, making the simple act of saying "hello" seem daunting. Yet, research shows this fear is common and something we can push through. Realize that most people appreciate genuine attempts at connection, especially in social environments. At the gas station, maybe not so much. So, know your settings and when and where starting a conversation is expected and normal vs a situation where starting one will catch the other person off guard or even be off-putting.

Case Study: Sarah's Shift from Fear to Curiosity

When I first met Sarah, she was several months into a new job at a midsize marketing firm. Bright, capable, and deeply thoughtful, Sarah excelled in her role behind the scenes: organizing timelines, proofreading campaign materials, and ensuring her team hit deadlines. But when it came to speaking up or starting conversations with coworkers, she froze. "I feel like everyone else already knows each other," she told me. "If I try to jump in, I'm afraid I'll interrupt or say something awkward."

Sarah's anxiety wasn't unusual. She was working in a company culture where spontaneous hallway chats and informal check-ins over lunch weren't just common - they were expected. In fact, during her onboarding, her manager encouraged her to "get to know everyone" and "build connections across departments." The problem wasn't a lack of willingness - it was fear. Sarah worried she'd come across as intrusive, or worse, be silently judged. For what, she didn't know.

We started by reframing her perception of workplace conversations. I asked her, "What if small talk isn't just fluff? What if it's actually the social glue that builds trust here?" That idea stuck. Together, we talked through how workplaces often function as social ecosystems, where connection helps people collaborate more easily and resolve issues before they escalate.

Then we moved into practical strategies. I didn't ask Sarah to suddenly become outgoing or bubbly. That wasn't her. Instead, we leaned into her natural strengths: observation, listening, and curiosity. I encouraged her to look for small openings, where she could ask a thoughtful question or show interest in someone's work. We brainstormed a few conversation starters she felt comfortable with:

- "I saw your name on the client deck. How did that pitch go?"

- "That lunch smelled amazing. Where did you order it from?"

- "I noticed you've been working on that project for a while. How's it going?"

To build confidence, Sarah practiced some of these lines aloud and even role-played with Voice ChatGPT. At first, she still felt nervous. But she quickly discovered that most people *wanted* to be engaged. They appreciated being asked about their work or day, as long as they weren't heads down in the middle of something urgent. "The first time someone lit up when I asked about their campaign," she told me, "I realized I'm not bothering them. I'm just being a person. A friendly social coworker"

Over time, those small steps added up. Sarah didn't become the loudest voice in the room, but she became a steady presence, someone others looked forward to talking with. She even found herself offering ideas in meetings and casually inviting a new coworker to join her for lunch.

Sarah's story is a powerful reminder that initiating a conversation at work doesn't require being an extrovert; it requires intention. When we shift from worrying about being judged to being genuinely curious about others, something opens up. The workplace starts to feel less intimidating and more human.

Discussion Prompt: Turning Curiosity into Confidence

Think about your own work environment. Are there moments where you've hesitated to start a conversation - maybe in the break room, before a meeting, or during a casual team chat? What were you feeling in that moment? What held you back?

Now, consider this: What might happen if you approached those same moments with curiosity instead of fear? What's one small, low-pressure conversation starter you could try this week, something simple, genuine, and rooted in interest?

Take a minute to reflect or jot down:

- A person you'd like to connect with at work

- A setting or time where a brief conversation might naturally happen

- One open-ended question you could ask to start that conversation

Remember: connection often starts with one small question. You don't have to be perfect, just present.

Preparation

Use the previous discussion prompt before any event or get-together you might attend. Arm yourself with conversation starters that work in various situations. Universal icebreakers like "What's the most exciting thing that happened to you this week?" or "What do you love most about your job?" can open doors to deeper discussions. Tailor these icebreakers to your environment.

For example, asking about someone's career path at a networking event can lead to insightful exchanges, while inquiring about someone's hobbies at a social gathering might uncover common interests.

Visualization techniques offer another powerful tool for reducing anxiety and boosting confidence. Close your eyes and see yourself approaching someone with ease and confidence. See the conversation flowing naturally. Envisioning positive outcomes can make them feel more attainable. Guided visualization exercises can walk you through successful interactions, helping your brain associate talking to new people with positive experiences. Many have found that visualizing these scenarios before stepping into social settings decreases their anxiety significantly, making them feel more prepared and capable.

To build confidence, **practice initiating conversations in low-pressure environments**. Coffee shops are great places to start. These settings provide opportunities to chat with strangers in a relaxed atmosphere, where low expectations and friendliness are the norm. Start small by making casual comments on what's happening in the store or the weather: things like a long line at the coffee shop, the heat, or an interesting event happening nearby. Such practice helps you become comfortable with initiating interactions and teaches you that most people are receptive to friendly overtures.

Reflecting on these experiences brings personal growth. After each interaction, take a moment to consider what went well and what could improve next time. Did you feel comfortable? Was the other person engaged? What could you do differently? Did you assume their DISC style and adapt your conversation based on that? Afterwards, do you think you guessed correctly? These reflections offer insights into your communication style and help pinpoint areas for improvement. Over time, you'll start noticing patterns, certain phrases that work better than others or specific topics that spark conversations.

At the end of the day, overcoming the fear of initiating conversations involves recognizing it and preparing yourself with the right mindset to tackle it. By using visualization techniques, reflecting, and practicing in low-stakes environments, you'll gradually find that initiating conversations becomes second nature. Ok, if not that far, at least easier.

Let's talk about another fear people have... what should I say?

Crafting Engaging Conversation Starters

Let's imagine you are at a party, drink in hand, standing awkwardly near the food table, eyeing the crowd. You want to join a conversation or start one with a stranger, but aren't sure how to begin. The key lies in crafting engaging conversation starters that pave the way for meaningful exchanges.

When you're unsure where to begin, start with universal topics. These are your safety nets, subjects almost everyone relates to and can easily discuss. Weather is a classic example. While it might seem mundane, it's a shared experience everyone can comment on. Mention the beautiful sunset or how surprisingly chilly it got, and watch as others chime in. Recent events also work well. Whether it's a big sports game or a trending news story, these topics invite opinions and stories. Make it a habit to read at least the news headlines. Even if you don't read the stories, looking at the headlines will let you know who just won the Super Bowl or what was the top movie at the weekend box office.

Shared activities, like attending the same event, provide natural jumping-off points. Observing your surroundings helps you find these commonalities quickly, what a beautiful old hotel the event is taking place in. Wasn't the keynote speaker inspiring? Did you notice the fantastic art on display? These observations help you find common ground swiftly.

But don't just stick to the generic. Personalize your approach to make your conversation starter more memorable and engaging. Tailor your opener to fit the context and the individual you're speaking with. Look around and use what you see as inspiration. Notice someone wearing a band shirt? Ask them about their favorite concert. Spot someone reading a book? Inquire about their thoughts on it. Personalized compliments or observations make people feel appreciated and noticed.

Once the ice is broken, keep the conversation flowing with open-ended questions. These questions require more than a yes or no answer, inviting the other person to share more about themselves. Instead of asking, "Did you like the event?" try, "What did you enjoy most about today?" This approach encourages a detailed response and naturally leads to deeper topics. Transitioning from openers to more substantial discussions involves listening carefully and picking up on cues that indicate interest or passion.

Humor is another powerful tool in your small talk arsenal. It can break the ice and make conversations more enjoyable. A well-timed joke or light-hearted remark can ease tension and bring smiles. Not a funny person by nature? Consider observational humor. Make a light-hearted observation about the long line at the buffet or a playful comment on how everyone seems to gravitate towards the dessert table. However, be mindful of context and audience when using humor. What might be funny in one setting could fall flat or even offend in another. Keep it light and relevant, focusing on inclusive jokes everyone can appreciate. Still don't think of yourself as a humorous person? That's ok, just shy away from a humorous opening.

Tennis Flow Conversation Method

The flow of conversation hasn't and doesn't always come easily to me. One great piece of advice I heard once was about relating a conversation to a game of tennis. And I still use this approach today. Here is how it works.

You start a conversation with someone, like hitting the tennis ball over the net to the other person. Now, they respond and hit the ball/conversation back to you. Here is the magic in this approach: you accept the conversation/ball by commenting on what they talked about (your comment should be a statement with a period at the end). Then you make another statement related to that topic, this time about yourself. And then finally, you return the ball/conversation to them by asking them a question. This accept, statement in response, statement about yourself, and then a question back to them method will help any conversation with any person flow smoothly. When you find the right tennis partner, or conversational partner, and they pick up this same rhythm, your conversation can last hours!

To enhance your skills in crafting conversation starters, consider keeping a mental or physical list of go-to topics and questions for different situations. This list serves as a handy reference when you need inspiration or when an awkward silence looms. Practice makes perfect, so seize opportunities to engage with others in low-pressure environments like casual meet-ups or social gatherings. Each interaction is a chance to refine your approach and discover what works best for you.

Reflection Section: Your Personalized Conversation Starter List

Try this exercise to create your '9 Go To's to Start Any Conversation!'

1. **Universal Topics:** List three universal topics you feel comfortable discussing. Examples include weather, recent sporting events, local news, movies, and best-sellers.

   - Universal Starter #1: _____

   - Universal Starter #2: _____

   - Universal Starter #3: _____

2. **Personalized Starters:** Think of three personalized conversation starters based on common observations. Examples include complimenting someone's unique accessory or commenting on a shared experience. Or even how you aren't good at this sort of event!

   - Personalized Starter #1: _____

   - Personalized Starter #2: _____

   - Personalized Starter #3: _____

3. **Open-Ended Questions:** Write three open-ended questions that encourage detailed responses. Examples include, "What inspired you to pursue your current career path?"

- ○ Open-Ended Starter #1: _____

- ○ Open-Ended Starter #2: _____

- ○ Open-Ended Starter #3: _____

By building this list, you'll be prepared for any social situation, confident in your ability to engage others with ease and authenticity. Then, as you gain experience, add to your list and fine-tune it. Here is another curated list from my history.

Universal Ice-Breakers: These work just about anywhere, at work, social events, even standing in line.

1. **"How's your day going so far?"** Simple, open, and invites a real answer beyond just "good."

2. **"That [item/clothing/book] looks interesting, what's the story behind it?"** Great for drawing attention to something personal and meaningful.

3. **"Have you done anything fun or different lately?"** Gets people talking about what they enjoy or are excited about.

4. **"I always find these things a little awkward, do you feel the same?"** Light vulnerability often makes others open up too.

5. **"What's something you're working on right now that you're really into?"** Works well with colleagues, creatives, or anyone passionate.

Work or Networking Event Ice-Breakers

1. **"So what brought you to this event today?"** A classic opener, polite and purposeful.

2. **"How did you get into your line of work?"** Most people enjoy talking about their path.

3. **"Is there a session or speaker you're looking forward to?"** Great for conferences or seminars.

4. **"What's one surprising thing people don't realize about your job?"** Invites storytelling and builds connection fast.

5. **"If you weren't doing what you do now, what do you think you'd be doing?"** Opens the door to dreams and side interests.

Social or Casual Gathering Ice-Breakers

1. **"How do you know [host's name]?"** A natural way to find common ground.

2. **"I just tried that appetizer, have you had it yet?"** Easy and event-specific, great near food tables.

3. **"This playlist is awesome, do you know who it is?"** Taps into shared taste and atmosphere.

4. **"I love your [jacket/shoes/bag/etc.], where'd you find it?"** Genuine compliments can open doors.

5. **"If you could teleport anywhere after this event, where would you go?"** Light, playful, and gets people dreaming.

Keeping Small Talk Authentic and Natural

When it comes to small talk, being genuine is your superpower. People can sense when someone is insincere, which often leads to awkward exchanges or a quick end to the conversation. Imagine attending a work event and striking up a chat with a colleague. Share something real instead of sticking to the typical "How's work?" routine. Maybe you mention how you've been learning guitar in your spare time and ask if they have any hobbies outside of work. This approach opens the door to a more genuine connection, rooted in authenticity. This approach focuses on you and your ability to speak from the heart, even during brief interactions. It might initially feel vulnerable, but it builds trust and makes your exchanges memorable. Vulnerability will make you stand out in the crowd and be the person people remember at the end of the day; however, an important caveat to this approach is that these people aren't your therapist. Don't just unload on them!

Active listening transforms small talk from a surface-level chat to a deeply engaging interaction. When you truly listen, it shows you value the other person's perspective, making them more open to sharing. Techniques like nodding and echoing sentiments demonstrate engagement. If someone mentions their love for travel, respond with curiosity: "I've always wanted to visit Italy. What was your favorite part?" This shows interest and can lead to unexpected connections, like discovering mutual friends or shared experiences.

Active listening involves more than just hearing words; it's about understanding the emotions behind them. By honing this skill, you create less superficial and more substantial conversations. There is no trick here. **You just have to listen and be present. Stop thinking about what you want to say.** Stop thinking about what you need to do next. Stop thinking about everything and just listen. Yes, it's hard! There are no tricks.

I will admit, this does not come easily or naturally to me. It is work and an effort for me to listen actively. It is hard. However, for my wife, this is who she is and her skill. Everyone is different, and you have to work from your current situation.

Did I mention this is hard? But it is one thing that will instantly set you apart from others.

Maintaining a positive attitude sets the tone for open dialogue and reduces tension. Even if you're having a rough day, approaching conversations with positivity can be contagious. Smiling, maintaining an open posture, and using encouraging words can help create a welcoming atmosphere. If negativity creeps in, manage those emotions by focusing on gratitude or shifting your mindset towards optimism.

Balancing talking and listening (like in our tennis approach) ensures that conversations remain dynamic and engaging. While it's tempting to dominate discussions, especially when you're passionate about a topic, it's equally important to encourage others to share. Redirecting conversations back to the other person is an art form in itself. If you monopolize the dialogue, gently steer it back by asking for their thoughts or reflections on what you've shared.

Another aspect of keeping small talk natural is **navigating awkward silences** with ease. Embrace silence as part of conversation instead of rushing to fill it.

These pauses can provide space for reflection or transition into new topics. If the silence lingers too long, have backup topics ready to bring up naturally (pull from your conversation starter list). Acknowledge awkwardness with light-hearted comments like "Oops, lost my train of thought there!" to diffuse tension and reset the conversation's flow.

Moving from small talk to meaningful dialogue involves recognizing cues indicating readiness for deeper engagement. Pay attention to verbal signals like thoughtful responses or non-verbal cues such as prolonged eye contact and nodding. These behaviors suggest a genuine interest in pursuing more substantive discussions. Transition smoothly with intelligent questions that bridge small talk into personal stories or experiences. Go deeper into yourself and your history when you have the tennis ball. Sharing of yourself fosters rapport and trust by revealing shared values or experiences.

As conversations evolve beyond small talk, invite them to share their perspectives and reflect on their experiences (the question part of our tennis analogy). Use open-ended questions to prompt them to open up further. These types of invitations deepen the dialogue while demonstrating your interest in the other person.

Navigating Awkward Silences with Ease

Silence in conversation often feels like an ominous cloud over a sunny day, creating an uncomfortable gap many are eager to fill hastily. But here's a surprising secret: silence is not the enemy; it can be your trusted ally. This void in dialogue provides a natural pause, offering a breather for those involved. Think of it as a space for reflection, allowing both participants to gather thoughts without undue pressure. Silence helps digest what's been said, appreciate nuances, and decide where to steer the conversation next.

Imagine being in a work meeting when a sudden hush falls over the room after a complex question is posed, a scenario that initially might appear intimidating. Instead of rushing to fill the perceived awkward gap, everyone takes a thoughtful moment to delve deeper into their thoughts. This deliberate pause often results in more insightful responses and richer discussions. Embracing these pauses as an integral part of the conversation can transform how you perceive them, not as awkward interruptions to be avoided, but as essential elements that enhance communication and understanding.

If you find yourself rushing to fill silences, do some self-reflection and ask why.

Using silence to transition topics requires a bit of finesse but can be incredibly effective if handled with care. A brief pause can subtly signal a shift in direction. During these moments, paying attention to your body language is crucial; a slight nod or a subtle change in posture can indicate you're ready to explore a new subject. Go back to your list of conversation starters.

Seamless transitioning involves discovering connections between what was just discussed and where you'd like to navigate the conversation next. For example, if you're in a discussion about travel and there's a lull, you could gracefully segue into talking about favorite destinations or sharing thoughtful travel tips that pique everyone's interest.

Sometimes, the most effective way to diffuse tension is by acknowledging it directly and with a light-hearted touch. Calling out the proverbial elephant in the room can help break the ice and reset the conversational tone. A gentle, humorous comment such as, "Well, that was a long pause," can ease the atmosphere and invite laughter. Humor works wonders in these situations, but maintaining a gentle approach is vital. By addressing any awkwardness openly, you demonstrate your comfort with imperfections, making others feel more at ease.

Navigating awkward silences with grace isn't about avoiding them; it's about transforming them into opportunities for deeper connection and understanding. By embracing silence as a natural and beneficial part of conversation, using it strategically to transition topics, having backup subjects on hand, and acknowledging any awkwardness with humor and openness, you become more adept at handling these moments with confidence and poise.

Silence is a powerful conversational tool that, when used wisely, can significantly enrich interactions, enhance understanding, and ultimately strengthen communication skills.

Moving from Small Talk to Meaningful Dialogue

While there's an innate familiarity and comfort in discussing the weather or sharing a brief anecdote about a weekend getaway, the truly rewarding and enriching interactions stimulate a form of deeper, more impactful conversation. To navigate this journey from basic pleasantries to meaningful dialogue, it is necessary to employ a keen sense of timing and a refined sensitivity to the subtle cues that beckon deeper exploration. Recognizing these cues requires understanding both the spoken word and the unspoken signals.

For instance, when someone nods with enthusiasm, maintains a steady, engaging eye contact, or subtly leans forward during your interaction, it denotes a heightened level of interest and readiness to delve deeper. More on body language later on. Likewise, if they choose to elaborate on a particular topic or offer a personal narrative, it is often a tacit invitation to amplify the dialogue.

However, one may question how exactly to transition without the conversation feeling contrived or uncomfortably intentional. This is where the art of asking thoughtful, open-ended questions comes into play. These questions gently guide the dialogue from superficial exchanges to conversations of substance.

For example, suppose the topic of weekend plans arises. In that case, a question like, "What's one thing you truly enjoy doing when you have some free time?" allows the individual to share insights into their personal life while maintaining a relaxed atmosphere. Tailoring these questions to suit the context is the idea, for there is a fine line between curiosity and intrusion.

How will you strike this balance? Practice and observation. If you ask a question and the other person is taken aback or hesitates, you may be going too deep. Redirect to something less personal and try again.

Sharing personal experiences first can serve as a kind of catalyst for the other person. When you share stories from your own life, you create a space for reciprocity, inviting others to contribute to the conversation in a similar way. Consider stories that highlight shared experiences or common values. Perhaps you both hail from modest rural towns or share a fervor for travel adventures. Go there first...but ensure your story is about the ongoing discussion. A narrative about overcoming workplace challenges could be compelling if career aspirations are the topic, yet might seem misplaced if discussing leisure pursuits such as hiking or reading.

Actively encouraging others to narrate their stories is equally significant. Prompting someone with phrases like "I'd love to hear more about that" or "What was that experience like for you?" invites them to engage on a deeper level and nurtures the art of reflective dialogue.

Why does this shift matter so profoundly? Moving beyond small talk can dramatically transform relationships, turning casual acquaintances into friends and partners. It creates genuine connections, where empathy and understanding thrive, and where every participant feels acknowledged and valued. Remember that meaningful conversation transcends mere words; it involves **attentive listening**, genuine **empathy**, and forming a deep-seated **connection** on a profoundly human level.

You should consider small talk the initial step in learning how to talk to anyone. When possible and in the appropriate context, seize opportunities for deeper interactions, leveraging thoughtful questions to steer the conversation. Share authentic stories that build rapport and invite others to share their experiences. These strategies not only hone your communicative skills but also enhance and deepen both personal and professional relationships.

Chapter Wrap: Your Small Talk Toolkit So Far

Small talk gets a bad rap, but as you've seen in this chapter, it's actually a powerful gateway to connection. Whether you're navigating nerves like Sarah or simply unsure how to start a conversation, the tools you've explored here can help you move from anxious to confident. You've learned that fear of starting a conversation is common and conquerable, especially when you shift your mindset from fear to curiosity. You've practiced using visualization techniques, created personalized conversation starters, and discovered how something as simple as a compliment or a question about someone's day can open the door to deeper engagement.

You now understand how to spot natural openings for small talk, tailor your approach to the context, and use tools like the tennis method to keep a conversation flowing. You've also explored how humor, open-ended questions, and active listening can elevate a surface-level chat into something far more meaningful. And perhaps most importantly, you've started to embrace awkward silences as part of the rhythm of conversation, not something to fear, but something to use.

Remember: small talk isn't about being witty or impressive, it's about being present, authentic, and curious. Start small. Use your 9 Go-To Starters. Pay attention to how others respond. And with each interaction, you'll grow more confident and more connected. This is where the real conversations begin.

Build the Life You Came For

What should you do next?

- **One Bold Move to Try This Week**
  This one could be scary. I know it will. This could be awkward. I know it will. DO IT ANYWAYS! Find one moment this week, at a coffee shop, work hallway, or waiting room, and initiate a quick/short conversation with someone you don't know well.

- Use a genuine, curiosity-based opener like:

  - "What's been the highlight of your week so far?"

  - "What's something you're looking forward to this week?"

  - "What's been keeping you busy lately, in a good way?"

  - "What do you usually do when you're not working?"

  - "Seen or heard anything interesting lately, podcasts, shows, anything?"

  - "Do you have any recommendations here?"

- **Then end the conversation and move on. Try this:**
  "It was really nice chatting with you. I'm glad we got to talk for a bit. Now, if you will excuse me, I have to get going, but I hope the rest of your [evening/event/day] goes great!" Well done!

CHAPTER THREE

— • —

MASTER THE SKILL THAT BUILDS INSTANT TRUST

ACTIVE LISTENING

Active Listening

Reflect for a moment on when you last experienced the profound sensation of truly being seen and heard. Was it during an intimate exchange with a close friend or while confiding in a trusted family member? In those moments, it felt as though time itself came to a standstill, enveloping you in an empowering aura of validation and understanding. That's the profound enchantment of active listening. It's a transformative experience that transcends the mere auditory processing of words, it's about immersing oneself fully and empathetically into the speaker's world, ensuring they feel genuinely seen and heard.

Active listening necessitates adopting a listener-centered approach, which is founded on providing your **absolute, undistracted focus** to the person speaking. This act of prioritizing them over all else serves as a signal of your genuine interest. **Eye contact**, in particular, emerges as a fundamentally crucial component here, as it conveys sincerity and intense engagement, while also encouraging the speaker to pour out their thoughts candidly. This non-verbal communication, expressed through a steady, attentive gaze, signifies profound interest and openness.

Eye Contact: Why It's Hard, and How to Get Better at It

Let's be honest: for something so small, eye contact can feel incredibly intense. If you've ever struggled to hold someone's gaze during a conversation, especially with someone new, you're not alone. Hello! That's still me today. Eye contact can stir up anxiety, self-doubt, and even shame. You might worry you're staring too much. Or not enough. Or that the other person can see right through you.

So, why is eye contact so uncomfortable for some of us?

For many, the insecurity comes from a fear of being truly seen. Eye contact is intimate. It signals presence. And **when we're unsure of ourselves**, or afraid we're being judged, that attention level can feel exposed. This is especially common for people who are shy, neurodivergent, socially anxious, or simply grew up in environments where eye contact wasn't modeled or encouraged. In some cultures, prolonged eye contact is considered disrespectful or confrontational, which adds another layer to the challenge.

The thing is, eye contact plays a huge role in how others perceive us. It implies confidence, trustworthiness, interest, and engagement. When you make eye contact, even briefly, you send a powerful signal: *I see you, and I'm here with you.* But if it's hard for you, that doesn't mean you're broken. It just means you need tools and practice.

How to Rethink Eye Contact

Rather than thinking of eye contact as a test of courage or a stare-down, try to think of it as a **connection tool**. You're not trying to lock eyes for an uncomfortable amount of time. You're simply creating brief moments of connection that make your listener feel seen and valued.

A helpful mindset shift: You're not being watched, you're **sharing presence**. This is a two-way interaction, not a performance.

Techniques and Exercises to Improve Eye Contact

1. Start Small and Safe

Practice making eye contact during low-pressure interactions, like with a barista, cashier, or someone you already feel comfortable around. Hold their gaze for 2–3 seconds when you say hello or thank them. These micro-moments build comfort over time.

2. Use the "Triangle Technique"

Rather than staring into someone's eyes the whole time, imagine a small triangle on their face: move your gaze gently between their left eye, right eye, and mouth. It helps you stay engaged without fixating or feeling locked in.

3. Aim for 50/70

In most one-on-one conversations, aim to make eye contact about **50–70% of the time**. That's enough to show interest without being overwhelming. During a group conversation, it's natural to shift your gaze around the room.

4. Look *through*, Not *at*

This sounds strange, but sometimes it helps to soften your focus. Look at the person, but don't *stare*. Instead of focusing on specific features, think about *being with* the person, not inspecting them.

5. Practice in the Mirror

It might feel awkward, but spend a few minutes a day making eye contact with your reflection while speaking. Try telling a short story or practicing a conversation opener. This helps build familiarity with your own presence.

6. Role-Play with a Trusted Friend (or ChatGPT Voice Mode!)

Ask a friend to help you practice casual conversation while focusing on making brief, steady eye contact. You can also try this in ChatGPT's voice mode, have a few back-and-forth exchanges, and intentionally work on your eye contact posture as you speak aloud. And where exactly is the eye contact with ChatGPT? The camera lens of course!

Here's a surprising strategy that actually works: even eye contact with a photo can boost your practice. On the next page, you'll see a pair of eyes, use them! Practice making strong, steady, intentional eye contact as if you're speaking to a real person. Strange? Maybe. Effective? Absolutely.

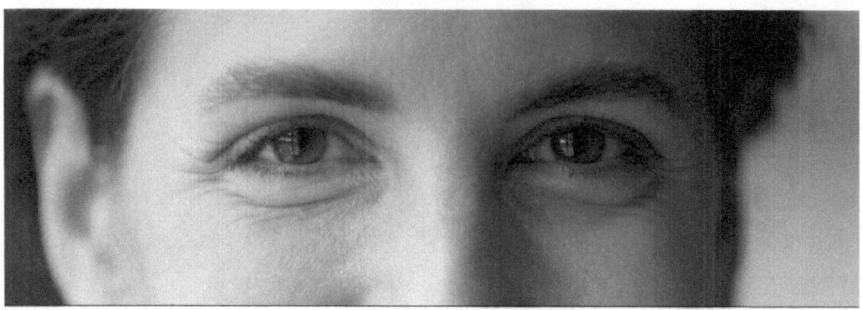

A Final Thought

You don't have to master eye contact overnight. Like every skill in this book, it's something you build through effort and grace. And remember: *your goal isn't to "look confident." It's to connect with another human being.* If your gaze wavers, that's okay. What matters is that you show up, and keep trying.

Techniques for Active Listening... continued

Affirmative gestures, such as consistent nodding, amplify your listening. They function as nonverbal cues of encouragement, reassuring the speaker to continue unraveling their narrative.

Further, **patience** is a cornerstone of active listening, a delicate art involving resisting the often-irresistible urge to interrupt. It demands allowing the narrator to articulate their views in their totality. Frequently, our instincts urge us to interject with our opinions, but cultivating patience means embracing those moments of silence, cherishing them until it's our turn to respond. Embracing this approach reflects respect for the speaker's narrative and provides ample time for us to process their words more ponderously. This patience can be nurtured through deliberate practices. Engage in conversations to practice silence, conscientiously allowing the speaker to steer the dialogue without interrupting. Over time, this discipline matures into an intuitive habit.

Reflecting upon and **summarizing the key points** delivered by the speaker operates as a powerful mechanism for confirming comprehension and showcasing deep attentiveness. When someone entrusts you with their thoughts, reciprocating with a synthesized recapitulation of what has been articulated validates their perspective and assures them of your grasp. Phrases like "So what I hear you saying is..." or "It sounds like..." function as a link to foster a stronger emotional bond and understanding. Embarking on the practice of summarizing intricate information in your own vocabulary guarantees mutual alignment and strengthens understanding between you and the speaker. Summarization is the key here. Otherwise, you are just parroting back what they said, which is far less impactful.

Eliminating external distractions is indispensable in establishing an environment that is receptive to the art of active listening. This one smacks me in the face! In our ever-connected, fast-paced world, it's incredibly shallow to be drawn away by the magnetism of buzzing phones or the hum of background conversations. Therefore, selecting an environment that is serene and comfortable for discussions significantly amplifies focus and immersion. Envision it as crafting the perfect backdrop for an unapologetically open exchange of ideas. Addressing digital interruptions is equally critical; actively consider disabling notifications or strategically placing your phone beyond sight during interactions, to forge a space free of diversions.

Interactive Element: Active Listening Checklist

To seamlessly weave these techniques into your everyday interactions, consider employing this straightforward checklist to guide your active listening endeavors.

Let's use the mnemonic: **"L.I.S.T.E.N."**

Each letter maps to a specific behavior that supports active listening:

- **L – Look** at the speaker (Maintain Eye Contact). Consistently engage in making intentional eye contact with the speaker, conveying genuine interest.

- **I – Indicate** engagement (Use Affirmative Gestures like nodding and smiling). Implement nods or subtle, reassuring smiles to demonstrate active engagement.

- **S – Stay Silent** (Practice Patience and don't interrupt). Prioritize allowing the speaker to conclude their narrative before offering your response.

- **T – Tell Back** what you heard (Summarize Key Points). Articulate back what you've comprehended to ensure mutual clarity and understanding.

- **E – Eliminate** distractions (Minimize Distractions and focus your attention). Opt for quiet settings and silent digital companions to maintain focus.

- **N – Notice** emotions and body language (bonus: tuning into unspoken cues shows true empathy)

By integrating these elements, you're embarking on a transformative journey towards becoming a significantly more adept listener. Through embracing these techniques, you're not simply acquiring listening skills; you're cultivating the dual arts of empathy and intentionality.

Speaking of empathy, let's talk about that next.

Developing Empathy Radar

Understanding how you feel, and why, can go a long way in helping you connect with others. You don't need to be an emotional genius or have a sixth sense. It just takes paying attention. The better you get at noticing your own reactions, when you feel frustrated, excited, nervous, or proud, the easier it becomes to recognize those same feelings in other people.

One way to build this awareness is by tracking what triggers strong emotions in your daily life. Nothing fancy. Just jot down a quick note in your phone or a notebook about what happened and how it made you feel. Over time, you'll start to spot patterns. That insight gives you more control and helps you respond, not just react, in conversations.

You can also build this skill by taking a few minutes each day to check in with yourself. Ask: "What am I feeling right now, and why?" No need to overthink it or judge it. Just notice it. The more often you do this, the easier it gets to stay grounded, and to pick up on what others might be feeling, too.

Once you've honed your emotional awareness, recognizing emotional cues becomes your next focus. People often reveal their feelings through subtle verbal and non-verbal signals. Tone of voice changes can indicate excitement or frustration, while facial expressions and body language often speak louder than words. Practice identifying these cues in everyday interactions. Role-playing scenarios with friends can help. For instance, ask a friend (or again ChatGPT voice) to express different emotions using only their voice or gestures, and try to identify each one. This exercise sharpens your ability to pick up on cues that might otherwise go unnoticed, enhancing your empathetic engagement.

ChatGPT Voice Prompt: Emotional Cue Practice
"Hi ChatGPT, I'd like to practice recognizing emotional cues. Can you role-play different emotional tones with me, using only your voice in your responses? For each round, say a short sentence while expressing a specific emotion like excitement, frustration, sadness, or boredom. Don't tell me which one, just act it out. After each one, pause so I can guess the emotion. Then let me know if I got it right and give me a little feedback before moving on to the next emotion."

Understanding others requires stepping into their shoes, a practice known as **perspective-taking.** This involves imagining yourself in someone else's situation to better grasp their feelings and motivations. Engage in exercises where you consider someone else's challenges or experiences from their viewpoint. Picture a colleague who seems stressed about a project deadline. Instead of seeing them as irritable, imagine their pressure and how it affects them. Reading stories about diverse experiences also broadens your perspective. When you immerse yourself in narratives different from your own, you gain insights into lives unlike yours, fostering more profound empathy.

Many struggle to express empathy authentically, especially when trying to balance genuine compassion with sincerity. It's central that your empathy feels real and not like a rehearsed script. Use language that conveys understanding and warmth. Simple phrases like "I can imagine how that feels" or "That sounds really challenging" can go a long way in making someone feel supported. The key is to listen actively and respond in ways that **reflect genuine care**. Remember to stay true to yourself; authenticity is felt on both sides of a conversation. If you naturally express empathy through humor, use it carefully to lighten the mood without diminishing the other person's experience.

Journaling Prompt: Enhancing Emotional Awareness

- **Reflect on a Recent Interaction:** Think of a recent conversation where emotions ran high. Write about your feelings during the exchange and what might have been driving them.

- **Identify Emotional Cues:** Note any verbal or non-verbal signals indicating the other person's feelings. What did their tone or body language reveal?

- **Explore Perspective-Taking:** Consider the situation from their point of view. What external factors might have influenced their emotions?

By practicing this daily, you not only start to become more empathetic but also evolve into a more connected and understanding communicator. You are developing your own type of empathy radar, not just for reading others but also for understanding yourself better, promoting a deeper connection with your own emotions and those around you.

When you build emotional awareness, notice subtle cues, put yourself in someone else's shoes, and respond with genuine empathy, your conversations become more real, personal, and meaningful.

Building Confidence Through Empathy

Empathy not only improves interactions with others but also boosts your own confidence. By understanding others' perspectives, you can approach conversations with less anxiety and more assurance.

Case Study: Mark Learns to Lead with Empathy

When I first met Mark, he was midway through a career pivot. He had just taken on a new role in a client-facing position after years of working behind the scenes in a technical support role. On paper, he had everything he needed to succeed: deep expertise, a calm demeanor, and a willingness to learn. But in person? Mark was visibly anxious in meetings. His voice shook when he spoke up. He often avoided eye contact. "I just never know what to say," he told me. "I overthink every word and replay it afterward, worrying I sounded stupid."

In our early conversations, we discovered that Mark's fear wasn't about a lack of knowledge, it was about a fear of being judged. Like many people, he was so focused on how *he* was coming across that he couldn't fully engage with the person in front of him.

So I asked him a question: "What if you stopped trying to be impressive and just tried to be curious?"

That's where we started. Instead of focusing on getting every word right, Mark began focusing on what *others* were feeling. In client calls, he made it a goal to pick up on tone, word choice, and emotional undercurrents. Was someone frustrated? Confused? Excited but unsure how to move forward? He started jotting down what he noticed, not just about the task at hand but also about how the other person *seemed* to be doing.

And something shifted.

"I realized I wasn't the only nervous one in the room," Mark told me. "Once I focused on the client's experience, what they might need, what might be stressing them out, I got out of my own head. The conversation wasn't about me anymore. That helped."

Empathy gave Mark a map. The better he got at reading others' emotions, the more confident he became in navigating each conversation. He started asking better questions, responding more calmly to tension, and even using moments of silence to let people share more. In time, those clients began seeking him out directly, not because he had the flashiest presentation, but because they felt understood.

Mark's confidence didn't come from pretending to be someone he wasn't. It came from turning his attention outward, toward connection. And it turns out, that's where the most powerful conversations start.

Discussion Prompt: Shifting the Focus Builds Confidence

Think about a time when you felt nervous in a conversation or social situation. Where was your attention, on yourself, or on the other person? It was on yourself, of course!

Now, imagine flipping that focus. What might have changed if you had tuned in to the other person's emotions, needs, or experience instead of your own insecurities?

Take a moment to reflect or jot down:

- A recent or upcoming situation where you feel uncertain or anxious

- One way you could shift your focus to the other person's experience

- A question you could ask or a sign of empathy you could show in that moment

Remember: sometimes the fastest way to build confidence isn't to "feel more confident", it's to get curious about someone else. That's where real connection (and growth) begins.

Empathy isn't just something that makes you a better communicator, it's something that makes you more confident, too. When you start seeing the world through other people's eyes, conversations feel less like a performance and more like a shared experience. You connect more deeply, listen more fully, and respond with more clarity. And the bonus? You stop second-guessing yourself so much.

Keep empathy in your toolbox as you grow, it's one of the most powerful tools you have for building trust, connection, and confidence in every part of your life.

Using Paraphrasing to Show Understanding

Here is a scenario. You are sitting across from a friend who's pouring their heart out about a recent breakup. They're sharing something deeply personal, and you want them to know you're truly listening. This is where paraphrasing comes into play. It's not just restating; **it's about showing you get it.**

When you rephrase what someone says, you offer validation, making them feel understood. It's like saying, "I'm here with you in this moment." Effective paraphrasing involves capturing **the essence of their message**. Instead of merely echoing back their words, like a parrot does. You instead focus on the meaning. This not only shows you've been listening but also validates their experience.

This is where understanding the difference between parroting and paraphrasing becomes important. Parroting is like a recording, repeating words without having to grasp the substance. Paraphrasing, on the other hand, captures the underlying meaning. It's about you hearing and then having to translate the speaker's thoughts into your own words while retaining the original intent.

Techniques to develop this skill involve actively listening for key points and emotions, then rephrasing them in a way that reflects your understanding. Imagine your friend shares their frustration about being overlooked at work. Rather than repeating, "You feel ignored," you might say, "It seems like you're feeling undervalued at your job." This approach affirms their feelings and encourages further dialogue.

Case Study: Vanessa Learns to Listen Differently

When I first started working with Vanessa, she told me she often felt helpless in conversations with friends, especially when someone was going through something hard. "I never know what to say," she admitted. "I want to be supportive, but I feel like I always end up giving advice or just nodding awkwardly."

Vanessa's a warm, thoughtful person by nature. The issue wasn't a lack of care, it was a lack of clarity on *how* to show that care. So, we worked on one skill that can completely transform emotional conversations: **paraphrasing**.

We began by talking through a real situation she'd recently experienced. A close friend had opened up about a painful breakup. While her instinct had been to say something like, "Yeah, that sounds really tough," she later realized she hadn't actually shown that she *understood* what her friend was feeling. "I was listening," she said. "But I wasn't reflecting anything back."

That's where we dug in. I explained the difference between parroting, just repeating someone's words back to them, and paraphrasing, which is about reflecting the meaning behind those words. Parroting might sound like, "You're upset because he left." But paraphrasing sounds more like, "It sounds like you're feeling blindsided and hurt, especially after investing so much in that relationship."

We practiced using everyday moments. I'd give her short, emotional statements, like a friend saying, "I just feel like no one at work sees what I actually do", and she'd try to rephrase it in a way that captured the emotion and perspective. Slowly, she started getting it.

"It's weird," she said at one point. **"Once I stopped trying to fix things and just tried to reflect what I heard, people actually opened up more."**

Vanessa now uses paraphrasing not just with friends, but in work meetings, with her partner, even when navigating tough conversations with her mom. It's given her a confidence she never expected, and the people in her life can feel the difference.

ChatGPT Voice Practice: Paraphrasing Emotional Moments

Now it's your turn to build this skill.

Use the voice feature in ChatGPT to simulate real emotional conversations. You'll practice hearing someone's message and reflecting it back, not word-for-word, but in your own language, with empathy.

> ### ChatGPT Voice Prompt: Paraphrasing
> "Hi ChatGPT, I want to practice paraphrasing in emotional conversations. Please play the role of a friend sharing a tough experience. Say something emotionally vulnerable, like you're talking about a breakup, stress at work, or feeling left out. After you share, pause and let me paraphrase what you said in my own words. Then give me gentle feedback, tell me if I captured the meaning correctly or missed something important. Let's do a few different examples together."

Final Thoughts on Paraphrasing

The power of paraphrasing extends beyond understanding, it builds trust and rapport. When people feel heard and understood, it lays the foundation for stronger relationships.

Guidelines for using paraphrasing to resolve misunderstandings focus on empathy and patience. When tensions arise due to miscommunication, approach the situation calmly and with an open mind. Start by acknowledging the other person's viewpoint before paraphrasing their statements.

Paraphrasing Cheat Sheet

How to Reflect Emotion, Not Just Repeat Words

What Paraphrasing *Is*:

- Restating what someone said using your *own* words

- Focusing on the *meaning* and *emotion* behind the message

- A way to show you're listening and that you *get it*

What It's *Not*:

- Parroting (just repeating their exact words)

- Giving advice right away

- Minimizing or dismissing their feelings

Sentence Starters for Paraphrasing

Try starting with one of these phrases:

- "It sounds like you're feeling..."

- "What I'm hearing is..."

- "So you're saying..."

- "It seems like what really hit you was..."

- "You're feeling [emotion] because..."

- "Let me see if I've got this right..."

As you practice these techniques regularly, notice how they enhance your ability to relate to others more deeply. With each interaction, you'll find yourself naturally integrating these skills into your repertoire, creating an environment where empathy thrives and relationships flourish.

Asking Questions

Case Study: Jordan Learns to Ask Instead of Assume

Jordan had always been one of those people who flew under the radar at work, not in a bad way, just quiet, steady, never ruffled. When we started working together, he'd recently been promoted into a project manager role at a mid-sized consulting firm, and suddenly everything felt different. "I used to just keep my head down and do the work," he told me. "Now I'm in meetings all day, and half the time I'm pretending I understand what people are saying."

He wasn't alone in that. Like a lot of smart, capable professionals, Jordan didn't want to interrupt the flow of a meeting or risk sounding like he wasn't following along. But all that nodding, smiling, and silent guessing? It was costing him clarity, and confidence.

One of the first things I asked was: "What if the smartest person in the room isn't the one who nods, but the one who asks the clearest question?"

That idea struck a chord. Together, we practiced what it looks like to ask **clarifying questions** in real time. Jordan learned how to say things like:

- "Just so I'm clear, when you say X, are you referring to the client deliverables or the internal version?"

- "That's helpful, can you walk me through how that ties into the Q3 targets?"

- "Can we back up for a second? I want to make sure I'm understanding your approach."

At first, Jordan was afraid these would make him seem slow or unprepared. But what he found was the opposite. People started turning to *him* to rephrase and summarize key points. He wasn't just understanding things better, he was helping *others* understand, too. And that made him feel like a true leader in the room.

"I always thought asking questions would make me look weak," he said. "Now I see it's the opposite. It shows I care enough to get it right."

Asking Clarifying Questions

When it comes to asking clarifying question, how you frame your question is essential. Finding that right **balance between curiosity and respect**. The goal is to encourage the speaker to express more without intimidation, thereby fostering a sense of openness rather than defensiveness. Open-ended questions are your steadfast allies in achieving this balance. They do not just solicit responses but rather expansive, insightful engagements.

For instance, instead of the straightforward and sometimes limiting inquiry, "Did you mean X?", you might instead opt for "Could you tell me more about how you arrived at that conclusion?" This not only elicits more detailed answers but also signals to the speaker your respect and genuine interest in their viewpoint. It's important to steer clear of leading questions which might inadvertently guide the conversation toward a presupposed direction. Instead, remaining anchored in neutrality allows for the free expression of thoughts, enabling the speaker to reveal their genuine perspectives uncolored by external bias.

Within many conversations lie hidden assumptions, those unspoken beliefs or expectations that subtly infuse dialogue with layers of intent and meaning. Utilizing questions to unearth these assumptions can be incredibly enlightening, both to the asker and the speaker. When someone makes a statement sparking your curiosity, a gentle, probing question such as "What makes you feel that way?" or "What led you to think that?" invites the speaker to pause, reflect, and articulate the underlying thought processes driving their statements. This approach provides a glimpse into their mindset and enriches your understanding.

ChatGPT Voice Practice: Mastering Clarifying Questions

Now let's help you build the same skill Jordan did, by practicing out loud.

Use the voice feature in ChatGPT to simulate conversation scenarios where things aren't 100% clear. You'll practice listening, spotting vague or incomplete information, and asking thoughtful clarifying questions.

> **ChatGPT Voice Prompt: Clarifying Questions Practice**
> "Hi ChatGPT, I want to practice asking clarifying questions in a conversation. Please act like a colleague or someone I'm meeting with. Start by saying something a little vague, confusing, or full of jargon, like in a meeting where I might not fully understand what's being said. After you speak, pause and let me ask a clarifying question. Then give me feedback on how clear and respectful my question was. Let's run through a few different scenarios."

An equilibrium in questioning and listening is a balance we must all find. An overabundance of questions may risk overwhelming the speaker, disrupting the flow of conversation. Observing subtle cues, such as hesitation or frequent pauses, can signal the need for enhanced listening versus probing more. Strategies for maintaining this delicate balance include keenly observing body language and tonal inflections, attuned to signs of comfort or discomfort. Encouraging a natural rhythm necessitates allowing silence to pervade moments for thoughtful reflection before pursuing another query.

Clarifying Questions Tip Card: Use These When You Need More Info

Basic Clarifiers

- "Can you walk me through that a bit more?"

- "When you say ____, what exactly do you mean?"

- "Just so I'm clear, are we talking about [X] or [Y]?"

To Dig Into Details

- "Could you explain how that works in practice?"

- "What would that look like step by step?"

- "Can you give me an example of what you mean?"

To Uncover Assumptions

- "What's the thinking behind that?"

- "What led you to that conclusion?"

- "What are we assuming to be true here?"

To Tie Things Together

- "How does that connect with what we discussed earlier?"

- "What's the end goal with this?"

- "Can you help me understand how this fits into the bigger picture?"

Watch Out For These Traps

- Don't ask yes/no questions when you need more insight.

- Avoid jumping in with your opinion, ask *before* offering ideas.

- Keep your tone neutral and curious, not confrontational.

Pro Tip: Say It With Confidence

You don't need to apologize for asking. Try:

- "I want to make sure I'm tracking with you."

- "Let me check my understanding here."

- "That makes sense, I'd love to hear more about..."

Chapter Wrap: Listening That Connects

This chapter is all about connection, the kind that goes deeper than small talk and makes **people feel truly seen, heard, and valued**. We explored how active listening isn't just about staying quiet, it's about staying present. Through eye contact, gestures, patience, and thoughtful reflection, you show others they matter. And when you do that, you open the door to real trust.

We also dove into the power of empathy, not as a fluffy buzzword, but as a practical tool that helps you communicate better *and* feel more confident. When you tune into what someone else is feeling, you stop overthinking your own performance and start building real relationships. Whether it's through paraphrasing, perspective-taking, or asking thoughtful, clarifying questions, empathy helps you shift the spotlight from insecurity to connection.

You don't have to master every technique overnight. But every time you slow down, listen closely, reflect honestly, and ask with curiosity, you're building the kind of communication that changes conversations and changes you.

Build the Life You Came For

What should you do next?

- In one conversation today, try combining these two powerful practices:

  - **Use the "Tell Me More" Prompt**
    When someone shares something with you, big or small, ask, "Tell me more about that." It signals genuine curiosity and encourages a deeper connection instantly.

  - **Mirror Back One Key Emotion**
    After they've shared more, reflect their emotion back with something like: *"It sounds like that was really [emotion] for you,"* or *"You seem [emotion] about that."* It's a simple way to build trust through empathy.

CHAPTER FOUR

— • —

THE HIDDEN LANGUAGE EVERYONE SPEAKS

NON-VERBAL COMMUNICATION

Body Language & The Power of Non-Verbal Communication

Case Study: Maya Reads the Room

When I first met Maya, she was stepping into a new leadership role after a recent promotion. Smart, sharp, and incredibly thoughtful, Maya had always done her best work behind the scenes, running numbers, building systems, keeping things organized. But with her new title came a new expectation: speak up, lead meetings, and present ideas in a room full of senior leaders.

In one of our early coaching sessions, she told me about a meeting that left her feeling defeated. "I prepped for days," she said. "I knew my plan was solid. But about halfway through, I completely lost my confidence."

I asked what happened.

She described standing at the head of a long conference table, walking her team through a proposed process change. Everything was going fine, until she locked eyes with Carl, one of the more seasoned VPs. "He was sitting across from me with his arms crossed, this half-frown on his face. He wasn't saying anything. Just... staring." Maya paused. "I couldn't tell if he hated the idea or was just bored. But it completely threw me."

That moment stuck with her, not because Carl had actually objected to her idea (he hadn't), but because the unspoken tension made her doubt herself.

So, we unpacked it.

We talked through what body language often signals, and what it sometimes doesn't. Arms crossed? Could mean defensiveness, yes. But also cold temperature. Or just a habit. The furrowed brow? Could be disagreement, or deep concentration. The key, I explained, is context. One gesture alone doesn't tell the whole story, but reading a combination of cues can give you a clearer picture. Did he lean forward during any part of her talk? Did he make eye contact, nod, or glance down at notes?

Then we practiced a few tools Maya could use in the moment:

- Noticing, but not immediately reacting, to body language shifts

- Asking clarifying questions to re-engage someone who seems disconnected

- Using open gestures herself to project calm and confidence

She also learned to use body language as a feedback loop. "Now when I see someone's posture shift, I don't spiral," she told me later. "I check in. Sometimes I say, 'Does that sound right to you?' or 'I'm curious what's on your mind.' That opens the door, instead of closing it."

Over time, Maya stopped fearing the silence in the room. She started to trust her own presence, and to read the nonverbal energy as one part of a much bigger communication landscape.

The next time Carl crossed his arms in a meeting, she didn't flinch.

She smiled, continued with her pitch, and afterward? He emailed her with a note: *"Well done today. Your idea's worth pursuing."*

Body Language

This is the silent power of body language, an unspoken mode of expression that resonates with profound significance even if no syllables are spoken. Mastering the subtle cues of body language can transform the way you connect with others, helping you naturally **project confidence, empathy, and authority without saying a word.**

At the core of effective body language lies posture, a powerful indicator of not only how you perceive yourself but also how others perceive you. **Standing tall, with shoulders back and head held high,** can exude a sense of confidence and command a measure of respect that reverberates within the room. By contrast, when you slouch or hunch over, even in moments of deep concentration, it might unintentionally signal insecurity or disinterest, regardless of your true intentions. Gestures play a pivotal role as well.

Open gestures, such as displaying your palms or keeping your arms relaxed by your side, denote openness, a willingness to engage, and approachability. Conversely, closed gestures, such as crossing your arms tightly or subtly turning your body away from the speaker, may indicate defensiveness or discomfort, creating an invisible barrier that can inhibit connectivity.

Body language doesn't have to be mysterious or overly complicated. You don't need to become an expert to start noticing some of the most common nonverbal signals. For example, crossed arms often suggest someone is feeling guarded or unsure, while leaning in shows interest and engagement. These small cues can help you read the room and respond with more understanding.

One helpful technique is mirroring, subtly matching someone's posture or gestures. It's a natural way to build connection and show you're in sync. Just be subtle about it, no copying movements like a mime.

And here's something important: sometimes people say one thing but their body says something else. That mismatch can tell you a lot. Like when someone says they're "fine," but their shoulders are tense and their smile seems forced. Paying attention to these signals helps you catch what's really going on, especially in conversations that matter. You're not looking for hidden secrets, just trying to better understand what someone might be feeling beyond their words.

If you want your body language to work for you, not against you, start being intentional about how you use it. Simple gestures, like using your hands to highlight key points during a presentation, can help make your words more impactful. Practicing an open stance, shoulders back, arms relaxed, can project confidence even when you're feeling unsure. The goal isn't to fake it, but to reinforce your message with how you show up physically. When your body matches your words, people are more likely to trust you and feel comfortable engaging in return.

Interactive Element: Body Language Awareness Exercise

1. **Observe Others:** Dedicate a day to consciously observing people's body language in various settings, meetings, social gatherings, or public spaces such as coffee shops or parks. Pay attention to common gestures, postures, and the subtle shifts in expression.

2. **Self-Reflection:** Engage in self-reflection regarding your own body language during interactions. Are there recurring patterns that emerge? How do others respond to the non-verbal signals you project, and do they align with your intentions?

3. **Practice Intentional Gestures:** Choose three distinct gestures that convey confidence and openness, perhaps adopting a relaxed stance, utilizing open palm gestures, or maintaining consistent eye contact. Practice integrating them naturally into conversations, observing discernible changes in how others react and interact with you.

Take your practice to the next level.

Practice Activity: Record Yourself and Review with ChatGPT

To improve how you use gestures in real conversations, try this practical exercise using video and ChatGPT's feedback feature. It'll help you spot what's working, and what might be sending mixed signals, so you can build more confident, intentional habits.

1. **Pick Three Gestures to Focus On** Choose three specific gestures that communicate openness and confidence. These could include:

   ◦ A relaxed, upright stance (not slouching or shifting nervously)

   ◦ Open palm gestures while speaking (instead of clenched fists or hiding your hands)

   ◦ Steady, comfortable eye contact when making a point

2. **Record Yourself** Using your phone or webcam, record a short video of yourself talking. It could be a mock introduction, a sample of explaining something you know well, or even a pretend conversation. Try to naturally integrate the three gestures you selected.

3. **Upload to ChatGPT for Feedback** Once recorded, upload your video to ChatGPT. Then say:

> **ChatGPT Voice Prompt: Body Language Practice**
> "Hi ChatGPT, I'm working on using confident body language in conversation. I've recorded a short video practicing three gestures, relaxed stance, open palms, and steady eye contact. Please give me feedback on how naturally and effectively I used them, and any suggestions for improvement."

• **Review and Reflect** Pay attention to the feedback, especially whether the gestures felt authentic or forced. Did they match your tone and words? Were they consistent throughout, or did they fade in and out?

• **Repeat and Refine** Practice again with slight adjustments. You might try adding a fourth gesture or working in front of a mirror before recording your next video. Over time, these movements will become more second nature and less like rehearsed theater.

When you start paying attention to body language in your everyday conversations, you'll get better at reading what's really going on, beyond just words. This awareness helps you connect more deeply, build trust more naturally, and communicate in ways that feel more genuine, even when nothing is being said at all.

More on Eye Contact

Eye contact holds a unique power in communication, influencing perceptions of confidence and trustworthiness. It's a connection that words alone often struggle to achieve (as anyone who has been in love can confirm). When you maintain eye contact, you signal engagement, making the other person feel valued and heard. Studies have shown that eye contact can increase persuasiveness, making your arguments more compelling and your presence more commanding.

Yet, not all eye contact is created equal. Cultural norms play a significant role in how eye contact is perceived, and what feels natural in one culture might be uncomfortable in another. For instance, in many Western cultures, direct eye contact is seen as a sign of confidence and honesty. However, in some Asian cultures, too much eye contact may be perceived as confrontational or disrespectful. Recognizing these differences is necessary when interacting in diverse settings. Pay attention to how people around you use eye contact and adjust accordingly. If you notice someone averting their gaze, it might be a cue to soften your approach.

Work to achieve a balanced approach to eye contact. Too much eye contact can feel intimidating, while too little might suggest disinterest. The key lies in finding a comfortable middle ground. Practice holding eye contact for just a few seconds longer than usual before glancing away. This brief extension can convey confidence without overstepping boundaries. Exercises involving mirrors or partners can help. Look into a mirror and practice different durations of eye contact to see what feels natural. Practice in low-stake / low-stress situations, again when ordering your coffee or in line at Chipotle. What feels comfortable but also engaging?

In professional settings, mastering the subtleties of eye contact can elevate your communication game. During presentations or negotiations, eye contact can project **authority and command attention**. Conversely, in more casual interactions, it can foster a sense of **warmth and approachability**. Consider how politicians or public speakers use eye contact, they sweep the room with their gaze, ensuring everyone feels included in the conversation. This technique creates a collective sense of engagement, fostering an inclusive environment.

Interactive Element: Eye Contact Reflection Exercise

1. **Observe and Reflect:** Spend a day observing how people use eye contact in various settings, workplaces, social gatherings, or public places like cafes or shopping centers. Focus on the people you admire and want to develop into. Note the differences and similarities in how they engage visually.

2. **Self-Assessment:** Reflect on your own use of eye contact during interactions. Are there patterns? Do you tend to make more or less eye contact depending on the situation? Consider how others respond to your gaze.

3. **Practice with Intention:** Choose specific interactions where you'll consciously adjust your eye contact, perhaps by holding it a bit longer during conversations with colleagues or softening it in more casual settings. Notice how these changes affect the dynamics of the interaction.

Eye contact is a powerful tool that enhances communication on multiple levels. Through practice you will master its nuances, and in doing so enrich your interactions, creating connections that are not only visible but also deeply felt by those around you.

Your Face Is Louder Than You Think

Facial expressions often conveying more than words ever could. Smiling is the universal sign of friendliness, breaking barriers and inviting connection – even bridging language barriers. Cross-cultural studies reveal the remarkable consistency in how these emotions are expressed and understood. Understanding these expressions allows you to navigate with ease, ensuring your messages are received as intended.

Case Study: Learning to Let My Face Speak Too

For years, I thought I was a pretty decent communicator, clear, intentional, and even a little witty when the moment called for it. But it wasn't until a colleague gave me some unexpected feedback that I realized I was missing one crucial piece: my face.

It happened during a presentation I was genuinely excited about. I had spent days preparing and felt confident in my ideas. After the meeting, a coworker I trust pulled me aside and said, "Your content was great, but you looked like you weren't enjoying it at all. You seemed tense."

I was surprised. On the inside, I had been fully engaged and proud of what I shared. But apparently, my face hadn't gotten the memo. That moment stayed with me. If I was passionate about something but looked flat or serious, how many other times had I unintentionally sent the wrong message?

That night, I stood in front of a mirror and talked through the opening of that same presentation. I noticed something immediately: my eyebrows were tight, my jaw slightly clenched. No wonder it didn't come across well. I tried again, this time letting myself actually smile when I hit a point I loved. I relaxed my face. I even let my eyes widen with enthusiasm instead of keeping them in "serious mode."

It felt awkward at first, almost like I was acting. But over time, I started integrating facial expressions more naturally into everyday interactions. I practiced small things first: a warm smile when greeting someone, an intentionally curious look when asking a question, a soft expression when listening to something emotional.

What I learned is this: facial expressions aren't extras in communication. They're central. When your face matches your intention, people connect with you faster and trust you more. I didn't need to become overly animated or fake, I just needed to be congruent.

Now, whether I'm leading a meeting, coaching someone, or even just chatting in the hallway, I'm more aware of what my face is saying. And that awareness has changed the way people respond to me. Smiles get returned. Tension drops. Conversations flow more easily.

Facial expressions are a link, one I didn't even realize I was neglecting. But once I stepped onto it, I found a whole new level of connection waiting on the other side.

Supercharge Your Message

Enhancing verbal messages with facial expressions can transform your communication from mundane to memorable. When you speak with enthusiasm, **let your eyes light up** and your **smile widen.** Your expression becomes an exclamation point on your words, amplifying your message and ensuring it resonates. Similarly, when conveying empathy, **soften your gaze** and **nod gently,** showing you genuinely understand and care.

Practicing expressive communication **in front of a mirror** can be surprisingly enlightening. Observe how your face naturally reacts to different emotions and consider how you might adjust these expressions to better align with your intended message.

In professional settings, managing facial expressions takes on added importance. You might find yourself in a tense meeting, where every raised eyebrow and pursed lip is scrutinized for hidden meaning. During difficult conversations, maintaining composure is key. Practice keeping a neutral expression when needed, preventing emotions from betraying your thoughts prematurely. Techniques such as focusing on controlled breathing or slightly redirecting your gaze can help maintain this composure. Recognizing that **not every emotion needs to be displayed** immediately allows for thoughtful responses and maintains professionalism.

Consider how politicians or public figures use expressions during speeches or debates, each smile or frown carefully calculated to convey sincerity or authority. In everyday interactions, this same awareness helps you during complex social dynamics, ensuring that your face mirrors the message you wish to convey.

Interactive Element: Expression Exercise

1. **Observe Faces:** Spend time observing facial expressions in various settings, during conversations with friends or in public places like cafes or parks. Note how expressions change based on context and interaction dynamics.

2. **Self-Reflection:** Reflect on your own facial expressions throughout a typical day. How do they shift in different situations? Are there patterns that emerge in specific contexts? If you walk pass a mirror, notice what your "resting" face is sending out to the world.

3. **Practice Expressiveness:** Choose specific interactions where you'll consciously adjust your expressions to match the tone, perhaps by softening your gaze when offering support or widening your eyes when sharing excitement. Notice how these adjustments affect the reactions of those around you.

4. **Want to Have Fun**: Want to see just how powerful facial expressions really are? Try this: in a safe, casual conversation with a friend, throw in a completely unexpected expression. If they're telling you something exciting, respond with a furrowed brow. Or deliver good news, with a dead-serious frown. Watch what happens. Chances are, they'll stop mid-sentence and ask, "Wait... are you okay?" That's how quickly your face can override your words. It's instant, instinctive, and impossible to ignore.

By tuning into the impact of facial expressions, you unlock a deeper, more human layer of communication, one where your presence speaks just as loudly as your words. With this awareness, every interaction becomes a chance to build trust, express authenticity, and create meaningful connection.

How You Say It Matters

Case Study: Finding My Voice, Literally

I used to think I was pretty clear when I spoke. I chose my words carefully, made my point, and tried to keep things efficient. But then one day, someone told me something that genuinely caught me off guard: "You know, sometimes it's hard to tell if you're excited or just going through the motions."

Ouch.

Of all people, this feedback came from my wife! We'd been talking about a project at work that I was genuinely excited about, something I had poured energy into for weeks. But apparently, I said it with all the emotional enthusiasm of reading a shipping receipt. Flat tone, no variation, totally monotone. That comment stuck with me.

So later that week, I decided to test it. I recorded myself talking, just a 60-second voice note where I explained something I was proud of. And sure enough, when I played it back, I couldn't believe how disconnected it sounded. My words said one thing, but my tone said something completely different. No rise, no warmth, no sense of personal connection. Just...flat.

That's when I realized how much tone and pitch matter. It wasn't that I didn't care, I did. But somewhere along the way, I had gotten so focused on "sounding professional" or "staying calm" that I stripped all the natural expression out of my voice.

So I started paying attention to how others talked. The way a friend's voice lifted when they shared good news. How a pause and drop in pitch could make a statement land with confidence. I started practicing, just a little at a time, adding energy to greetings, softening my tone when showing empathy, using vocal variation to emphasize key points.

It wasn't about being performative. It was about aligning how I *felt* with how I *sounded.*

Now, when I speak, whether I'm presenting, catching up with a friend, or coaching someone through a tough moment, I try to bring my full voice with me. Not just the words, but the meaning behind them.

Tone and pitch used to be invisible to me. Now, they're some of my most important tools.

Tone & Pitch

These often-overlooked components of spoken discourse, function as subtle yet potent tools that enrich our interactions, imbuing them with depth and layered significance. They can dramatically alter the perception and reception of a message, crafting the crucial distinction between sarcasm and sincerity.

A **buoyant tone** transforms a simple greeting into a heartfelt welcome, radiating warmth and friendliness. In stark contrast, a flat or monotonous delivery might unintentionally express a lack of interest or even apathy, changing the undertone of the conversation entirely. Similarly, pitch possesses the remarkable **ability to influence our perception** of authority and confidence. Numerous studies have shown that lower pitches tend to exude a sense of **power and surety**, endowing your words with a sense of finality and assurance. However, raising your pitch can signal **uncertainty or pose a question**, even when that's not the intended meaning.

A rising intonation at the end of a sentence can signal a question or imply doubt, subtly inviting validation or agreement from your listener. Conversely, a descending pitch as you finish can emphasize authority or convey firm belief, leaving little room for misinterpretation. These patterns are not arbitrary; they are deeply embedded in our communication habits and provide valuable insights into the speaker's emotional state or intent.

By adapting your tone and pitch to align with various situations, you can significantly improve your effectiveness in communication. Experimenting with vocal modulation by reading aloud or reciting passages imbued with different emotional undertones allows you to observe and refine how tone and pitch can substantially alter perception. Let's try it!

ChatGPT Voice Practice: Finding the Right Tone

Voice Prompt to Speak into ChatGPT

"Hi ChatGPT, I'm working on improving my tone and pitch when I speak. Can we practice together? I'll say a few short phrases, and I'd like you to tell me how my tone comes across, like if I sound enthusiastic, bored, confident, or unsure. After each phrase, please give me gentle feedback and suggest how I might adjust my tone or pitch to better match my intention. Let's do a few rounds together."

Optional Phrases to Try Saying Out Loud During the Practice:

1. "I'm really excited about this idea."

2. "That's something I've been thinking a lot about."

3. "I'm not sure how to move forward."

4. "Thanks for meeting with me today."

5. "This part is especially important."

These lines will give you a starting point to test how they *sound*, not just what they say. It's a great way to bring more warmth, confidence, and intentionality into their everyday conversations.

Tone and pitch are dynamic elements of communication. Your ability to leverage these vocal tools will enrich conversations and attract people to you.

Chapter Wrap: Speaking without Words

Communication isn't just about what you say, it's about how you show up. In this chapter, we explored the often-overlooked power of non-verbal cues: body language, facial expressions, tone, pitch, and eye contact. These subtle signals influence how your words are received and how connected people feel to you.

You learned how to read common body language cues, how to adjust your posture and gestures for more impact, and how facial expressions can either enhance or contradict your message. You learned how tone and pitch add emotional weight to your words and how mastering eye contact helps build trust. **The big takeaway:** Non-verbal communication isn't about performance, it's about alignment. When your body, face, and voice match your message, you come across as more genuine, more confident, and more human.

Build the Life You Came For

What should you do next?

- **Observe Three People Today (Silently)**
  Choose three people to observe (in person or on video) and note their posture, eye contact, gestures, and tone. Try to guess their mood or message before you hear their words.

- **EXTRA CREDIT EXERCISE: Record Yourself During a Conversation (or a Mock One)**
  Use your phone to record a video of yourself talking, then watch it back with no sound. What does your body language say? Are your expressions, posture, and gestures aligned with your message?

CHAPTER FIVE

— • —

HOW TO BE BOLD WITHOUT BEING LOUD

CONFIDENCE & ASSERTIVENESS

Confidence-Building Strategies

Let's be real, this chapter might be the hardest one yet.

It definitely was for me. Self-reflection hasn't always been my strength, and if you're like me, looking inward can feel uncomfortable or even overwhelming. But this chapter isn't about perfecting how you talk to others, it's about getting more comfortable with yourself. And that's where real transformation begins. **Don't skip this part.** The way we show up in conversations starts with the way we see ourselves.

Transforming Social Anxiety into Social Strength

Case Study: How I Turned My Social Anxiety Into a Strength

I still remember one particular networking event like it happened last week. It was held in the lobby of a downtown hotel in Minneapolis, dim lighting, name tags on lanyards, the soft clinking of glasses (at least they served alcohol... right!), and a buzz of polite small talk all around. I had driven there straight from work, sat in the parking ramp for ten full minutes, debating whether to walk in or turn around and go home. I was sweating, my heart was pounding, and my stomach felt weird. All trying to convince me to go home.

But I went in anyway.

At that point in my life, social anxiety was a quiet but constant presence. I didn't dread people, I dreaded being judged. The awkward silences. The fear of saying the wrong thing. Not knowing what to say. The feeling that I didn't really belong. And walking into a room full of confident-looking strangers felt like walking into a place I didn't belong in and wasn't supposed to be.

What helped me shift was a coaching conversation I had just weeks earlier. I had been working with a woman named Sarah who asked me a powerful question: "What if you stop trying to impress people, and instead focus on just being curious?" Interesting! I didn't need to be the most interesting person in the room. I just had to be present, and interested. This isn't the first time this idea has come up for us!

So that night, I tried something new. Instead of scanning the room for someone to impress, I looked for someone who seemed just as out of place as I felt. I found a guy standing by the coffee station, fidgeting with his name tag. I walked over and said something simple: "I never know what to say at these things. So I'll just say hi, my name is Jared."

He laughed. And just like that, the tension broke. Thanks Patrick, you had more of an impact on me than you will ever know!

We ended up having a great conversation, nothing earth-shattering, but genuine. And I left that night not feeling like I had conquered social anxiety entirely, but like I had chipped away at it just enough to try again.

That moment taught me something important: confidence isn't about eliminating anxiety. It's about showing up anyway. Each time I stepped into another event, whether a meetup, a team dinner, or even just a Zoom call, I practiced that same mindset. I gave myself permission to be me, to not have it all figured out, and to connect from a place of curiosity rather than performance.

Over time, the fear shrank. Not disappeared, but shrank. And now, those once-paralyzing moments have become opportunities. Opportunities to connect, to learn, to stretch. Social anxiety didn't vanish, it became something I learned to move through, one authentic interaction at a time.

Techniques

To tackle social anxiety, consider **exposure techniques**, which involve gradually facing your fears in controlled settings. Start small, perhaps with a brief chat at a local café, then gradually progress to larger settings. This method builds resilience over time. Imagine first attending small gatherings of friends where you feel safe, then progressing to more significant social events. This step-by-step approach nurtures confidence. Stories of individuals who've embraced exposure highlight its transformative power.

Reframing anxiety as excitement can help. The physiological symptoms of anxiety, like a racing heart, are remarkably similar to those of excitement. By mentally shifting your perspective, you can transform nervous energy into positive anticipation. Techniques like cognitive reframing help here, allowing you to reinterpret those butterflies in your stomach as the thrill of opportunity. Before attending an event, practice telling yourself, "I'm excited to meet new people today," rather than focusing on potential discomfort. Positive affirmations like "This is my chance to shine" can shift your mindset from dread to delight.

In the moment, **managing anxiety** with practical techniques can be necessary. **Breathing exercises** work wonders for calming nerves. Take slow, deep breaths, inhaling for four counts and exhaling for four counts, to center yourself before stepping into a new setting. **Visualization practices** also prepare your mind for success. Picture yourself walking confidently into a room, engaging easily in conversations, and leaving with a sense of accomplishment. These mental rehearsals set the stage for real-life triumphs.

Progressive Muscle Relaxation (PMR): A Mind-Body Reset

Progressive muscle relaxation is one of the simplest and most effective techniques I've found for calming both the body and the mind, especially before high-stakes interactions like presentations, networking events, or tough conversations. It's a practice I use often, especially in those quiet minutes before walking into a room where I need to show up as my best self.

Here's how it works: You start by focusing on one muscle group at a time, usually beginning with your toes. You tense those muscles for about 5–10 seconds, just enough to feel the tightness, and then release them slowly, allowing that tension to melt away. Then you move up: calves, thighs, stomach, chest, shoulders, arms, neck, jaw, even the muscles around your eyes. It's a full-body reset that leaves you grounded and far more present.

What's powerful about PMR is not just the physical relaxation, it's what happens mentally. As you tune into each part of your body, you shift your attention inward. You break the loop of anxious thoughts and re-anchor yourself in the present moment. And when your body feels safe and still, your mind usually follows.

Interestingly, this practice isn't limited to psychology or wellness circles. It has deep roots in certain martial arts disciplines, especially those that focus on internal balance and controlled breathing, like Tai Chi and Aikido. In both practices, there's an emphasis on full-body awareness, softening tension, and moving from a relaxed center.

What I love about this connection is the mindset it encourages: relaxation isn't weakness. In fact, in many martial traditions, true strength comes from being relaxed but alert, not stiff or rigid. That idea has changed the way I think about confidence. It's not about puffing up or powering through. It's about being grounded, breathing deeply, and moving from a place of calm control.

Personally, I like to use a short PMR session before important conversations. I'll sit somewhere quiet, maybe in my parked car or even a bathroom stall if I have to, and do a quick scan of my body. Am I clenching my jaw? Tensing my shoulders? Holding my breath? Bit by bit, I let go. And by the time I walk into the room, I'm fully confident in myself.

Additional Exercises for Boosting Self-Esteem

Setting achievable social goals is a tactic to build confidence incrementally. Start with small, manageable objectives like initiating a conversation with a colleague or joining a new group activity. These short-term goals act as stepping stones, gradually expanding your comfort zone without overwhelming you. Celebrate each success, no matter how minor it seems.

Did you manage to strike up a chat with someone new? That's a win! Recognizing and celebrating these small victories builds momentum and reinforces your ability to tackle more significant challenges. Whether it's treating yourself to a favorite snack or sharing your achievement with a friend, acknowledging progress fosters motivation and self-assurance.

Positive self-talk is another key element in building self-esteem. **The way you talk to yourself** shapes your mindset and impacts your confidence. Replace negative internal dialogues with affirmations that uplift and empower. Try telling yourself, "I am capable and resourceful" or "I approach challenges with confidence." These affirmations may feel unnatural initially, but repetition reinforces their message, gradually reshaping your self-perception. To challenge negative thoughts, ask yourself if they are based on fact or assumption. Often, we hold ourselves back with unfounded fears. Reframing these thoughts into positive statements helps shift your mindset and encourages a more optimistic outlook. **Never talk to yourself differently than you would your friend.** We are too hard on ourselves in situations where we would have compassion for a friend facing something similar.

With each step forward, you'll find yourself growing more comfortable in your skin and more adept at handling whatever social challenges come your way until ultimately you cultivate an unshakeable sense of self-assurance that permeates every interaction.

Overcoming the Fear of Rejection

Rejection. There was a season in my life when rejection felt like a punch to the gut, every time. Not just professionally, but personally too. A "no" didn't feel like feedback. It felt like proof that I wasn't good enough. And while I could give great advice to friends about staying positive and "not taking it personally," I wasn't exactly applying that same grace to myself.

One experience stands out more than most. I had applied to speak at a conference I really cared about. I had spent weeks working on the proposal, fine-tuning my pitch, and visualizing what it would feel like to be up there on stage sharing my message. I hit send on the application, hopeful, but also terrified. I kept refreshing my inbox for days, waiting.

When the rejection came, it was a two-line email. "Thank you for your submission. Unfortunately, we've decided to go in another direction."

That was it.

My heart sank. All that effort, all that hope, and I didn't even make the shortlist. I sat there staring at the screen for a long time, completely deflated. The spiral started almost instantly: *Maybe I'm not good enough. Maybe I don't have anything worth saying. Maybe they saw right through me.*

Eventually, I remembered a coaching tool I had used with someone else not long before. A reflection exercise around rejection. Funny how we're so good at offering tools to others, and so bad at remembering to use them ourselves.

So I grabbed a notebook and started writing. I forced myself to move beyond the emotion and look at the experience more objectively. *What did I learn from this process? What parts of my pitch could I improve? What might have made someone else's submission stand out more? I looked at the final speaker line up and reviewed why they may have been chosen over me. And based on that, what I would do differently next time.*

And that started to shift things.

Instead of seeing that email as a final verdict on my worth, I began to see it as part of the process. I reminded myself of something I had once told a friend: "Rejection is redirection." Maybe that stage wasn't the right one. Maybe something better was coming. And maybe this was just one more repetition in building the muscle of resilience.

I applied again the next year, same event, better pitch. I didn't get in that time either.

But the third time? Maybe we will see!

Now, I don't pretend rejection doesn't sting. It still does. But I've learned that it doesn't define me. It informs me. And more than anything, it pushes me to keep growing, refining, and showing up anyway.

Rejection isn't the end. It's a fork in the road. And sometimes, the better path is the one you only find after you've been told no.

Supportive Relationships

Surrounding yourself with a supportive network is equally important on this journey. Friends, mentors, spouses, or colleagues can offer encouragement and valuable perspectives when facing rejection. Seek out those who uplift and challenge you to see beyond immediate setbacks. Engaging in networking opportunities can expand this circle of support. Consider joining groups or attending events where like-minded individuals gather. These connections provide emotional backing and open doors to new possibilities.

Building supportive relationships **requires intentional effort**. Reach out to friends or mentors when you need a listening ear or advice. Their external perspectives can shed light on aspects you might overlook. Networking events offer more than just professional connections; they often foster genuine friendships based on shared interests and goals. Choose gatherings that align with your passions to meet people who resonate with you.

Facing rejection doesn't have to be life defining. It shouldn't be. Rejection is just another experience in life's expedition, offering insights and building your resilience. As you build a network of supportive individuals, you'll find comfort in knowing you're not alone in this process.

By integrating these strategies into your life, you empower yourself to step forward with confidence, ready to face whatever comes your way. The fear of rejection diminishes when viewed through the lens of opportunity and learning.

Being Assertive

Assertiveness isn't about being loud, forceful, or demanding. It's about standing in your own voice, calmly, clearly, and with self-respect. When you're assertive, you're able to express your needs, opinions, and boundaries in a way that respects both yourself *and* the other person. It's the sweet spot between passive and aggressive. And for many of us, finding that middle ground takes real work.

Let's be honest: if you're not used to being assertive, speaking up can feel physically uncomfortable. Your chest might tighten. Your voice might shake. You may worry that you're being "too much" or fear upsetting someone. That's totally normal. For people who've spent years people-pleasing or avoiding conflict, assertiveness can feel unnatural.

But here's the truth and an overused analogy: being assertive is a muscle. And like any muscle, it gets stronger with practice.

What Assertiveness Feels Like

When you're being assertive, it might feel unfamiliar, but it also feels clean. Grounded. There's no need to dominate or defer. You simply say what you mean. You don't apologize for your needs, and you don't bulldoze anyone else's.

Over time, this clarity brings a sense of internal alignment, your outer communication starts to reflect your inner values.

Starting Small

Building assertiveness starts with small choices:

- Saying no when you mean no.

- Making a request instead of hoping someone will read your mind.

- Correcting a miscommunication instead of letting it slide.

These small moments build the foundation for more confident communication in bigger, higher-stakes conversations.

Simple Scripts

You don't have to wing it. Try using this sentence structure:

"I feel [emotion] when [situation] because [reason]. What I'd like is [assertive request]."

Example:

"I feel frustrated when meetings run long without an agenda because I struggle to stay focused. What I'd like is for us to outline key points at the beginning, would that be okay?"

Scripts like this help you anchor your message in *you*, your emotions, your experience, without blaming or attacking others. They shift the energy from confrontation to clarity.

Let's try some more.

1. When someone asks you to take on extra work you can't handle

- *Passive:* "Um, sure... I guess I can try to fit it in somehow."

- *Assertive:* "I'm at full capacity right now and wouldn't be able to give it the attention it deserves. Can we discuss prioritizing or reassigning?"

2. When a friend constantly cancels on plans

- *Passive:* "No worries, maybe next time."

- *Assertive:* "I feel disappointed when plans get canceled last minute. I value our time together, can we find a time that works better and stick to it?"

3. When someone interrupts you during a conversation

- *Passive: [lets it go and doesn't finish the point]*

- *Assertive:* "I'd like to finish what I was saying first, then I'm happy to hear your thoughts."

4. When you're given vague feedback at work

- *Passive:* "Okay, thanks. I'll try to do better."

- *Assertive:* "Thanks for the feedback. Could you give me a specific example so I can better understand what to adjust?"

5. When your meal at a restaurant isn't what you ordered

- *Passive:* "It's fine, I'll just eat it."

- *Assertive:* "I actually ordered the grilled chicken, not the fried. Would it be possible to get the right one?"

Final Thought

Being assertive doesn't mean you'll never feel nervous. It means you choose to speak anyway. You trust that your needs matter, and that being honest and respectful is better than staying silent and stewing in frustration. The more you practice, the more your confidence grows. Not because every conversation is perfect, but because you're showing up, being real, and learning to stand in your own voice.

Practice with Voice AI

Now it's your turn to build this skill in a safe, judgment-free space. You can use ChatGPT's voice feature to simulate real conversations and practice sounding more clear, direct, and respectful.

> **ChatGPT Voice Prompt: Assertive Communication Practice**
> "Hi ChatGPT, I want to practice assertive communication. Please play the role of someone I need to speak to, maybe a coworker who's interrupted me, a friend who's overstepped a boundary, or someone I need to ask something from. Give me a short scenario. Then pause so I can respond assertively. After I speak, please give me feedback on how clear and respectful I sounded. Let's do a few examples together."

Chapter Wrap: Calm, Clear, and Confident

Confidence doesn't come from having all the answers, it comes from showing up anyway. In this chapter, we explored how true self-assurance is built not by eliminating fear or anxiety, but by learning to move through it with awareness and courage. Whether it's transforming social anxiety into curiosity, managing nerves with breathing or muscle relaxation, or standing firm with assertive communication, each tool is designed to help you feel more grounded in your own voice.

You learned:

- How to shift from performance to presence in social situations

- Practical tools like exposure therapy, reframing anxiety, and progressive muscle relaxation to regulate your nervous system

- The power of rejection as a growth opportunity, and how to extract insights rather than take it personally

- Why self-talk matters, and how to challenge the harsh inner critic with compassionate affirmations

- How assertiveness feels and how to practice it with real-world examples and role-playing scripts

This chapter wasn't just about talking to others, it was about how you talk to yourself. Confidence is a muscle built in small moments: choosing to speak when it's uncomfortable, stepping into a room when it's easier to hide, and advocating for your needs with clarity and calm. The more you practice, the more natural it becomes. Not perfect. Not polished. But **real**. And that's where your true presence begins.

Build the Life You Came For

What should you do next?

This one sounds easy, but it will be harder than you think.

- **In one conversation this week, practice the "Power Pause."**
  Before responding, while making eye contact, take a deep breath, count silently to three, and then speak with intention.

  You'll not only feel more grounded, but your words will carry more weight.

CHAPTER SIX

—·—

THE SECRET SAUCE TO MAGNETIC CONVERSATIONS

STORYTELLING

S torytelling is how we've made sense of the world for thousands of years. It's part of who we are.

Why Storytelling Works

Long before we had microphones or group chats, we had stories. Around campfires, in crowded village squares, whispered in temples, or passed from parent to child at bedtime, *storytelling* was how we made sense of the world. It's one of the oldest human traditions, etched into our DNA.

Stories do more than entertain, they help us remember. They carry lessons, values, warnings, and hopes. They bypass logic and speak straight to the emotional core. A fact might inform you, but a story? It *moves* you.

That's why storytelling is so powerful in everyday communication. It turns data into meaning, strangers into allies, and small moments into lasting impressions. When you share a story, not just a point, you invite people in. You give them something to relate to, remember, and feel. And that's where connection truly begins.

Crafting Your Personal Narrative

Case Study: Derrick Finds His Voice Through Storytelling

When Derrick first came to me for coaching, he was working as a mid-level manager at a logistics company in St. Paul. Sharp guy. Super reliable. Great at systems and execution. But every time he had to speak in front of a group, whether it was a team meeting or a quarterly business review, his confidence evaporated.

"I just don't think I'm cut out for public speaking," he told me. "I'm not that guy who commands a room. I freeze up. I ramble. People don't really remember what I say."

What struck me most wasn't the fear, it was how convinced he was that he had *nothing worth sharing*. That, to me, was the real issue. Derrick didn't need a TED Talk voice or a flashy PowerPoint deck. He needed a connection to his own story.

So that's where we started.

In one session, I asked him to tell me about a moment in his career when he felt truly proud. He hesitated. Then he shared this story about a time when he stayed overnight during a snowstorm to help keep operations running. Most of his team couldn't get in, but he and one warehouse associate named Luis showed up and managed to get the entire delivery schedule back on track by hand. No systems. No help. Just grit.

He lit up telling that story. I could see it: the spark, the emotion, the quiet pride. And when he finished, I just said, "*That's* what people need to hear. Not just what you do, but *why* it matters."

Over the next few weeks, I worked on helping Derrick build out a few more of those stories. Not flashy or over-polished, just *real*. We talked about structure, how to open strong, build a turning point, and land the story with a takeaway. We worked on delivery, sure. But more importantly, we worked on *belief*. The belief that his experiences *were* worth sharing, and that his voice had value.

Eventually, Derrick was invited to give a five-minute "culture spotlight" at a regional leadership meeting. He told the story about the snowstorm. No slides. Just him, standing in front of 75 people, sharing a slice of his story.

People came up to him afterward. They said things like, "That reminded me of my own first winter on the job," or "I'll never look at dispatch the same way again." That moment changed things for Derrick. He realized that storytelling wasn't about impressing people, it was about *connecting* with them.

Since then, Derrick's spoken at a few conferences in the logistics industry. He's not famous. He's not trying to be. But he's respected. And when he speaks, people *listen*, because his stories come from the heart.

Now when I talk to new clients about the power of storytelling, I think of Derrick. He didn't become a speaker by mastering stagecraft. He became one by finding his voice and having the courage to share what was real.

Let's build your story.

Reflection Exercise: Crafting Your Personal Story

Your story matters, not just because it's yours, but because it holds the power to connect, inspire, and resonate. This exercise will walk you through shaping a meaningful personal narrative you can use in conversation, networking, or public speaking.

1. Identify Key Life Moments

Think about three experiences that helped shape the person you are today. These don't have to be dramatic, just real.

- **Event 1:** What happened? How did this shape your personal growth?

- **Event 2:** What lesson did you learn? What changed in you?

- **Event 3:** How does this experience reflect something universal, like courage, loss, resilience, or hope?

Tip: These don't have to be career-related. Often, everyday moments, moving to a new place, failing at something important, having a hard conversation, make the best material.

2. Structure Your Story

Use the classic three-part arc to give your story shape and flow.

- **Beginning:** Set the scene. Where were you? Who was there? What was the situation?

- **Middle:** Introduce the challenge or turning point. What decision had to be made? What internal or external struggle was present?

- **End:** What happened next? What insight did you gain or how did the experience end?

Tip: Even if the situation is still ongoing, you can share what you've learned so far.

3. Add Color With Descriptive Details

Choose one of your events and bring it to life with sensory language.

- **What did it look like?** (Colors, setting, people)

- **What sounds were present?** (Laughter, silence, background noise)

- **What emotions were stirred in you?** (Pride, fear, hope, surprise)

Tip: You don't need to over-dramatize. A small detail like "my hands shook as I opened the email" can be incredibly powerful.

By weaving together meaningful moments, a clear structure, and vivid details, your personal story becomes more than just a memory, it becomes your connection point, one that lets others see you, feel something with you, and remember what you said long after the conversation ends.

Using Storytelling to Connect and Engage

But not all stories can be told the same way. We must tailor our storytelling techniques to suit different contexts. For example, casual storytelling can lighten the mood at a social gathering and make interactions feel more personal. At a barbecue with friends, you could recount a travel mishap, which will lead to laughter and set the tone for relaxed conversation.

However, storytelling takes on a different form in professional settings. During presentations or meetings, your aim might be to persuade or inspire. Here, structuring your narrative with clear goals and outcomes is key. Incorporating relevant data alongside personal anecdotes helps maintain credibility while keeping your audience engaged.

Humor and Relatability: The Secret Sauce of Great Storytelling

If storytelling is a human connection, then humor and relatability are the rhythm and melody. They're what bring your stories to life, making them not just heard, but felt, remembered, and shared.

Let's start with **humor**. A well-timed, well-placed joke doesn't just make people laugh, it lowers defenses, eases tension, and makes you instantly more approachable. Think back to a time when someone commented on a shared struggle, like surviving a chaotic Monday morning, forgetting someone's name two seconds after hearing it, or navigating the wild world of office Zoom calls. You probably smiled, maybe laughed. And more importantly, you probably thought, *"Yep, I've been there."*

That's the power of humor, it reminds us we're not alone.

Relatability does the same thing, but in quieter, more lasting ways. When someone tells a story that mirrors our own lived experience, even slightly, it sticks. Why? Because we see ourselves in it. Whether it's about starting a new job, moving to a new city, or fumbling through small talk at a party, relatable stories build connections. They say, *"Me too."* And those two words are often all it takes to create a connection.

But storytelling isn't a solo performance, it's an invitation. A great story opens the door for dialogue. It pulls people in and gives them a way to step forward, not just as listeners, but as participants. Try asking a simple question during your story:

- "Has anything like this ever happened to you?"

- "What would you have done?"

- "Anyone else feel like that sometimes?"

Suddenly, the room isn't just hearing your story, they're living it with you.

This interactive approach works wonders in both casual and professional settings. For example, share a brief story about a time you botched a presentation, and then ask your audience if they've ever had a moment where things didn't go as planned. You'll not only get nods of empathy (and probably a few laughs), but you'll also spark meaningful dialogue that deepens trust.

Humor and relatability also help stories land in high-stakes settings. Nervous about telling a personal story at a networking event or in a team meeting? Start small. Use a light anecdote everyone can relate to, like trying to gracefully sip coffee during a serious Zoom call, only to spill it all over yourself. People won't remember every word you say, but they'll remember how you made them feel. And laughter, paired with shared experience, creates emotional glue.

Here's the key: don't force it. Humor shouldn't feel like a stand-up routine, and relatability isn't about crafting the perfect "aha moment." It's about being human. Vulnerable. Real.

When your stories reflect real emotions and universal experiences, when they make people smile, nod, or lean in, you're not just talking. You're connecting.

So as you craft your stories, ask yourself:

- "Where's the moment people will say, 'Me too'?"

- "Is there room for a little laugh?"

- "What question could I ask that invites someone else in?"

Because storytelling isn't just about sharing your voice, it's about making space for others to share theirs, too.

Worried that you don't have a story to tell? Hold that thought until the end of this chapter.

Balancing Facts and Emotion in Your Stories

Let's say you're sharing a story about a significant work achievement. You could bombard your audience with facts and figures, but without emotion, it's just a data dump. The true magic of engaging communication happens when you weave statistics with feelings, creating a narrative that captivates and persuades. However, integrating facts with emotional elements requires finesse.

Start by **identifying the core message** or emotion you want to convey, then support it with relevant data. For instance, when discussing a project's success, highlight how it positively impacted the team or improved processes, not just the bottom line. This approach not only informs but also resonates on a personal level.

In addition, using emotion effectively can significantly **bolster your credibility**. When you speak with genuine passion, showing that something truly matters to you, it naturally draws people in. **Authenticity is key** here. Share why a topic ignites your enthusiasm or concern, and let that emotion shine through. The blend of **fact and emotion** demonstrates genuine commitment and authenticity, making your message more compelling and memorable.

However, there's a fine line between engaging storytelling and **over-embell-ishment**. Avoid stretching the truth to make a story more appealing; it risks eroding trust and credibility. Focus on subtle embellishments that enhance the narrative without altering reality. For instance, describing a hectic day at work as "a whirlwind of activity" adds color without distorting facts. Authenticity in storytelling involves staying true to your experiences while using creative language to engage your audience.

Crafting a narrative flow that maintains interest requires careful attention to pacing and clarity. A well-structured story unfolds naturally, guiding listeners through emotional highs and factual clarity. Storyboarding techniques can help organize your thoughts, ensuring each element contributes to the overall message.

Storyboarding is a powerful technique used to organize your story before you tell it. Whether you're sharing a personal experience, giving a presentation, or preparing a speech, storyboarding helps you map out the key beats, what happens, in what order, and why it matters. You might use sticky notes, index cards, or a digital tool to lay out each part of your story.

Begin with an engaging opening that captures attention, then build tension through conflict or challenges. Use facts strategically to support key points without overwhelming your audience. As the story progresses, balance emotional peaks with factual anchors, allowing listeners to connect both intellectually and emotionally.

To maintain interest throughout your narrative, vary the pacing to match the story's rhythm. Use pauses to emphasize important points or allow emotions to sink in. Consider how filmmakers use pacing, quickening during action scenes, and slowing for emotional moments. Similarly, adjust your storytelling pace to match the themes you're exploring. This dynamic approach keeps audiences engaged and invested in the outcome of your narrative.

When integrating facts into your storytelling, consider how they complement rather than compete with the emotional elements. For example, a story about a charitable initiative might include statistics on funds raised, but it should center on the human impact, how those funds changed lives. Grounding facts within an emotional context creates a holistic narrative that resonates deeply with listeners.

Balancing fact and emotion is particularly crucial in professional settings. Presentations that rely solely on data risk becoming dry and forgettable, while those infused with emotion capture attention and leave lasting impressions. Consider using visuals or infographics to support factual elements visually while maintaining focus on the emotional core of your message.

As you hone your storytelling skills, remember that balance is key. **Facts provide credibility; emotions create connection**. Together, they form a powerful duo that engages hearts and minds alike. Whether sharing personal anecdotes or professional achievements, strive for narratives that inform and inspire through this harmonious blend of fact and feeling.

Adapting Stories for Different Audiences

If colleagues and clients surround you at a company event, the stories you tell in this setting might differ greatly from those you share with close friends over coffee. Understanding your audience's needs and expectations is the first step in crafting stories that resonate.

Consider their preferences, cultural backgrounds, and what they value. Audience analysis techniques can guide you in tailoring your stories. Survey your audience's interests or observe their reactions to previous interactions. This awareness helps shape a narrative that aligns with their expectations, making your story heard and felt.

Different audiences perceive the same story in unique ways. What entertains one group might bewilder another. For instance, a humorous anecdote about office mishaps might delight peers but could confuse clients unfamiliar with your workplace dynamics. Recognizing these differences ensures your storytelling hits the mark every time.

Adjusting language and style for the audience. When speaking to a broad audience, simplifying language can enhance comprehension. Avoid jargon or complex terms that might alienate some listeners. In contrast, a more formal tone might be appropriate for professional environments where clarity and precision are valued.

Incorporating relevant themes and context into your stories enhances their impact. Researching your audience's interests and demographics can reveal themes that resonate deeply with them. For instance, if speaking to young professionals, themes of innovation and career growth may hold significant appeal. Crafting a story that reflects shared values or experiences creates a connection rooted in commonality. Whether it's discussing the challenges of balancing work and personal life or the excitement of embarking on a new project, aligning your narrative with your audience's experiences makes it more relatable and engaging.

As we wrap up this chapter on storytelling, remember that the power of a well-told story lies in its ability to transcend differences and unite us through **shared experiences**.

Interactive Exercise: Build a Story That Connects

Let's talk all we learned and put it together.

Everyone has a story worth sharing. Use this section to dig deep and reflect. This exercise helps you uncover one of yours and craft it into something that resonates with others.

Step 1: Choose a Real Moment That Mattered

Think of a specific experience that shaped you. It doesn't have to be dramatic, just real. Try one of these prompts to get started:

- A time you overcame something hard

- A moment that changed your perspective

- An unexpected success or failure

- A time you had to make a tough decision

Jot it down in one sentence: **"The time I _____."**

Step 2: Use the Three-Part Story Arc

Structure gives your story flow. Use this template to guide your outline:

- **Beginning – Set the Scene** Where were you? What was happening? Who else was there?→ *"I was working at ____, and it was the end of Q4..."*

- **Middle – Introduce the Conflict** What challenge, obstacle, or turning point happened? How did you feel?→ *"I was overwhelmed, uncertain, and totally stuck..."*

- **End – Find the Resolution** What changed? What did you learn?

What's the takeaway? → *"Looking back, that moment taught me..."*

Step 3: Add Relatability and Emotion

Stories connect through shared experiences. Now ask yourself:

- What part of this story will make someone say, *"Me too"*?

- What emotion do I want them to feel, hope, humor, courage, relief?

- Is there a small, funny, or human detail I can add?

Example:

"I stood outside the door rehearsing my pitch for the seventh time, then spilled coffee down my shirt before I even walked in. Classic me."

Step 4: Make It Conversation-Ready

Your story doesn't have to be long. Try boiling it down into 2–3 sentences you could share at a dinner table or team meeting. Keep it real, keep it warm.

Try this template:

"There was a time when _____. I struggled with _____, but I learned _____. Now, I try to _____ whenever I face something similar."

Optional: Practice With ChatGPT

ChatGPT Voice Prompt: Storytelling Practice

"Hi ChatGPT, I'm practicing storytelling. I'll tell you a short personal story I want to use in conversation or a talk. After I share, please give me feedback on clarity, emotional impact, and how engaging it sounds. Ready?"

Chapter Wrap: Speak So People Feel It

Storytelling is one of the most powerful tools in communication, it helps us connect, inspire, and be remembered. In this chapter, you learned how to craft personal narratives using key life moments, structure, and vivid details. We explored why stories work, from their roots in oral tradition to their ability to evoke emotion, foster connection, and make facts memorable. Through humor, relatability, and interactive engagement, you can make your stories resonate in both casual and professional settings. You also learned how to adapt your storytelling for different audiences and balance emotion with data. Whether you're sharing a moment over coffee or presenting in front of a room, your story, told with authenticity and care, can leave a lasting impact.

Build the Life You Came For

What should you do next?

- **Craft Your Go-To Story Library**
  Write down three short personal stories that reflect key values (like resilience, curiosity, or humor). Practice reciting them out loud to ChatGPT until you feel confident.

- **Extra Credit: Use a Story to Answer "How's Your Day?"**
  Next time someone asks this everyday question, reply with a 30-second story instead of "Good" or "Busy." Make your answer memorable and human. And related to your actual day!

Chapter Seven

— • —

How to Say Hard Things Without Making It Worse

Conflict & Criticism

Strategies for Managing Conflict Gracefully

When Silence Was Louder Than Words

I'll never forget the tension in that meeting room. The kind where no one raises their voice, but the air feels like static. Tight, crackling, about to snap.

It was a Thursday afternoon, and I was coaching a client named Michelle, a director at a regional healthcare company. Michelle is smart, driven, and incredibly capable, but also someone who carries the weight of her team's performance like it was tattooed on her skin. That day, she invited me to attend a leadership meeting as an observer. What she didn't know was how much that hour would reveal.

The meeting was about missed deadlines on a new reporting system rollout. Michelle opened with a question that seemed harmless enough: "Can someone help me understand why we're still behind on Phase Two?" Silence. People looked around the table, fiddled with pens, and avoided eye contact. Finally, Raj, one of her project managers, spoke up. His tone was clipped. "Frankly, I don't think the expectations were ever clear."

You could feel the room shrink.

Michelle stiffened. "We've had three planning meetings," she replied, her voice sharp. "I thought we *were* clear."

That moment stuck with me, not because anyone yelled or stormed out, but because no one felt safe enough to speak freely. The rest of the meeting limped forward, but the real conversation never happened.

Afterward, Michelle and I debriefed over coffee in her office. I asked her point-blank, "What do you think Raj was *really* reacting to in that moment?"

She paused, then said, "I don't know. Maybe he thinks I'm too controlling. Or maybe he's just not paying attention." That's when I invited her to dig deeper. "What if it's not about you or him? What if it's about something neither of you said out loud?"

We broke it down. The root cause wasn't laziness or disrespect; it was unmet expectations and miscommunication. Michelle had assumed her clarity was enough, and Raj had interpreted her leadership style as micromanagement. Neither had said it directly, but it was all there. In the tension, the clipped words, the silence.

Over the next few weeks, we worked together on de-escalation techniques. Michelle practiced what we called her "verbal reset switch." When conversations got heated, she'd say, "Let's take a breath, I want to make sure I'm hearing you clearly." It was simple. Respectful. Disarming.

She also committed to a new listening habit: before offering her opinion, she'd summarize the other person's point of view. "So you're saying the timeline felt rushed, and that made it harder to plan resources, did I get that right?" That small habit changed everything. Her team started to open up. Tensions softened. Raj even admitted during a follow-up that he'd misread her tone and appreciated her effort to meet him in the middle.

What started as a near-silent standoff became a turning point, not because anyone won the argument, but because Michelle learned how to slow the boil before it spilled over.

That's the thing about conflict: it's rarely about what's said. It's about what's underneath. And when you're willing to pause, listen, and lead with curiosity, you turn conflict into clarity.

Interactive Exercise: Conflict Reflection and Reset

Use this space to process a recent moment of tension, not to relive the frustration, but to reframe it with new tools.

1. Identify the Moment: Think back to a recent situation that left you feeling tense, defensive, or misunderstood, whether at work, home, or elsewhere. *What happened on the surface? Who was involved? What was said or done?*

2. Look Beneath the Surface: Just like Michelle learned, most conflicts aren't about what's said but what's *unspoken*. *What expectations might have gone unmet? Were emotions involved that weren't expressed directly? Could miscommunication have played a role?*

3. Rewind and Reimagine: If you could go back, how might things have gone differently? Try applying one or more of these techniques:

- A **verbal reset**, like: "Can we pause for a moment? I want to make sure I'm really hearing you."

- A **summary statement**, like: "It sounds like you're saying X, do I have that right?"

- A **curious question**, like: "What would have made this easier for you?"

Write out a revised version of how the conversation could have unfolded using these tools.

4. Reflect on the Shift: How would the tone of that moment have changed? How might the other person have responded if they felt seen and heard instead of judged or dismissed?

By walking through this process, you're not just analyzing a past conflict, you're building a blueprint for navigating future ones with more empathy, awareness, and confidence. The goal isn't perfection. It's progress. One calm reset, one clarified assumption, one "I hear you" at a time.

Voice Practice: Navigating Conflict with Clarity and Calm

Use this prompt to practice handling tense conversations. You'll get a simulated conflict scenario where you can respond using the de-escalation and listening tools from this chapter.

> **ChatGPT Voice Prompt: Managing Conflict Practice**
> "Hi ChatGPT, I want to practice managing conflict in conversation. I will readout a topic and then the start of the scenario. Please role-play the other person. After I respond, give me feedback on how well I used de-escalation, listening, and clarity. The headline topic is [create your own or choose one from the list below] and the scenario is [create your own or read the script]."

Conflict Role-Play Scenarios for Voice Practice

1. Missed Deadline at Work

"Hey, I was really counting on your part of the project being done by Friday. Because it wasn't, I had to scramble to finish things myself. I'm frustrated."

2. Friend Feels Ignored

"You haven't responded to my texts lately, and honestly, it feels like you're avoiding me. Did I do something wrong?"

3. Roommate or Partner Overstepping

"I know you meant well, but moving my stuff without asking really crossed a line for me. Can we talk about it?"

4. Feedback Delivered Harshly

"In that meeting, I felt like you shut down my idea without really listening. I was embarrassed."

5. Team Member Feeling Undervalued

"I've been doing a lot behind the scenes lately, but no one seems to notice. It feels like my work doesn't matter."

Pro Tip: Try practicing with different tones, confident, calm, empathetic. You'll start to build muscle memory for moments that usually catch you off guard. And remember: you're not trying to "win" the conversation, you're practicing how to *listen, stay grounded,* and *respond with purpose.*

Embracing Criticism Without Losing Yourself

I still remember the meeting, conference room 5C, third floor, fluorescent lights buzzing a little louder than usual. I had spent two solid weeks preparing a detailed analysis for our quarterly planning session. I felt good about it. No, actually, I felt proud. Everything was on time, well-sourced, and neatly visualized. I had even rehearsed how I was going to walk through the key slides.

Then came the moment.

About ten minutes into my presentation, right after I walked through the second key recommendation, one of my colleagues, let's call him Ben to protect his "innocence," cleared his throat and said, "I'm not sure this data shows the full picture. It feels a little thin, especially around the regional breakdown."

It hit me like a punch to the stomach.

The room went still. I could feel the heat rise in my neck and ears, and that little voice in my head, "*You missed something. You messed this up. Everyone sees it now.*" I wanted to push back; to defend the hours I had poured into that deck. My first instinct was to say in a strong, biting tone, "Actually, Ben! I think the data's solid," and move on. Ignoring his stupid comment (yes, the wound still exists for me).

But something stopped me.

It was a coaching conversation I'd had just a few weeks earlier with a woman named Kim, a sharp, perceptive professional I had the pleasure of mentoring. In one of our sessions, she'd shared how she used to shut down anytime she received feedback in meetings. "It felt like I was being attacked," she said. "Like they were questioning *me,* not just my work. It was always personal for me." We worked on reframing feedback as data, not judgment, on staying curious instead of defensive.

And in that meeting, with Ben's comment hanging in the air, I took my own advice.

I paused, took a breath, and said, "Thanks, Ben. That's a fair point. Where do you think I could build it out more? Are there specific regions you had in mind? You dumb a**! (No, I really didn't say that last part out loud.)

That shift to curiosity over defensiveness changed everything, even though it was not easy. What we do is personal to us. We do feel attacked. We do take offense at it. But what matters to you here? Defending yourself? Or adding value?

Ben responded immediately with ideas. A couple of others chimed in. Instead of turning into a tug-of-war, it became a collaborative discussion. And I walked out of that meeting not just with my ego intact, but with a stronger product to refine. Even more surprising? Two people messaged me later that day and said, "I appreciated how you handled that feedback. It set a great tone."

Here's what I've learned since then: **Criticism is inevitable**. But how we respond? That's where the growth lives.

Not all feedback is right, but that doesn't mean it's useless. I've made it a habit now to ask follow-up questions, thank people for their perspective, and note what's useful, even when it stings. I've practiced this in coaching sessions, in voice notes to myself, even in awkward team moments. And slowly, my internal dialogue has shifted. I don't see feedback as a threat or an attack against me, I see it as a tool.

So the next time criticism shows up, I don't brace for impact. I lean in.

Because confidence isn't about getting it perfect, it's about being open to getting better.

Interactive Exercise: Criticism Reflection & Reframe

Objective: This exercise helps you reflect on a real moment of criticism, either recent or memorable, and practice responding in a way that fosters growth, not defensiveness.

Step 1: Recall a Recent Criticism

Think of a moment when someone gave you feedback that felt uncomfortable, maybe even painful.

- What was the situation? (e.g., a work presentation, a team meeting, a personal conversation)

- Who gave the feedback, and what exactly did they say?

- How did you feel in the moment, emotionally and physically?

- How did you respond at the time?

Jot down a few quick bullet points for each.

Step 2: Identify the Trigger

Now ask yourself:

- What *specifically* triggered my defensive reaction?(e.g., fear of looking unprepared, embarrassment in front of peers, feeling misunderstood)

- Was the feedback attacking *me*, or was it addressing my *work* or behavior?

Often, criticism feels personal even when it isn't. The goal here is to name what made it feel so charged.

Step 3: Reframe the Moment

Let's practice a mental reframe:

- What part of the feedback was **valid or helpful**, even if it stung?

- What follow-up question could I have asked to better understand the feedback?

- What could I say next time that shows openness and professionalism?

Write a reframe sentence using this structure:

"In that moment, I felt [emotion], but now I see that the feedback was really about [issue]. Next time, I could respond by saying, '[curious or collaborative response].'"

Example: "In that moment, I felt embarrassed, but now I see that the feedback was really about clarifying expectations. Next time, I could respond by saying, 'Thanks for flagging that, what specifically could be clearer for you?'"

Voice Practice: Receiving Feedback with Curiosity

This voice prompt allows you to *role-play receiving criticism* in a calm, constructive way using ChatGPT's voice feature.

ChatGPT Voice Prompt: Criticism Practice

"Hi ChatGPT, I want to practice receiving constructive criticism with curiosity and professionalism. Please play the role of a coworker or manager, giving me feedback. Start with a scenario something like feedback on a report or presentation (or use what you created from the interactive exercise). Deliver one piece of constructive criticism. Then pause so I can respond. After I speak, please give me feedback on how curious and open my response sounded, and how I might improve. Let's try a few rounds."

Turning Disagreements into Productive Discussions

Let's be honest, disagreements can feel like emotional quicksand. One moment you're discussing a difference of opinion, and the next you're knee-deep in frustration, talking in circles, each person defending their position like it's a hill to die on. But here's the thing: disagreement doesn't have to equal conflict. And conflict doesn't have to equal damage.

If the previous sections helped you identify the **roots of tension** and taught you to approach **criticism with curiosity**, then this next step is about turning friction into forward motion. Because, believe it or not, some of the most productive, relationship-strengthening conversations begin with a difference of opinion.

It starts with a mindset shift: Instead of aiming to "win" the conversation, aim to understand and build. That doesn't mean giving in. It means stepping into the discussion with a clear goal: to find shared ground and work from there.

Find the Shared Goal Beneath the Surface

Most heated disagreements are actually rooted in something you *agree* on, you just haven't named it yet. A delayed project timeline, a disputed strategy, and a clash of values at home usually point to a mutual desire: success, respect, fairness, and progress. Try this: next time you feel the conversation heading off the rails, pause and ask yourself, *What's the outcome we both want?*

It might sound like:

- "I think we both care a lot about getting this right. Can we take a second to talk about where we're aligned?"

- "I want this to work as much as you do. Maybe if we find what we agree on first, we can move from there."

That shift, **from adversaries to partners,** is often all it takes to change the entire dynamic.

Speak From Experience, Not Accusation

It's tempting to go into defense mode in tense moments and start assigning blame. But nothing shuts down a conversation faster than finger-pointing. That's where "I" statements come in. They allow you to express your experience without implying judgment or fault.

Try swapping:

- Instead of- "You never listen to my ideas."

- Try – "I feel frustrated when I don't feel heard in meetings, I want to contribute but I'm not sure how to break through."

This shift changes the emotional temperature of the conversation. You're not launching an attack, you're opening a door.

Keep the Dialogue Open With Curious Language

One of the easiest ways to de-escalate a disagreement is to stay curious. It's hard to stay angry at someone who genuinely wants to understand you. Instead of shutting down or pushing back, try language that signals openness:

- "Can you help me understand your perspective on this?"

- "What's most important to you in this situation?"

- "Would you be open to exploring a few ideas together?"

These phrases signal that you're not just looking to prove a point, you're looking to solve something *together*.

Build Solutions Collaboratively

Once emotions have cooled and clarity has returned, it's time to shift toward solution mode. This is where brainstorming can be your superpower. The goal isn't to force agreement, it's to generate ideas that serve the **shared goal** you identified earlier.

Try saying:

- "What if we each share two ideas and build from there?"

- "Let's list out all the options before we decide which one fits best."

This moves the conversation away from opinion-based standoffs and into a creative, forward-looking space. People are far more willing to compromise when they feel heard, and far more energized when they helped build the solution.

Interactive Exercise: "I" Statement Conversion

Let's put this into practice:

1. **Recall a Recent Disagreement:** Think of a conversation where things felt tense, defensive, or unproductive. Write down what you *wanted* to say in the moment, even if it was reactive or blunt.

2. **Reframe with "I" Language:** Rewrite your original statement using the "I feel... when... because... what I'd like is..." structure.

Example:

- Original: "You made me look bad in that meeting."

- Reframed: "I felt undermined when my part wasn't acknowledged. It's important to me that our team's efforts are seen. Could we make space to clarify next time?"

Voice Practice Prompt: Navigating Disagreement

> **ChatGPT Voice Prompt: Handling Disagreements Practice**
> "Hi ChatGPT, I want to practice handling disagreements constructively. Please give me a scenario where I might clash with someone's opinion, like a coworker rejecting my idea or a friend misunderstanding my intent. Pause so I can respond using an 'I' statement and neutral language. Then give me feedback on how I came across and how I could say it with more clarity or care. Let's do 2 or 3 rounds together."

By approaching disagreement with empathy, shared purpose, and thoughtful language, you don't just defuse conflict, you build trust. These moments become proof points that you're someone who can be counted on, not just when things are easy, but when it matters most.

Communicating Assertively: Without Crossing the Line

By now, you've explored how to navigate conflict, respond to criticism gracefully, and turn tension into progress. But there's one final skill that ties it all together: **assertive communication**, the kind that lets you speak up clearly and confidently, without slipping into aggression.

Here's the truth: assertiveness is not about volume or dominance. It's about clarity. It's the ability to express your needs, set boundaries, or offer feedback while still showing respect for the other person's perspective. When done well, assertiveness builds trust, not tension.

The challenge? **It's easy to confuse assertiveness with aggression.** Especially when emotions are running high.

Let's take a simple example. If someone says,

- "I feel this deadline isn't realistic for me," they're being **assertive**. But if they snap,

- "You're making this impossible!" crosses into **aggression.** Blame replaces dialogue, and respect gets sidelined.

The difference is subtle but powerful: assertiveness centers on one's own experience, while aggression points fingers. One opens doors, while the other shuts them.

Practicing the Balance

Finding that middle ground takes self-awareness and repetition. Role-playing real-world scenarios, whether with a coach, a friend, or even ChatGPT's voice feature, can help you build confidence. Practicing responses before you need them gives you a blueprint for the moments that matter.

Start by choosing a few common situations where you've felt unsure how to respond, maybe when someone dismisses your idea in a meeting or pushes past your boundary. Write down what you wanted to say. Then rewrite it through the lens of assertiveness: firm, respectful, and focused on your needs, not their faults.

Here's a mini framework:

- **Aggressive**: "You always talk over me."

- **Passive**: "It's fine, never mind."

- **Assertive**: "I'd like to finish what I was saying first, I want to make sure I communicate my point."

Assertiveness is not about being *nice*. It's about being **clear and kind** at the same time.

Staying Grounded in the Moment

Of course, even the best language can lose its power if it's delivered with tension or heat. That's why **composure is key**.

Think of your presence like the eye of a storm, calm, steady, and unmoved, even when emotions swirl around you. Tools like deep breathing, pausing before you speak, or visualizing yourself staying grounded can help you maintain calm in high-stakes moments.

Personally, I've discovered that a brief three-second pause can make a huge difference. It gives your brain time to catch up with your emotions. It tells the other person: "I'm here, I'm calm, and I'm thinking this through." And it almost always leads to a better outcome.

Assertiveness That Builds Connection

The final piece of this puzzle is **respect**, not just for yourself, but for the person across from you.

Great communicators don't dominate conversations or overpower others. They foster understanding and connection. You can hold your ground *and* acknowledge someone else's point of view. That might sound like:

- "I understand where you're coming from, and here's how I see it differently."

- "I appreciate the work you've done so far, can we explore a different approach?"

This kind of language communicates confidence *without shutting anyone down*. It sets the tone for solutions, not standoffs.

Because here's the truth: **assertiveness isn't about getting your way, it's about making sure your voice is part of the way forward.**

Chapter Wrap: When Conversations Get Uncomfortable

As we close this chapter, let's bring it all together:

When you approach conflict with calm, receive criticism with curiosity, and assert yourself with respect, you turn challenging conversations into powerful ones. You become the kind of communicator people trust, not because you always agree with them, but because you show up with clarity, courage, and care.

And that's what real confidence sounds like.

Build the Life You Came For

What should you do next? This is another hard one.

- **Have a Low-Stakes Difficult Conversation**
  Identify a small but honest conversation you've been putting off (like giving a roommate feedback or setting a boundary at work). Practice starting it with curiosity and clear intent. Begin with: "Hey, can we talk about something that's been on my mind?"

  Try rehearsing the conversation with ChatGPT first. Get some of your nerves out by rehearing it several times. Then, go for it!

Chapter Eight

—·—

How to Not Accidentally Offend People

Communicate with Different Cultures

Understanding Cultural Contexts in Communication

Let's role-play. You're at an international conference, and you've just entered a room buzzing with conversations in multiple languages, each carrying its own rhythm and flair. You're excited to connect, yet a bit unsure of how to navigate this new situation. Should you shake hands? Bow? Dive straight into your point or ease in with small talk?

This is where cultural context becomes your best guide, not just to avoid missteps, but to build relationships.

Culture shapes communication in ways we often don't realize. It's not just about language, it's about *how* things are said, *what's* left unsaid, and *why* people speak the way they do. The pauses. The eye contact. The emotional tone. All of it flows from invisible cultural blueprints.

Take context, for example. In **high-context cultures,** like Japan, Brazil, or many Arab nations, much of the meaning is carried between the lines. What isn't said can be just as important as what is. People expect you to read the room, understand shared norms, and interpret subtle cues. Silence can speak volumes.

In **low-context cultures**, like the U.S., Germany, or Australia, clarity is king. Directness is valued, and people tend to say exactly what they mean. There's less reading between the lines and less tolerance for ambiguity.

Now layer in **collectivism vs. individualism**. In **collectivist societies** like India or South Korea, communication often prioritizes group harmony. You may notice more deference, fewer interruptions, and a careful avoidance of conflict. In **individualistic cultures**, like the U.S. or the Netherlands, conversations may lean toward personal achievement, self-expression, and even healthy debate.

Then there's **power distance,** the degree to which a culture respects hierarchy. In **high power-distance cultures** like Mexico or Russia, formality and titles matter. People may not speak as openly in front of higher-ups. In **low power-distance cultures** like Sweden or New Zealand, everyone's voice tends to carry equal weight, and even interns might feel comfortable challenging the CEO.

Finally, consider **uncertainty avoidance,** how comfortable a culture is with ambiguity. Countries like Greece or Japan tend to prefer rules and structure, especially in professional settings. Others, like Singapore or the U.K., are more at ease with uncertainty and flexible plans.

These frameworks aren't about boxing people in, they're about opening up. Understanding the forces shaping how someone communicates makes you a more empathetic and effective conversation partner.

And here's the beauty of it: you don't need to master every custom to make a strong impression. Just staying curious, asking questions, and showing a willingness to learn sends a powerful message, *I see you, I respect where you're coming from, and I want to meet you there.*

That's what makes cross-cultural communication not just possible, but powerful.

Country	Context Style	Individualism vs Collectivism	Power Distance	Uncertainty Avoidance
United States	Low-context	Individualist	Low	Moderate
Germany	Low-context	Individualist	Low	High
Japan	High-context	Collectivist	High	High
Brazil	High-context	Collectivist	High	High
India	High-context	Collectivist	High	Moderate
China	High-context	Collectivist	High	Moderate
Mexico	High-context	Collectivist	High	High
Denmark	Low-context	Individualist	Low	Low
Russia	High-context	Collectivist	High	High
Singapore	Low-context	Collectivist	Low	Low

Table of Selected Countries

Respectful Engagement Across Cultures

When "OK" Isn't Okay: Navigating Symbols Across Cultures

When we communicate, it's easy to assume everyone sees the world through a similar lens. But the reality is, meaning lives in context, and context changes across cultures. What feels like a harmless gesture or expression to you might carry a completely different (or even offensive) meaning to someone else.

Take hand gestures, for example. A thumbs-up might feel like a universal "Great job!" to many Americans, but in parts of the Middle East, West Africa, or South America, it can be interpreted as rude or dismissive. The classic "OK" hand sign? Perfectly friendly in the U.S., but in countries like Brazil or Turkey, it has vulgar connotations. Even a simple nod, which typically means "yes" in many places, might be interpreted as "no" in Bulgaria or parts of Greece.

I remember a client once telling me about a moment on an international video call where she gave a thumbs-up to close a conversation. The silence that followed wasn't agreement, it was discomfort, what she meant as encouragement had been taken the opposite way.

These aren't just etiquette missteps, they can shape trust and rapport. And they remind us: communication isn't just about what *you* say, it's about how it's *received*.

That's why cultural awareness matters. Taking the time to learn the norms, gestures, and unspoken cues of those you interact with doesn't just prevent misunderstanding, it shows respect. And in any conversation, respect is what opens the door to real connection.

Cultural Sensitivity

Before engaging with a culture different from your own, take some time to dig into its norms and values. This doesn't mean becoming an expert overnight, but rather knowing enough to show respect and understanding. A simple search or chat with someone from that culture can offer invaluable insights. Avoiding stereotypes is crucial; each individual is unique, and no one wants to be reduced to a cliché.

In Italy, a simple handshake may suffice for a greeting, while in India, a respectful namaste might be more appropriate. Such nuances in etiquette can significantly impact communication effectiveness. Understanding cultural etiquette is like learning the unspoken rules of a new game; it helps you play more effectively. For example, in many Asian cultures, addressing someone by their first name immediately might seem overly familiar and disrespectful. Instead, using titles and surnames showcases respect for hierarchy. In contrast, American culture often embraces first-name bases even in professional settings. These distinctions highlight the importance of adapting your approach based on context. Awareness of such formalities helps avoid awkwardness and demonstrates your commitment to respectful communication.

Curiosity is your best ally when exploring new cultural landscapes. Genuine interest not only enriches your own experience but also fosters goodwill with those you interact with. Ask open-ended questions about cultural traditions or practices. Questions like "What's the story behind this festival?" or "How do you celebrate special occasions?" can spark engaging conversations that allow others to share their heritage proudly. Expressing curiosity signals respect and appreciation for different cultures, opening the way for meaningful connections.

However, even with the best intentions, cultural misunderstandings may arise. Managing these moments with grace is essential for maintaining harmony and respect. If you find yourself in a cultural faux pas, a sincere apology goes a long way. Suppose you mistakenly use an inappropriate gesture in Brazil; acknowledging the error and asking for clarification shows humility and willingness to learn. Humor can also help diffuse tension, lightheartedly admitting, "I guess I need to brush up on my cultural etiquette!" can ease discomfort while demonstrating your openness to correction. Remember that everyone makes mistakes; it's how you handle them that matters most.

Adapting Across Cultures: Communication Without Borders

The first time I coached a team with members from four different countries, I realized just how much our communication habits are shaped by culture and how easily things can go sideways without even realizing it. I said something I thought was crystal clear. Two people nodded. One looked confused. And another said, "I think we may be talking past each other." They were right.

These differences aren't obstacles. They're signals. Learning to recognize and adapt to them is a skill that strengthens every relationship, especially in today's global world.

Here are a few key dynamics that matter when you're communicating across cultures:

- **Direct vs. Indirect Communication** In places like Germany or the Netherlands, people tend to be blunt, saying what they mean, clearly and without fluff. In contrast, many Asian and Middle Eastern cultures prefer indirectness, where suggestions, pauses, or body language fill in the blanks.

- **Individualism vs. Collectivism** In the U.S., people are often encouraged to speak up and share their unique viewpoint. In collectivist cultures like Japan or India, harmony and group consensus are prioritized. Understanding this can help you interpret silence or deference not as disinterest, but as a sign of respect.

- **Power Distance** Some cultures (like Mexico or the Philippines) maintain strong respect for hierarchy. Titles and formality matter. In others, like Sweden or Australia, you'll find more egalitarian norms and casual communication regardless of role.

- **Personal Space and Gestures** A friendly pat on the back may feel warm in Brazil but invasive in the UK. Even gestures like the "OK" sign or a head nod carry different meanings depending on where you are.

The key is curiosity. Ask. Observe. Learn.

You can't learn about every culture in one book. Learn when the need arises. If you plan to head out of the country, research and practice with AI to help you understand and get ready for the trip.

The Role of Empathy

At the heart of all this is empathy. When you try to see the world through someone else's cultural lens, even if just a glimpse, you build trust. You turn difference into dialogue. That might mean adjusting how you speak, yes. But it doesn't mean losing your voice. It means tuning it for resonance.

When you stay open, ask questions, and listen deeply, cross-cultural communication becomes less about getting it right and more about getting real, with people who see the world differently than you do.

Chapter Wrap: When Worlds Talk

Effective communication across cultures isn't about memorizing customs; it's about staying curious, respectful, and open. From reading between the lines in high-context cultures to adapting your gestures, tone, and personal space, a successful cross-cultural connection starts with empathy and a willingness to learn. By recognizing the invisible forces that shape how people speak, listen, and relate, you build connections, not barriers. And when you lead with humility and curiosity, you don't just avoid missteps, you invite meaningful connection.

Build the Life You Came For

What should you do next?

- **Learn One Cultural Greeting or Custom**
  Choose a country, culture, or colleague's background, and research a basic greeting or social norm. Use it appropriately this week to start a conversation or build connection.

  It's a small gesture that often goes a long way. If this seems odd or out of character for you and them, just let them know you wanted to learn more about their country. Then ask them if this is still a relevant greeting or custom in their culture today.

Chapter Nine

— • —

How Mindfulness Can Fix Your Awkward Moments

Mindful Listening

Practicing Mindful Listening

L et me take you to a familiar scene.

You're sitting at a bustling café, steam rising from your mug, chairs scraping on tile, the background hum of conversations rising and falling like waves. Across from you, a friend leans in to speak. And in that moment, something shifts. The rest of the world fades into a soft blur. You're not just hearing them, you're *with* them. Every word, every pause, every shift in their expression holds your full attention.

That's the heart of **mindful listening**.

While *active listening* is a valuable skill, it focused on techniques like nodding, paraphrasing, or making eye contact. *Mindful listening* goes a step deeper. It's not just about *doing* the right things; it's about *being* fully present. No agenda. No rehearsed response. Just awareness.

When you're mindfully listening, you're not preparing your next point. You're not mentally cataloging advice. You're quieting the mental noise, your to-do list, your opinions, your inner critic, and tuning in completely. **It's presence with a purpose**. And in a world constantly nudging us to move faster, it's a radical act of respect.

I once worked with a client, let's call him Jordan, who was a rising star at his company. Smart, articulate, driven. But his peers often described him as "distracted" or "distant" in one-on-one meetings. When we dug deeper, we uncovered the issue: he was listening to respond, not listening to *understand*. He'd nod, smile, interject with "Got it", but his mind was already chasing the next bullet point. Once Jordan started practicing mindful listening, the shift was immediate. His team opened up. His relationships deepened. And the phrase "you really listened" started showing up in his performance reviews.

How to Listen with Presence

Start small. Put your phone face down. Take a breath before responding. Make eye contact, not like you're scanning for signs of life, but as if you're anchoring yourself to this moment. Let your body language say, *"I'm here. I'm listening. You matter."*

Notice the other person's facial expressions, posture, and tone. Is there hesitation behind their words? Are they leaning in or pulling back? A raised eyebrow, a deep sigh, these quiet cues often speak louder than anything verbal.

Practice with someone you know well. Ask a simple question, "How's your day been?" and challenge yourself to listen (no, REALLY listen) for the emotion behind the answer. Is it stress? Pride? Disappointment? Don't fix. Don't solve. Just observe.

And here's the tricky part: don't judge. Don't jump to conclusions. Don't mentally file their story into categories of "right" or "wrong." Curiosity is the engine of mindful listening. Let phrases like *"Tell me more"* or *"That's interesting, how did that feel?"* keep the door open.

Mindful Listening Is a Practice

You won't always get it right. You'll zone out. You'll interrupt. You'll catch yourself drifting into mental multitasking. That's okay. Like meditation, mindful listening is about noticing when you've left the moment, and gently returning.

In fact, keeping a short **Reflective Listening Journal** can accelerate your growth. Try this:

Interactive Element: Reflective Listening Journal

- **Recall a Conversation**: Write down a recent conversation where you tried to stay present. What verbal and non-verbal details stood out?

- **Spot the Gaps**: Did distractions creep in? Did you judge, interrupt, or drift? What triggered it?

- **Set a Micro-Goal**: Identify one thing you'll try differently in your next conversation. Maybe it's pausing for three seconds before replying. Maybe it's noticing tone more closely.

Over time, you'll begin to experience what so many others have: that *mindful listening doesn't just change how others feel, it changes how you show up.* You start hearing more than just words. You hear emotion. You hear need. You hear *people*.

And when people feel heard, they trust. They open up. They invite connection.

Because being fully present with someone, even for five minutes, isn't just a skill. It's a gift.

Staying Present in the Moment

Have you ever been in a conversation where time seemed to slow down, not because you were bored, but because you were fully there? The world faded just a bit. You weren't thinking about what to say next or what you had to do afterward. You were simply present. That's the kind of attention mindful communication asks of us, not perfection, just presence.

Being present sounds simple, but in practice, it's anything but. Our minds love to wander. A ping on your phone, a half-formed worry about tomorrow's deadline, even the mental loop of rehearsing your next sentence, it all pulls you out of the moment. That's why mindfulness starts with intention.

One of the easiest ways to ground yourself is through your breath. Before you walk into a meeting or pick up the phone, take one full breath in. Hold it. Then let it out slowly. Feel the air move. Let your shoulders drop. This kind of pause doesn't just settle your nervous system, it clears the clutter so you can actually show up.

Pair that breath with your senses. Notice the chair beneath you. The sound of the other person's voice. The way their expression changes when they hit a nerve or share something meaningful. These small anchors help you stay rooted right where you are, instead of drifting into distraction.

It's tempting to believe multitasking makes us more efficient, but when it comes to communication, it usually does the opposite. Checking your email while listening to a friend talk about something important sends a subtle message: "You don't have my full attention." And people can feel that, even if you don't say it. Instead, try putting your phone on silent and turning it face down. Close the tab with your inbox. These tiny shifts create sacred space for connection. They say, "I'm here. You matter."

One powerful tool to stay present is the **mindful pause**. That little beat before you speak. That breath after someone finishes talking. It gives you time to truly absorb what's been said, and it shows the other person you're not just waiting for your turn, you're with them. Yes, silence might feel awkward at first. But in reality, it's one of the most generous things you can offer in a conversation.

And then there's observation. Not just listening to words, but noticing tone, facial expressions, posture. Is their voice tight with stress? Are they leaning in with interest, or pulling back with discomfort? *These micro-signals tell stories*. When you train yourself to see them, you begin to understand not just what's being said, but what's being felt.

I once worked with a leader who thought he was a great listener. And in many ways, he was, he made time, gave feedback, asked thoughtful questions. But he didn't realize how often his eyes darted to his watch in meetings. When a team member finally pointed it out, he was surprised. "I didn't even know I was doing that," he told me. But his team meetings started to feel different once he brought that habit into awareness and made a conscious effort to stay fully present, no watch, no phone. More honest. More human.

That's the secret of mindfulness. It's not about being perfectly still or endlessly patient. *It's about being willing to return to the breath, to the moment, to the person in front of you, again and again.*

So next time you're in conversation, ask yourself:

- Am I here right now?

- Am I listening with all of me: eyes, ears, heart?

- Am I open to what this moment is offering?

Mindful presence isn't something you master in one sitting. It's a practice. But it's a practice that changes everything, from how you speak, to how you lead, to how you love.

Using Mindfulness to Manage Conversation Anxiety

I've been there. About to step into a room filled with people, and suddenly, a wave of anxiety crashes over me. Heart racing, palms dripping, and a million thoughts of self-doubt start to invade my thoughts. It's called conversation anxiety and mindfulness offers a powerful tool to manage it.

Recognizing anxiety triggers involves tuning into your body's signals. Take a moment to scan your body and emotions. This practice isn't just about noticing discomfort; it's about acknowledging it without judgment. People often find that identifying these triggers gives them a sense of control.

Resetting With the Breath

Let's talk about one of the simplest, and most powerful, tools you have to calm your nerves in the moment: your breath.

Not the kind of breath you take on autopilot, like while scrolling your phone or rushing between meetings. I'm talking about conscious, intentional breathing. The kind that grounds you. The kind that reminds your body: *you're safe*.

Imagine you're at a networking event. The room hums with conversation, laughter, and clinking glasses. You feel your heart start to race. That familiar squeeze in your chest. The swirl of thoughts: *Do I belong here? What should I say?*

Here's what you do: pause. Let your feet feel the floor. Then slowly inhale through your nose, filling your lungs, not just your chest, but down into your belly. Hold for a moment. Then exhale slowly, fully, as if you're letting out a long sigh of relief. Try a rhythm like this: inhale for four counts, hold for four, exhale for six.

Do that just a few times, and your nervous system starts to shift. You're not just "taking a breath", you're flipping the switch from fight-or-flight to calm and focused.

This kind of mindful breathing sends a clear message to your brain: *I'm okay right now. I can handle this.* And it works whether you're standing in a crowd or sitting quietly before a presentation.

Want to take it a step further? Pair your breathing with a calming mental image. Picture yourself in a place that makes you feel safe, maybe a quiet forest trail, or the rhythm of waves lapping the shore. Let that scene fill your mind as you breathe. It's not about escaping reality, it's about steadying yourself in it.

These aren't just tricks. They're tools, practices you can return to anytime stress hijacks your focus. With just a few breaths, you give yourself a reset. And sometimes, that's all you need to come back to the moment with clarity and confidence.

Creating Space for Thoughtful Responses

Let's be honest, when emotions run hot, so do our replies. You've probably been there: mid-argument, and your brain is already crafting the perfect comeback before the other person even finishes their sentence. But here's the thing: those fast, reflexive responses are often more about winning than understanding.

What if instead, you paused?

Not forever. Just long enough to take one mindful breath. Just long enough to ask yourself, *"What's really happening here?"* That small pause, barely a few seconds, can change everything. It creates a beat of clarity, a buffer between impulse and intention. And in that space, you get to choose your response, not just react.

This practice is a cornerstone of mindful communication. And it's deceptively simple: **pause, breathe, respond.**

I once worked with a guy who used to steamroll meetings. Smart guy, but every conversation felt like a ping-pong match. We worked on one thing: slowing down. Taking three seconds before speaking. It wasn't easy, at first, he said the silence felt unbearable. But then he noticed something: people opened up more. His responses carried more weight. He wasn't just heard, he was respected.

That's the power of a pause.

Instead of rushing to fill every gap, let silence do some of the work. It's not awkward, it's thoughtful. It tells the other person, *"I'm actually thinking about what you just said."* In fact, some of the best communicators I've met are masters of the pause. They let a moment breathe. They listen until the end. Then they speak, with intention.

Try this: in your next conversation, **count to three silently before responding** (again, not the first time we've seen the pause come into play), especially if you feel defensive. Or paraphrase what you heard before offering your view:

- *"So what I'm hearing is..."*

- *"That makes sense. Here's how I'm seeing it..."*

These habits send a subtle but powerful message: *I respect you. I'm not here to win. I'm here to connect.*

And don't stop when the conversation ends. One of the best ways to grow in this area is to reflect afterward. Ask yourself:

- Did my pause help or hurt the flow of dialogue?

- Did I listen fully, or was I just waiting to speak?

- Could I have said less, and meant more?

Writing these reflections down helps make them stick. You'll start to spot patterns in your communication, when you get triggered, when you rush, when you speak with clarity. Awareness creates choice. And choice leads to better conversations.

Interactive Exercise: Your Response Reflection Journal Use this tool to strengthen your pause muscle and sharpen your intention.

1. Rewind a Conversation: Think of a recent interaction where emotions ran high or the stakes felt important. What did you say? How quickly did you respond?

2. Replay with a Pause: If you could do it again, where would you insert a pause? What might you have said differently? Write a version that includes space and reflection.

3. Set a Goal: Pick one conversation this week where you'll practice a mindful pause before responding. What cues will you use to remind yourself to pause?

Creating space isn't about slowing everything down to a crawl, it's about making room for intention. And in that room, better conversations are born.

Chapter Wrap: The Power of Pause & Presence

Mindfulness transforms the way we communicate, not by adding complexity, but by stripping it away. This chapter explored how mindful listening differs from simply being "active," it's about presence without agenda, curiosity without judgment. Whether it's staying grounded through your breath, setting aside distractions, or pausing before you speak, mindfulness allows you to connect with others more authentically. When you breathe through anxiety, give your full attention, or choose your words with care, you shift the entire energy of a conversation. The tools we explored, like the Reflective Listening Journal and the mindful pause, aren't about slowing things down just to be polite. They're about creating space for clarity, connection, and respect. In the end, mindfulness isn't just a personal practice, it's a relational one. And each time you choose presence, you invite deeper understanding and more meaningful communication.

Build the Life You Came For

What should you do next?

- **Try the "Anchor to the Moment" Trick**
  During a stressful conversation, lightly press your fingers together under the table or notice the texture of your chair. These tactile cues bring you back to the present moment.

- **Extra Credit: Do a One-Minute Breathing Reset Before Your Next Conversation or Meeting**
  Set a timer, close your eyes, and focus on your breath for 60 seconds before you go to your next meeting, enter that room, or make that phone call.

  This helps ground you and clears mental clutter before you speak.

CHAPTER TEN

— • —

HOW TO BE THE PERSON PEOPLE WANT TO TALK TO

TRUST & VULNERABILITY

Moving Beyond Surface-Level Interactions

Let's do a visualization practice. See yourself at a friendly gathering, the kind where people chatter around comfortably decorated spaces, each holding a drink or nibbling on small bites (a networking event or at a friend's house for a large social gathering).

The conversations bounce gently from one person to the next. The air is filled with a casual hum. Still, when listening carefully, you find the exchanges are shallow, hovering around benign subjects like weather patterns, local sports, or casual weekend plans. There's a lack of depth that tinges the conversation with an unspoken dissatisfaction, a subtle yearning for more profound dialogue.

You may have encountered this often: the unmistakable signs of a dull conversation include superficial questions and lifeless answers. These exchanges resemble white noise, always present and mildly pleasant, **yet ultimately forgettable**. Recognizing this is our first step in bringing life and a deeper connection. Recognizing this enables you to intentionally guide the conversation toward more meaningful topics. When discussions focus on facts and small talk, **they rarely fulfill**, leaving both parties with a nagging sense of incompleteness, a feeling of "does this conversation really matter?"

The standard "**How was your day?**" acknowledges the person's existence but doesn't make the person feel important. If you want to go deeper, try asking something more grounded and relatable, like, "**What made you smile today?**"

or "Was there anything that totally threw you off today?" These kinds of questions give people permission to be real, not just polite. They open the door to conversations that go beyond surface-level. Timing matters, too. Save the deeper questions for when the other person seems settled or at ease. And above all, ask with curiosity, not obligation. When people sense you're genuinely interested, not just passing time, they're far more likely to open up.

Want to invite someone to open up? Start by sharing a bit of your own story. It doesn't have to be dramatic, just real. A small moment from your day, a challenge you're working through, or something that made you pause and think. When you go first, you create space for others to meet you there. It's less about impressing and more about connecting. A story about learning patience during a hard season or finding unexpected joy in something small can be surprisingly powerful. When you speak from your values, about growth, love, resilience, you give the other person a chance to see themselves in your story. That's where connection starts.

And when it's their turn to share? Don't just listen for the words. Listen for the emotion underneath. Lean in. Nod when it matters. Hold eye contact, not to perform, but to be present. Echo back something they said to show you really heard it: "That sounds frustrating," or "It makes sense you'd feel that way." This kind of presence isn't just good communication, it's how we say, without saying, "You matter. I'm with you."

Interactive Element: Going Beneath the Surface

Let's put this into practice with a quick reflection:

1. **Revisit a Recent Conversation** Think back to a chat that stayed on the surface. Maybe it was full of small talk, or you walked away feeling like nothing real was said. Jot down when and where it happened, and who it was with.

2. **What Held It Back?** Now dig a little. What kept that conversation from going deeper? Were you both distracted? Were the questions too generic? Was there an opportunity to share something more personal that you held back on?

3. **Map Out a Do-Over**If you could go back, what would you try differently? Maybe ask a question with more heart behind it, like "What's been on your mind lately?" instead of "How's work?" Or share something small but real about your own day to open the door for honesty.

4. **Set an Intention for Next Time**Pick one person in your life, a friend, coworker, family member, and set a goal to go one layer deeper in your next conversation. What's one meaningful question you could ask? What's one piece of your story you could offer?

Even one honest moment can shift the tone of a relationship. When you reach beyond surface talk and bring your real self, you often find the other person is just waiting for permission to do the same.

Building Trust Through Consistent Communication

Case Study: Micah and the Broken Coffee Dates

Micah was the kind of friend everyone liked, warm, funny, generous with his compliments. But if you asked his closest friends how reliable he was, you'd get a different story.

I first met Micah during a professional workshop I led on relationship dynamics and communication. He was in his early thirties, a UX designer with a quick wit and a slight restlessness to his energy, like he was always half-ready to bolt to his next meeting or idea. Afterward, he approached me with a question that stayed with me: "How do you rebuild trust when you didn't realize you were breaking it?"

Micah had been struggling with a pattern. He'd make plans with friends and cancel last minute. Not just once or twice, but habitually. "It's not that I don't care," he said. "I just get overwhelmed. Work deadlines pile up, or I hit a social wall, and it feels easier to back out than to push through."

The turning point came with his friend Karina. They'd known each other since college. She had always been patient with his flakiness, until she wasn't. After he no-showed for a third coffee meetup (the kind they used to joke was "therapy with foam"), she sent a short text: *"I care about our friendship, but this feels one-sided lately."*

Micah was crushed. Not because Karina was wrong, but because she was finally saying what others hadn't.

In our follow-up coaching conversation, we unpacked the issue. Micah didn't see himself as unreliable, but to others, that's exactly how he came across. His intentions were good, but his actions were inconsistent. Trust wasn't being lost because of any one event, it was eroding drip by drip, like a faucet left leaking.

We worked on a few simple practices:

- **Clearer commitments:** Instead of "Let's hang soon," he'd offer: "Can we grab coffee next Thursday at 10? I'll block it now."

- **Follow-through rituals:** He began setting weekly check-ins with two close friends, even if just to say, "Thinking of you." It helped him stay present in the relationship, not just reactive.

- **Owning mistakes quickly:** When he slipped up again, and he did, he called, not texted. "I messed that up. I want to fix it."

A few months later, Micah shared a win: Karina had invited him to her birthday dinner. "I think we're good now," he smiled. "Not perfect, but good."

Reflection

Micah's story is one many of us can relate to, where our intentions outpace our actions. It's not about being flawless; it's about showing up consistently and communicating clearly. Trust isn't built through grand gestures. It's built in the small, ordinary moments when we mean what we say and follow through, even when it's inconvenient.

Which leads to vulnerability.

The Importance of Vulnerability in Conversations

Cassie's Unscripted Moment

Cassie was one of those people who had everything "together." Or at least, that's what she wanted everyone to believe.

She worked in project management at a fast-growing healthcare startup, where she was known for her calm demeanor and razor-sharp follow-through. In meetings, she was always prepared, always professional. If you asked her how she was doing, her answer was usually, "Great, just busy." She was dependable, polished, and quietly guarded. Even in casual workplace conversations, Cassie knew how to steer clear of anything that might feel too personal.

I met her during a workshop I led on emotionally intelligent communication for emerging leaders. She sat near the back, arms crossed at first, nodding politely but saying little. Until halfway through the session, we did a small-group activity called *"The Moment That Changed Me."* The goal was simple: share a real-life moment that shaped who you are, not your résumé, but your *human story*.

Cassie went third in her group. And for a moment, she hesitated.

Then, with her voice low but steady, she shared how two years ago, she had been passed over for a promotion she had quietly but desperately wanted. "I didn't just want the title," she said. "I wanted to feel seen. Like I mattered."

Her colleagues leaned in.

She went on to explain how she'd worked long hours for months, often sacrificing personal time to meet deadlines. But in the end, she said, "I wasn't vocal about what I wanted. I thought if I just kept my head down and delivered, they'd notice. They didn't."

It was the first time many of her peers had seen Cassie not as the buttoned-up team lead, but as a real person. One with disappointment, self-doubt, and grit.

What made her story so powerful wasn't that she was flawless, it was that she wasn't. It was how she ended her share that stayed with me: "I used to think vulnerability made you look weak. But not speaking up was what really made me feel invisible. I'm working on that."

In the weeks after the workshop, Cassie told me she started having different kinds of conversations with her team. Instead of glossing over stress or avoiding hard topics, she started naming them, sometimes clumsily, but honestly. "I've been surprised by how many people opened up in return," she said. "Once I showed a little of what's behind the curtain, they did too."

Reflection

Cassie's story is a reminder that vulnerability isn't about over-sharing or dramatic confessions, it's about showing up as the person you really are. That moment in the workshop wasn't planned, polished, or strategic. But it was real. And it changed the way her team saw her, and how she saw herself.

Vulnerability doesn't always come naturally, especially in environments that prize competence and control. But when it's used with care, it creates a kind of connection that no amount of credentials or confidence can manufacture. Cassie didn't lose respect when she shared her disappointment, she gained it.

Reflection Exercise: Building Trust, One Step at a Time

1. **Choose a Relationship That Matters**Think about a relationship in your life, personal or professional, where trust feels a little off. Maybe it's been strained by mixed signals, missed check-ins, or a lack of clarity.

2. **Pinpoint a Small Shift**What's one thing you could do consistently that would build trust over time? Maybe it's following through on a promise. Maybe it's checking in weekly. Maybe it's simply being more direct about your intentions. Write it down and make it realistic.

3. **Track the Ripples**Over the next few weeks, pay attention. What shifts? How does the other person respond? Keep a short journal or voice memo after interactions. Notice if the tone softens, the openness grows, or the conversations deepen.

Trust isn't built in bold declarations, it's built in the small, steady signals we send again and again. And when we practice showing up consistently, with clarity, empathy, and follow-through, we lay the foundation for something deeper.

Finally, let's explore how these habits come together to create relationships that can last a lifetime.

Cultivating Long-Lasting Relationships

Strong relationships aren't built in big, dramatic moments, they're built in the small, steady ones. A check-in text. A regular coffee. A quick laugh shared at the end of a long day. Like a garden, they need tending, just enough sun, a little weeding, and attention when it matters.

When you show up consistently, you're sending a message: "You matter. I'm here." That might look like a monthly dinner with your parents, or celebrating a friend's new job with a handwritten note instead of just a text. These rituals don't have to be grand. **They just have to be real.**

And then there's change. Life happens, moves, job shifts, growing kids, shrinking schedules. Relationships that last are the ones that bend without breaking. They adapt. A friendship that once meant daily texts might become a monthly phone call. A partner's new job might change your dinner routine. But when the bond stays rooted in respect and care, it grows in new directions.

Gratitude keeps those bonds strong. It's not about grand gestures, it's the "thanks for always listening" at the end of a call, the "I appreciate you" dropped in the middle of a hectic week. These small expressions add up. They remind people they're seen. And that builds trust.

So, if you want relationships that go the distance, start here:

- Show up with consistency.

- Celebrate what matters, big or small.

- Stay flexible when life shifts.

- Say thank you more often.

Lasting connections aren't just about being close. They're about choosing each other, again and again, in the quiet ways that matter most.

Up next, we'll explore how to carry these same principles into your professional world, because the relationships that sustain us don't stop at the office door.

Building Rapport with Colleagues and The Boss

Some of the most critical connections we build are the ones we navigate daily with colleagues and supervisors. And just like friendships, these relationships thrive on trust, empathy, and a little intentional effort.

Start with the small things. A quick shout-out in a meeting. A message that says, "I noticed the way you handled that client, really well done." These aren't just nice gestures; they're culture-shapers. Every time you recognize someone's contribution, you reinforce that they matter. It lifts morale, sets the tone, and builds an environment where people want to show up, for each other as much as for the work.

Language matters, too. Switching from "I did this" to "we pulled this off together" changes everything. It sends a message that success is shared, not hoarded. It creates room for collaboration, not competition. And when wins are celebrated as team efforts, whether that's a spontaneous donut run after a big project or a lunch toast to hitting a milestone, it cements the idea that no one's in this alone.

And while warmth and informality are powerful tools for building trust with peers, communicating with superiors often calls for a little more intentionality. That doesn't mean becoming robotic or overly stiff, it just means adjusting your tone with care. A message to your manager can still sound human: "Hope you're having a great week. I wanted to follow up on..." goes a long way toward keeping things respectful but personal.

Part of emotional intelligence is knowing how to code-switch between the hallway catch-up and the boardroom briefing. That means knowing when it's time to share your weekend Netflix binge and when it's time to pivot back to deadlines and project goals. Being able to flex between friendly and professional signals maturity, and helps keep boundaries clear, especially in close-knit teams.

Appreciation is one of the most underused tools in the workplace. Not vague pats on the back, but real, specific acknowledgment. Instead of "Great job," try, "Your analysis on the Q3 report clarified our direction, I really appreciated how clearly you laid it out." That kind of feedback doesn't just affirm the work, it affirms the person behind it. And if you want to go the extra mile? Handwritten notes, check-in texts, or spontaneous "coffee on me" moments build connection in unexpected but meaningful ways.

Of course, building rapport doesn't mean blurring boundaries. Work friendships work best when they're balanced with professionalism. A little laughter in the break room? Absolutely. But if it stretches into a half-hour vent session while emails pile up, it starts to erode trust instead of build it. Keep the rhythm light but grounded, check in, share something human, and return to focus when needed.

In the end, the best workplace relationships aren't built on grand gestures, they're built on moments of consistency, clarity, and care. When you show up with presence, give credit generously, speak with respect, and balance warmth with professionalism, you help create a culture where everyone feels seen, supported, and encouraged to bring their best.

And just like in our personal lives, those kinds of relationships don't just help us get through the day, they make the work more meaningful.

Chapter Wrap: Why They'll Want to Talk to You Again

True connection goes beyond surface-level small talk, it's about showing up with presence, trust, and vulnerability. In this chapter, we explored how to spark deeper conversations by asking meaningful questions, sharing small but honest pieces of ourselves, and listening for what's said *and* unsaid.

Through real-life stories like Micah's journey to rebuild trust and Cassie's powerful moment of vulnerability, we saw how consistency and authenticity strengthen bonds over time. We also examined the importance of rituals, adaptability, and gratitude in sustaining long-lasting relationships.

Finally, we turned our focus to the workplace, where building rapport with colleagues and superiors means balancing warmth with professionalism, recognizing others genuinely, and adjusting our tone with emotional intelligence. Whether in personal or professional settings, connection grows through intention, follow-through, and a willingness to be real.

Build the Life You Came For

What should you do next?

- **Create a Mini-Ritual for One Key Relationship**
  Choose a friend, partner, or coworker and commit to something small but consistent: a weekly check-in text, Friday coffee, or a monthly lunch.

  Setup a calendar reminder or an alarm so that you don't forget.

CHAPTER ELEVEN

— · —

HOW IT ALL COMES TOGETHER: PRACTICE IN REAL SITUATIONS

COMMUNICATION IRL (IN REAL LIFE)

Putting It All Into Practice

You've done the reading, the reflecting, and maybe even a few of the Chat-GPT Voice exercises. But now it's time to step into the real world, the place where your communication skills truly come alive.

In this final chapter, we're shifting from theory to practice by guiding you through a series of realistic scenarios drawn from both personal and professional life. These aren't hypothetical case studies or abstract advice; they're everyday moments where clear, compassionate, and confident communication can make all the difference.

For each scene, you'll be invited to drop in, observe what's unfolding, and consider how you'd respond. It's time to move from learning to doing and see just how far your growth can take you.

Your Turn: Real-Life Scenarios to Practice What You've Learned

These eight scenes are grouped into two categories, personal life and professional settings, but the lessons inside each one can often apply across both.

In your personal life, you'll explore what it means to:

1. Introduce yourself confidently to someone new at a coffee shop

2. Join a conversation at a house party

3. Navigate a tense family dinner conversation

4. Have "the talk" with a romantic partner about future goals

At work, you'll practice how to:

1. Connect at a networking event with confidence

2. Present a new idea in a team meeting

3. Request clarification from a manager without sounding incompetent

4. Give feedback to a peer who missed a deadline

Each scene is designed to help you practice the full range of skills we've covered, from building trust and staying present to using your voice with intention and adapting to different dynamics.

Let's jump in.

Personal Life Scenarios

Scenario #1: Introducing Yourself Confidently at a Coffee Shop

Setting the Scene

It's a rainy Tuesday afternoon. You've carved out a quiet hour between meetings and errands, so you settle into your favorite corner of a local coffee shop. You've got your drink, a seat by the window, and the gentle hum of espresso machines and indie music around you.

As you glance up from your notebook, someone sits nearby, someone who looks familiar, or maybe just interesting. They're wearing a t-shirt from an event you attended last year, and they seem friendly. This is the kind of moment where connection could spark, if you choose to step into it.

Your Character

You're someone who has been working on your confidence. You've read this book, done the exercises, and practiced mindful communication. But this is still the kind of moment that tests your nerves. The stakes are low, but they *feel* high. What if you say the wrong thing? What if it gets awkward?

Still, you remind yourself: connection starts with a hello.

The Challenge

You want to introduce yourself to this person in a way that's:

- Confident but not overbearing

- Friendly but not forced

- Engaging while staying authentic

You've got a few seconds to observe, gather context, and go.

Key Communication Skills in Action

This scenario is an opportunity to apply multiple concepts from the book:

- **Chapter 1:** Consider their possible DISC profile. Do they seem outgoing (I)? More reserved and observant (S or C)?

- **Chapter 2:** Use an engaging, context-relevant opener, something related to the shirt, the weather, or the vibe of the coffee shop.

- **Chapter 3:** Practice active listening and empathy once they respond.

- **Chapter 4:** Use open body language, gentle eye contact, and a friendly tone.

- **Chapter 5:** Channel your self-talk to manage any lingering anxiety or fear of rejection.

- **Chapter 6:** If the conversation deepens, share a short, relevant personal story.

- **Chapter 9:** Use a mindful breath before speaking. Stay present. Let go of the outcome.

Step-by-Step Flow

1. **Observation & Opener:** You take a breath, smile, and say: *"Hey, is that shirt from the Summit last year? I went too, it was wild seeing so many people in one place who all geek out about the same stuff."*

2. **Response Handling:** They smile. "Yeah! First time I've been, felt like I found my people." You nod and ease in: *"Totally. I'm [your name], by the way. I remember coming home feeling like my brain was on fire, in a good way."*

3. **Listening & Follow-Up:** As they respond, you maintain eye contact, notice their tone, and ask a follow-up: *"What drew you there in the first place?"* This invites them to share more, and it moves you beyond small talk.

4. **Connection Point**: If the moment feels right, you share a quick story of how you ended up at the event too, maybe something that connects to your current goals. You're not trying to impress, just relate.

5. **Closing the Loop**: After a few minutes of good chat, you say: *"It's been really nice chatting. If you're ever back here again around this time, say hi. Or... we could grab coffee again sometime?"*

You've offered connection without pressure. Mission accomplished.

Time to Reflect

- What internal voice popped up as you considered introducing yourself?

- What helped you stay grounded in the moment?

- How did the other person's body language or tone guide your choices?

- Would you try something different next time?

Record Your Notes & Thoughts on this Scenario Below

Scenario #2: Joining a Conversation at a House Party

Setting the Scene

It's a Saturday evening, and your friend has invited you to a laid-back house party. String lights are glowing on the patio, music hums low in the background, and a mix of laughter and clinking glasses fills the air. You don't know many people here, but that was part of the reason you came to meet new ones.

You're holding a drink, scanning the room. In the corner of the kitchen, a small group of three people are deep in conversation, animated but friendly. You catch a few phrases, they're talking about a recent documentary you've seen too. You'd like to join in. You just haven't yet figured out how.

Your Character

You've been working on overcoming social hesitation. You're no longer content staying on the sidelines of the room. You want to practice being proactive, finding connection, and adding something thoughtful, not barging in, not standing awkwardly at the edge waiting forever.

You take a breath. This is the moment.

The Challenge

You want to join a small group conversation in a way that is:

- Smooth and natural

- Respectful of the group's dynamic

- Engaging without being disruptive

You need to read the room, find a gap, and ease in with authenticity.

Key Communication Skills in Action

This scenario gives you a chance to pull together several skills from the book:

- **Chapter 1:** Observe personalities: who's leading, who's reacting, who's quieter?

- **Chapter 2:** Find a natural hook or shared interest.

- **Chapter 3:** Practice empathy by listening before speaking.

- **Chapter 4:** Use body positioning, posture, and eye contact to signal interest.

- **Chapter 5:** Channel self-assurance with your internal script ("I belong here.").

- **Chapter 6:** When the timing feels right, contribute a short, personal story or insight.

- **Chapter 9:** Stay grounded with a mindful breath. Focus on presence, not performance.

Step-by-Step Flow

1. **Position Yourself**: You walk over with casual confidence, standing close enough to signal interest but not interrupt. You smile and nod as someone finishes a point.

2. **First Entry**: You wait for a natural break, then say: *"Hey, sorry to jump in, but I caught you talking about the new David Attenborough doc, 'Planet Earth III,' right? I just watched the glacier episode. Insane."*

3. **Gauge Response**: One person grins: "Right? That scene with the walruses? Wild." Another gestures you in closer.

4. **Establish Connection**: You take a small step in, laugh, and say: *"Exactly. I kept thinking, 'How did the camera crew even survive that?'"*

5. **Contribute Without Dominating**: As the conversation picks up, you share a 20-second story about how that documentary inspired your last hiking trip, or why you can't watch the deep-sea episodes at night. Keep it short, real, and light.

6. **Follow the Flow**: You listen just as much as you speak. You react, ask

a question: *"So what's your take, do these kinds of shows actually change behavior, or just entertain us?"*

7. **Blend In Naturally**: After 10 minutes, you're just another voice in the circle. You've earned your place by showing interest, not by forcing it.

Reflection Questions

- What subtle cues helped you know the group was open to being joined?

- What internal stories or fears did you have to challenge in this moment?

- How did you balance speaking up with not overstepping?

- What would you do differently next time to improve your timing or phrasing?

Record Your Notes & Thoughts on this Scenario Below

Scenario #3: Navigating a Tense Family Dinner Conversation

Setting the Scene

It's Sunday night at your parents' house. The table is set with comfort food, and extended family is gathered, siblings, an aunt visiting from out of town, a cousin home from college. At first, the conversation is light: football scores, travel updates, how good the potatoes turned out this time.

But then, like it has before, things shift. Someone brings up a controversial topic. It might be politics. Or parenting choices. Or a family decision that's still a little raw. Voices rise, body language stiffens. You can feel the tension thickening the air like humidity before a storm.

You're mid-meal, and everyone's now walking the line between casual banter and outright conflict.

Your Character

You're someone who cares about keeping peace, but you're also tired of sitting silently when things get uncomfortable. You've been working on finding your voice, not to "win," but to offer calm, to redirect where you can, and to set boundaries when needed.

You're not here to escalate. You're here to show up with clarity, empathy, and confidence.

The Challenge

You want to navigate the tension in a way that:

- De-escalates rising conflict

- Protects your boundaries without shutting people down

- Creates space for real conversation, or a graceful redirect

You'll need to stay grounded, listen carefully, and choose your words with care.

Key Communication Skills in Action

This scenario is a chance to draw on several skills:

- **Chapter 1:** Recognize personality types. Who's speaking with dominance? Who's withdrawing? Who's trying to mediate?

- **Chapter 3:** Use paraphrasing and empathy to validate feelings without endorsing hurtful views.

- **Chapter 4:** Pay close attention to body language, yours and others'. Stay open but firm.

- **Chapter 5:** Use assertive (not aggressive) communication to share your views or request a change of subject.

- **Chapter 7:** Apply conflict resolution tools, stay calm, reframe inflammatory comments, and pause before reacting.

- **Chapter 9:** Take a mindful breath. Stay present, even if the emotions swell.

Step-by-Step Flow

1. **Notice the Shift:** Your uncle just said something that made your sister bristle. She crosses her arms. You see your dad stiffen. The tone in the room has changed.

2. **Ground Yourself:** You take a silent breath. Feel your feet on the floor. Remind yourself: I can speak with calm.

3. **Step In Thoughtfully:** You lean forward and say, gently but clearly: "Hey, I know we all care about this topic, but it feels like the temperature at the table just went up a notch. Can we take a second?"

4. **Validate, Don't Escalate:** Your aunt says, "Well, I just think people need to be honest." You nod and respond: "I hear that. And I think we all want to feel heard here. Maybe we can slow it down a bit?"

5. **Set a Boundary or Reframe:** If needed, you add: "I'd love for us to

keep this dinner enjoyable. We don't have to solve everything tonight."

6. **Redirect with Care:** You offer a shift: "Actually, speaking of being honest, I saw that movie you recommended last week. It really surprised me, can we talk about that?"

7. **Check for Connection:** Watch the room. Shoulders start to relax. A few people glance at you with appreciation. The tension softens. You didn't "fix" everything, but you helped the moment shift.

Reflection Questions

- What signals helped you recognize the shift into tension?

- What helped you stay grounded rather than reactive?

- Where did you find the balance between protecting peace and speaking honestly?

- What would you do differently next time in tone, timing, or approach?

Record Your Notes & Thoughts on this Scenario Below

Scenario #4: Having "The Talk" with a Romantic Partner About Future Goals

Setting the Scene

It's a quiet evening at home. You and your partner just finished dinner, the dishes are drying in the rack, and you're curled up on the couch with a blanket and low music playing. It's comfortable, maybe even a little too comfortable. Because lately, something's been on your mind.

You've been together for a while now, and while things feel good, you're starting to wonder: Are we aligned on where this is going?

You've dropped hints before. "Where do you see yourself in five years?" "Would you ever want kids?" But you've never really had *the* talk. The one where you lay out your hopes, fears, and vision for the future, and ask your partner to do the same.

It's time.

Your Character

You've grown in your ability to communicate clearly and calmly, even when stakes feel high. You want this conversation to be honest, open, and productive, not a pressure campaign or a guessing game. You've been working on vulnerability, listening with presence, and speaking with clarity.

This moment calls for all three.

The Challenge

You want to express your goals and get clear on your partner's without:

- Triggering defensiveness

- Losing your composure

- Avoiding or sugarcoating hard truths

You're hoping to create shared understanding, and maybe take a next step together.

Key Communication Skills in Action

This scenario calls on the best of what you've learned:

- **Chapter 1:** Be aware of your partner's communication style, do they need time to process? Are they more indirect or expressive?

- **Chapter 3:** Use empathy and active listening to understand their views fully before reacting.

- **Chapter 4:** Watch for nonverbal cues, are they leaning in or checking out?

- **Chapter 5:** Speak assertively about your needs without guilt or apology.

- **Chapter 6:** Share your own story or fears to frame the conversation in honesty and warmth.

- **Chapter 7:** Stay grounded when emotions rise. This isn't a confrontation, it's a collaboration.

- **Chapter 9:** Use mindful pauses and breathing to stay present. Don't rush it.

Step-by-Step Flow

1. **Set the Stage:** You pick a time when you're both relaxed and not distracted. You start with vulnerability: "I've been thinking a lot lately about where life is heading, and I want to check in with you about how we're both feeling."

2. **Lead with Openness:** You offer your thoughts first, not as an ultimatum, but as a window: "I've realized I'm someone who's starting to think about building something long-term, maybe marriage, maybe a family. I don't need answers right now, but I want us to start that conversation."

3. **Invite, Don't Interrogate:** You pause, then gently ask: "How do you

see things? What feels clear to you, and what still feels uncertain?"

4. **Listen Without Jumping In:** As they respond, you nod, reflect back what you hear: "So it sounds like you're open to all of that, but just not sure on the timeline yet. Is that right?"

5. **Hold Space for Differences:** You don't panic if you're not 100% aligned. You say: "It's okay if we're in different places right now. What matters to me is that we're talking about it honestly."

6. **Co-Create Next Steps:** End with something collaborative, not con-clusive: "Would it feel okay if we kept checking in about this every few months? I don't want to pressure either of us, but I do want us to be intentional."

Reflection Questions

- What made this conversation feel vulnerable?

- How did you balance honesty with kindness?

- Where did you sense alignment or disconnection, and how did you respond?

- What tools helped you stay grounded and open?

Record Your Notes & Thoughts on this Scenario Below

Work Life Scenarios

Scenario #5: Connecting at a Networking Event with Confidence

Setting the Scene

It's a midweek evening, and you've arrived at a local professional networking mixer hosted at a downtown co-working space. There's a buzz of polite conversation, small name tags, free drinks, and light hors d'oeuvres. You're here because you want to meet people in your industry, make meaningful contacts, and maybe find opportunities that don't show up on job boards.

You scan the room, some clusters of people already deep in conversation, others sipping quietly while scrolling on their phones. You're not the only one who feels a little awkward, but you're ready to push past that.

This is your moment to make a connection.

Your Character

You've worked hard on building your confidence in social situations. You've practiced managing nerves, making introductions, and following up with intention. You're not looking to impress everyone, you're here to be real, curious, and memorable.

You know what you bring to the table. Now, it's time to walk up and say hello.

The Challenge

You want to start conversations that feel natural and lead to real professional rapport. That means:

- Breaking the ice without sounding rehearsed

- Being memorable without oversharing

- Asking questions that spark genuine dialogue

Key Communication Skills in Action

This scenario pulls together tools from across the book:

- **Chapter 1:** Read the room, notice posture, energy levels, openness.

- **Chapter 2:** Use small talk as a doorway, then go deeper.

- **Chapter 3:** Listen with curiosity. Reflect back to build connection.

- **Chapter 4:** Mind your nonverbal cues, confident posture, steady eye contact.

- **Chapter 5:** Use self-talk to reinforce your confidence: "I belong in this room."

- **Chapter 6:** Have one or two personal stories that frame your professional journey.

- **Chapter 9:** Stay present. Don't mentally rush to "networking outcomes", stay human.

Step-by-Step Flow

1. **Pick Your Spot:** You notice someone standing alone near the snack table. You walk over casually, make eye contact, and offer a warm, simple opener: "Hey, I don't think we've met yet, I'm [Your Name]. Mind if I join you?"

2. **Start Light:** You ease in with something casual but sincere: "These events always feel a little awkward at first, do you come to these often?"

3. **Find a Hook:** As you both share what brought you here, you pick up on a point of overlap: "Oh, you're in UX? I'm in product, so I'm always curious about how teams collaborate across those roles."

4. **Build the Bridge:** You listen well, ask good follow-ups, and share a short story of a recent work moment: "We just rolled out a feature last month that taught us a lot, remind me to never skip user testing again."

5. **Make It Mutual:** You close the loop with a friendly question: "What's been the most interesting part of your work lately?"

6. **Leave a Door Open:** As the conversation winds down, you smile and say: "This has been awesome, I'd love to keep in touch. Are you on LinkedIn?"

Reflection Questions

- What small cues helped you pick someone approachable?

- How did you feel before and after introducing yourself?

- What made the conversation feel genuine rather than transactional?

- How might you follow up to nurture this connection?

Record Your Notes & Thoughts on this Scenario Below

Scenario #6: Presenting a New Idea in a Team Meeting

Setting the Scene

It's Tuesday morning, and you're sitting in a weekly team sync with five colleagues and your direct manager. The team has been working on optimizing internal workflows, and the conversation so far has been dominated by familiar voices. You've had an idea brewing, something you think could save hours of time across departments, but you haven't pitched it yet.

You've tweaked the idea, built a basic outline, and practiced your delivery. Now you're ready to speak up, not just to be heard, but to add value.

The conversation slows. Your manager says, "Anyone have ideas we haven't tried yet?"

This is your moment.

Your Character

You're thoughtful, solution-oriented, and ready to be more visible. You've been building confidence in your communication skills, and now you want to present your idea in a clear, compelling way without dominating the room, or feeling like you're overstepping.

You take a breath. Time to contribute.

The Challenge

You want to present your idea in a way that is:

- Clear and easy to follow

- Confident without being overbearing

- Open to feedback and collaboration

Key Communication Skills in Action

This scenario draws on several book chapters:

- **Chapter 1:** Consider personality styles in the room, who prefers data, who prefers vision?

- **Chapter 3:** Show empathy by framing the problem in terms of shared team pain points.

- **Chapter 4:** Use tone, posture, and pacing to hold attention and show confidence.

- **Chapter 5:** Rely on self-talk and preparation to overcome fear of judgment.

- **Chapter 6:** Anchor your pitch in a brief, relevant story or example.

- **Chapter 7:** Be ready for questions or pushback, respond with curiosity, not defensiveness.

- **Chapter 9:** Stay grounded with breath. Be present, not rushed.

Step-by-Step Flow

1. **Anchor Yourself:** You plant your feet, take one steady breath, and lean forward slightly to signal you're about to speak.

2. **Start With the Pain Point:** "I know we've all been feeling the friction with how requests move between teams, especially when priorities shift."

3. **Introduce Your Idea:** "I've been thinking about a lightweight solution that could help streamline that. What if we created a shared request tracker that resets each week, so we can see what's urgent, what's in progress, and what's dropped?"

4. **Offer an Example:** "I saw something similar at my last company, and it helped different teams stay aligned without a ton of overhead. It took 10 minutes to update, but saved hours of follow-up emails."

5. **Invite Feedback:** "I know this might need tweaking, but I'd love to get thoughts or see if anyone's tried something like this."

6. **Hold the Space:** You listen. You nod. You field a question with openness: "Great point, I hadn't thought of that, but maybe there's a way to address it by..."

7. **Wrap With Clarity:** "Happy to put together a one-pager or test a version with a smaller group if that's helpful."

Reflection Questions

- What did you do to prepare that made the pitch feel stronger?

- How did you read the room before and during your presentation?

- What part of your communication helped others engage or build on your idea?

- How might you follow up to keep the momentum going?

Record Your Notes & Thoughts on this Scenario Below

Scenario #7: Requesting Clarification from a Manager Without Sounding Incompetent

Setting the Scene

It's Thursday afternoon and your manager just wrapped up a fast-paced check-in meeting. Before everyone logged off, she quickly outlined next steps for a new project you'll be supporting. But here's the thing: you're not totally clear on what she meant by "follow the revised submission structure" or "coordinate with external contacts before initiating."

You don't want to seem like you weren't paying attention, or worse, like you're in over your head. But you also know that guessing is a gamble you can't afford. The project kicks off tomorrow. You need clarity.

You open your email, draft a Slack message, then pause. You want to ask the right way.

Your Character

You're capable, curious, and committed to doing your best work. You've been working hard to build trust with your manager, and you want to show initiative, not confusion. But you also want to make sure you understand exactly what's being asked before taking action.

You're ready to speak up, without selling yourself short.

The Challenge

You want to ask for clarification in a way that:

- Demonstrates attention and accountability

- Avoids sounding passive or unprepared

- Maintains confidence and professionalism

Key Communication Skills in Action

This scenario calls on:

- **Chapter 1:** Know your manager's style, does she value brevity, formality, or details?

- **Chapter 3:** Use clarifying questions to avoid assumptions.

- **Chapter 4:** Choose your tone carefully, friendly, but clear.

- **Chapter 5:** Push past fear of looking weak; focus on getting it right.

- **Chapter 7:** Use assertive communication without sounding defensive or self-deprecating.

- **Chapter 9:** Take a breath, stay calm, and stay present while asking.

Step-by-Step Flow

1. **Calm the Inner Critic:** Before reaching out, take a mindful breath and remind yourself: asking questions is a sign of diligence, not incompetence.

2. **Start With Context and Accountability:** "Hi Jenna, I wanted to follow up on today's meeting, I've been reviewing the notes and prepping for tomorrow's kickoff."

3. **Clarify With Specificity:** "I want to double-check I understand your direction around the 'revised submission structure.' Would that be the new format we discussed last week, or something different?"

4. **Add Ownership:** "I just want to be sure I'm aligned before moving forward, happy to adjust if I've misunderstood anything."

5. **Keep It Light but Direct:** "Appreciate your time, and let me know if you prefer a quick chat instead."

6. **Gauge the Response and Respond Promptly:** If she replies quickly with an answer, thank her and recap it to show clarity. If she suggests a

quick sync, be ready to show you've done your homework.

Reflection Questions

- How did you approach your manager in a way that felt confident?

- What language helped you ask without sounding unsure of yourself?

- What assumptions did you avoid by seeking clarity early?

- What might you do differently next time to prevent confusion upfront?

Record Your Notes & Thoughts on this Scenario Below

Scenario #8: Giving Feedback to a Peer Who Missed a Deadline

Setting the Scene

It's Monday morning. You're halfway through your coffee when your project management dashboard reminds you of a key deliverable that was due last Friday. It's still not in.

The task belonged to your teammate, Sam, a colleague you generally get along with. But this isn't the first time a deadline has slipped. You've shouldered extra work to keep things moving, and while you've let it slide before, the pattern is starting to affect the whole team.

You want to say something. You *need* to say something. But you don't want to damage the working relationship, or sound like you're pointing fingers.

Your Character

You value collaboration and accountability. You're not trying to micromanage, but you also don't want your own reputation, or the project, to suffer because of someone else's delay. You've been working on being more assertive, especially in tough conversations.

You've decided: you're going to bring it up directly, respectfully, and constructively.

The Challenge

You want to give feedback that is:

- Honest without being confrontational

- Focused on behavior, not personality

- Clear about impact and expectations

Key Communication Skills in Action

This moment taps into:

- **Chapter 1:** Consider Sam's style, will he respond best to directness or a softer approach?

- **Chapter 3:** Use paraphrasing and empathy to keep things collaborative.

- **Chapter 5:** Channel confidence to initiate the conversation instead of avoiding it.

- **Chapter 7:** Apply assertive communication, name the issue, stay kind, stay firm.

- **Chapter 9:** Ground yourself with a mindful breath before you begin.

- **Chapter 10:** Preserve rapport while holding clear boundaries.

Step-by-Step Flow

1. **Start With Empathy and Clarity:** "Hey Sam, can we chat for a minute about the client handoff doc? I know last week was packed, so I just wanted to check in."

2. **Acknowledge the Human Side:** "I totally get that things can pile up. We've all been there."

3. **Name the Impact, Not the Person:** "When the file didn't come through Friday, it put a bit of a crunch on today's prep. I had to scramble to rework my part, and I'm trying to avoid that pattern becoming the norm."

4. **Invite a Solution:** "What's a good way for us to stay in sync next time? Maybe a quick status check the day before?"

5. **End With Reconnection:** "I really value working with you, and I know we're both trying to do our best work. I just wanted to be open about what I'm seeing."

Reflection Questions

- What helped you approach this conversation without shaming or blaming?

- How did you balance honesty with empathy?

- Did your language focus more on behavior than on character?

- How did your feedback open the door to better collaboration?

Record Your Notes & Thoughts on this Scenario Below

Chapter Wrap: Turning Lessons into Life

This chapter was your proving ground.

We moved from learning the principles of confident, empathetic, and effective communication into actually living them, through moments that feel just like the ones you'll encounter in the real world.

From striking up a conversation with a stranger at a coffee shop to navigating a tense family dinner... from pitching an idea in a team meeting to giving hard feedback to a colleague, you've now walked through scenarios where communication *isn't theoretical*, it's personal, messy, human.

Each situation asked you to draw on what you've learned:

- Understanding different personalities and adapting your style

- Using body language and tone with intention

- Staying grounded with mindful pauses

- Asking better questions, telling better stories

- Balancing assertiveness with empathy

- Building trust through consistency, vulnerability, and care

These aren't just communication *tips*. They're *tools*. And you now have them.

The goal isn't to become perfect in every conversation. It's to show up more present, more aware, and more human. To step into connection, even when it feels uncertain. To move through discomfort with curiosity, not avoidance. And to build relationships that are deeper, stronger, and more real.

Keep practicing. Revisit these scenarios. Use the voice prompts. Reflect, refine, and return.

Because the more you practice showing up as your full, thoughtful, grounded self, the more every conversation becomes a chance to lead, to grow, and to connect in a way that lasts.

Build the Life You Came For

What should you do next?

- **Pick One Scenario and Try It in Real Life**
  Choose the scenario that feels most relevant or challenging, and commit to reenacting it in your daily life this week. Whether it's starting a conversation at a coffee shop or giving feedback to a peer.

  - **Practice with Voice ChatGPT Three Times**
    Use Voice Mode to role-play the scenario three different times and in three different ways. Repeat the conversation, tweak your responses, and focus on improving your opener, tone, or confidence.

  - **Then go do it IRL (in real life)**

Your Voice Could Help Someone Find Theirs

Leave a Review to Help Someone Else Begin

If you've made it here, you've done something big. You didn't just flip through a book; you invested in yourself. You learned to listen more deeply, speak more clearly, and connect more honestly. That deserves to be celebrated.

And now, you have a chance to pass that value along. Would you take 60 seconds to leave a review?

Seriously, that's all it takes. A few words about what this book meant to you, how it helped, or why you'd recommend it. Your review isn't just a pat on the back, it's a beacon for someone else.

Someone like you. Someone who needs encouragement. Someone who's still trying to find their voice. Your review might be the thing that helps them take that first step.

Leave the review where you found this book!

You don't need to write a novel. Just be real. That's what this book is about, anyway. Thank you for reading. For showing up. For doing the work.

It Doesn't End Here

A s we close this book, take a breath and take a moment.

You've done something meaningful: not just read about communication, but taken real steps toward becoming more present, more authentic, and more connected. That was the heart of this book's mission: to offer a practical, modern manual for mastering conversations that matter.

Whether you picked this up because small talk felt draining, because work meetings left you doubting your voice, or because you wanted to connect more deeply with friends and family, you now have tools to carry into every room, every relationship, every moment.

Together, we've walked through:

- How to understand different personality styles using <u>DISC</u> (Chapter 1)

- How to navigate <u>small talk</u> with confidence and ease (Chapter 2)

- How to listen with <u>empathy</u> and respond with clarity (Chapter 3)

- How <u>nonverbal cues</u> and tone speak louder than words (Chapter 4)

- How to build inner <u>confidence</u> and overcome the fear of rejection (Chapter 5)

- How to tell <u>stories</u> that build connections with people (Chapter 6)

- How to handle <u>difficult conversations</u> without losing yourself (Chapter 7)

- How to <u>navigate culture</u> and context with respect and awareness (Chapter 8)

- How <u>mindfulness</u> transforms how we show up in every conversation (Chapter 9)

- And how trust, <u>vulnerability</u>, and consistency create real, lasting connections (Chapter 10)

Then we put it all into action.

In Chapter 11, we brought everything to life through realistic, <u>everyday scenarios</u>, from introducing yourself at a coffee shop to giving feedback at work. These were designed so you could *see* the skills in motion, and start using them right away.

So now what? Now, the book ends. But the practice begins.

You don't need to master every concept at once. Communication is a lifelong skill. The best way to grow is by doing, by trying, reflecting, adjusting, and trying again. Use the voice ChatGPT prompts. Revisit the reflection questions. Pick a scenario and walk through it again, imagining yourself a little more confident each time.

Celebrate the progress you've already made. Maybe you've started listening with more intention. Maybe you've asked better questions this week, or spoken up in a meeting you used to avoid. That matters. Every small win compounds over time.

And most of all: stay curious. Curious about others. Curious about yourself. Curious about what a great conversation can unlock.

Because your voice matters. Your presence matters. And the world needs more people who know how to connect, not just talk.

So go forward. Ask the question. Share the story. Take the breath.

And step into the next conversation with confidence, clarity, and care.

And then share back with me at:

Jared@professionalskillspublishing.com

REFERENCES

10 personal narrative examples to inspire your writing.(n.d.). Reedsy. https://blog.reedsy.com/personal-narrative-examples/

15 digital communications trends that will remainimpactful in 2023. (2022, December 20). Forbes Communications Council. https://www.forbes.com/councils/forbescommunicationscouncil/2022/12/20/15-digital-communications-trends-that-will-remain-impactful-in-2023/

5 effective communication skills in meetings. (n.d.).Aprio Board Portal. https://aprioboardportal.com/news/5-effective-communication-skills-in-meetings/

5 strategies for cross-cultural communication acrossglobal teams. (2023, October 3). Wells, R. https://www.forbes.com/sites/rachelwells/2023/10/03/5-strategies-for-cross-cultural-communication-across-global-teams/

5 techniques to build rapport with your colleagues.(2021, September). Harvard Business Review. https://hbr.org/2021/09/5-techniques-to-build-rapport-with-your-colleagues

7 tips on using humor in conversation. (2009,December 1). Small Talk, Big Results. https://smalltalkbigresults.wordpress.com/2009/12/01/7-tips-on-using-humor-in-conversation/

8 effective networking strategies for professionals.(n.d.). Indeed. https://www.indeed.com/career-advice/career-development/networking-strategies

9 types of nonverbal communication. (n.d.). VerywellMind. https://www.verywellmind.com/types-of-nonverbal-communication-2795397

Active listening: Definition, skills, & benefits.(n.d.). Simply Psychology. https://www.simplypsychology.org/active-listening-definition-skills-benefits.html

Adapting your influential story for different audiences-and cultures. (2022, May 6). Forbes Coaches Council. https://www.forbes.com/councils/forbescoachescouncil/2022/05/06/adapting-your-influential-story-for-different-audiences-and-cultures/

Addressing the root cause of social anxiety. (n.d.).D'Amore Mental Health. https://damorementalhealth.com/addressing-the-root-cause-of-social-anxiety/

Are there universal facial expressions? (n.d.).Ekman, P. https://www.paulekman.com/resources/universal-facial-expressions/

Assertive vs. aggressive: What's the difference?(n.d.). Manhattan CBT. https://manhattancbt.com/assertive-vs-aggressive/

Building trust through better communication. (n.d.).Whitaker, N. LinkedIn. https://www.linkedin.com/pulse/building-trust-through-better-communication-nathan-whitaker-arisc

Clarifying questions will help you be a better listener.(2023, March). Psychology Today. https://www.psychologytoday.com/us/blog/the-adaptive-mind/202303/clarifying-questions-will-help-you-be-a-better-listener

Cognitive restructuring techniques for reframing thoughts.(n.d.). PositivePsychology.com. https://positivepsychology.com/cbt-cognitive-restructuring-cognitive-distortions/

Creative conversation-starters for networking events.(n.d.). Grace, A. https://abbygraceblog.com/networking-conversation-starters/

Discovering your unique communication style as an EA.(n.d.). EA Campus. https://theeacampus.com/blog/discovering-your-unique-communication-style/

How to communicate effectively with any Myers-Briggs®personality type. (n.d.). Stiegler, S. https://www.psychologyjunkie.com/communicate-effectively-myers-briggs-personality-type/

How to develop empathy: 10 best exercises for adults.(n.d.). PositivePsychology.co m. https://positivepsychology.com/empathy-worksheets/

How to give and take constructive criticism (withexamples). (n.d.). Bet-terUp. https://www.betterup.com/blog/how-to-give-and-receive-constructive -criticism-at-work

How to handle receiving constructive criticism.(n.d.). The Muse. https://www.th emuse.com/advice/taking-constructive-criticism-like-a-champ

How to practice active listening: 16 examples &techniques. (n.d.). PositivePsycho logy.com. https://positivepsychology.com/active-listening-techniques/

How to skip small talk and have deep conversations.(2015, December). Business Insider. https://www.businessinsider.com/how-to-skip-small-talk-and-have-de ep-conversations-2015-12

Mindful listening: 7 tips to practice it every day.(n.d.). PsychCentral. https://ps ychcentral.com/lib/mindful-listening-exercise

Pathos and persuasion: Why emotions are critical forinfluencing others. (n.d.). UNC Executive Development. https://execdev.unc.edu/pathos-and-persuasion -why-emotions-are-critical-for-influencing-others/

Social anxiety disorder: Symptoms, tests, causes &treatment. (n.d.). Cleveland Clinic. https://my.clevelandclinic.org/health/diseases/22709-social-anxiety

The benefits of vulnerability. (n.d.). PsychiatricAssociates. https://psychassociat es.net/the-benefits-of-vulnerability/

The best 15 SMART goals to improve communication skills.(n.d.). Elevation Vibe. https://elevationvibe.com/blog/smart-goals-to-improve-communication-skills/

The impact of making eye contact around the world.(2015, February). World Eco-nomic Forum. https://www.weforum.org/stories/2015/02/the-impact-of-mak ing-eye-contact-around-the-world/

The impact of tone in communication. (n.d.).Campbell, L. L. LinkedIn. https://www.linkedin.com/pulse/impact-tone-communication-dr-li sa-l-campbell--heouc

The importance of active listening. (n.d.). Gift of Life Institute. https://www.gif toflifeinstitute.org/the-importance-of-active-listening/

The importance of pauses & silence in effective communication. (n.d.). Speakeasy, Inc. https://www.speakeasyinc.com/the-power-of-the-pause-making-silence-w ork-for-you/

The power of communication: The principle of paraphrasing. (n.d.). Listen-able. https://listenable.io/web/articles/lessons/b1bd0b6e/4876/the-principle -of-paraphrasing/

The power of feedback: A catalyst for growth in leadership and employee development. (2024, July 18). Forbes Business Council. https://www.forbes.com/councils/forbesbusinesscouncil/2024/07/18/the-pow er-of-feedback-a-catalyst-for-growth-in-leadership-and-employee-development/

The psychological power of storytelling. (2011, January). Psychology To-day. https://www.psychologytoday.com/us/blog/positively-media/201101/the -psychological-power-storytelling

What is the importance of body language in communication? (n.d.). Modern-Gov. https://blog.moderngov.com/why-is-body-language-important-in-comm unication

Why emotions are critical for influencing others. (See: Pathos and persuasion...) UNC Executive Development. [Duplicate title treated earlier]

THE ESSENTIALS OF PUBLIC SPEAKING

MASTER POWERFUL STRATEGIES TO COMMAND THE STAGE, SPEAK CONFIDENTLY, AND DELIVER THE SPEECH EVERYONE REMEMBERS, EVEN WITH FEAR & ANXIETY

PROFESSIONAL SKZ PUBLISHING

CONTENTS

 # FREE BONUSES

Take advantage of this unique opportunity to guide and motivate you further on your public speaking journey. We're excited to present a specially curated collection of materials, each designed to enhance and amplify your oratory prowess. Embark on this enhanced learning experience to truly elevate your public speaking skills.

Click the link or scan the QR code now to claim your bonuses!

epsbonus.professionalskillspublishing.com/book

 #### Bonus #1: **Powerful Speeches to Model**

Dissect the artistry of 12 of the most iconic speeches delivered by the world's top influential speakers. These masterpieces, available on YouTube, are a goldmine of techniques and styles to emulate and learn from.

 #### Bonus #2: **Understand Your Audience**

Our 3 uniquely tailored ChatGPT prompts will help enhance audience engagement and save time on your research, ultimately elevating your speech.

 #### Bonus #3: **Capture their Attention!**

Check out our curated list of 48 speech topics, each with 3 sub-topics, designed to spark your creativity, springboard you forward, and ensure your passion and the audience's interest align.

Bonus #4: **Speech Roadmaps**

You will also receive 13 detailed outlines to structure your presentations flawlessly – whether a keynote, wedding toast, or asking for a raise- ensuring your audience remains captivated from start to finish.

 Bonus #5: **BONUS CHAPTERS!**

Plus, as a special bonus, delve deeper into the art of persuasion and engagement with 2 exclusive bonus chapters, adding layers of depth and insight to your public speaking repertoire.

- Storytelling: Your Secret Weapon
- The Digital Stage: A New Era

Don't miss out on this opportunity.

Click the link or scan the QR code now to claim your bonuses and continue your journey to becoming an unforgettable speaker!

epsbonus.professionalskillspublishing.com/book

INTRODUCTION

I magine stepping onto a stage and feeling a surge of exhilaration instead of a wave of anxiety. Standing in front of the crowd, imagine feeling right at home with your shoulders free of tension, confident, and relaxed.

Picture yourself delivering your speech with such conviction that the audience hangs onto every word. Throughout your speech, you exude an unwavering sense of self-confidence and boldness, captivating your audience with your passionate and authentic voice that speaks directly to their hearts. As you end your speech, the audience showers you with resounding applause. Who wouldn't? You were simply amazing!

This is the vision of public speaking you deserve, even if it is not the one you have right now. Would you believe 75% of people fear public speaking (Souers, 2022)? Indeed, it is a universal dread that has haunted many of us at some point or other in our lives. That rush of anxiety, the racing heartbeat, the dry mouth– they are all too familiar.

However, did you know this fear can hold you back in more ways than you might imagine? For one, the fear of public speaking can hinder your chances of a promotion by a staggering 15% (Zauderer, 2023). Make no mistake - it's a roadblock between you and the opportunities you deserve.

However, here's the catch: 90% of speech anxiety arises from insufficient preparation (Zauderer, 2023). The fear of public speaking, often known as glossophobia, is far more conquer- able than you might have ever thought. The nerves that come with standing before an audience are a challenge shared by many, and it's now time to address them head-on.

Do not let the fear of public speaking sabotage your next career move, your wedding toast, or your pitch for that ground- breaking startup. Look, I know it's easier said than done. The butterflies in your stomach seem almost uncontrollable, and the prospect of standing in front of an expectant crowd feels like an insurmountable feat.

Nevertheless, here is a secret - a secret that has been shaping the art of persuasion, communication, and audience engagement for centuries: **Aristotle**.

In the following pages, you will discover the wisdom of the famous Greek philosopher who has profoundly impacted the world of public speaking and communication. Aristotle's five rhetorical secrets are the keys to unlocking your potential as a captivating speaker. They include the following:

- **Understanding your audience:** Tailor your message to resonate with your listeners.

- **Ethos, pathos, logos:** Master the balance between credibility, emotion, and logic.

- **Structure and organization:** Craft your speech for maximum impact and coherence.

- **Language and style:** Choose your words and delivery method with precision.

- **Delivery and presence:** Command the stage with confidence and charisma.

SHARING IN YOUR STRUGGLES

Experiencing the paralysis of public speaking needs no explanation. Choking when confronted with a tough question from a potential investor or your boss is par for the course when fear takes hold. And who hasn't felt their knees weaken as they stand before a room, about to deliver a heartfelt wedding toast?

I get it - really. I understand the catalyst that led you to pick up this book. It's not just about the title - it's about the desire to tackle social anxiety, conquer the fear of public speaking, and finally overcome stage fright. You are at a critical juncture in life where endless possibilities await. And guess what? Seizing that promotion, persuading investors to back your startup, or leaving an indelible mark with your next toast are *all* within your grasp once you master the steps.

In the coming chapters, you will find shortcuts to success that will transform your speaking prowess.

This book is grounded in the profound influence of Aristotle's rhetorical framework on modern-day speaking. As such, you will soon see how these age-old techniques remain as relevant today as they were centuries ago.

Imagine walking into any room and effortlessly capturing everyone's attention. Envision swaying colleagues, students, investors, bosses, and even your family and friends with your words. Picture a life where you are armed with the tools to prepare any speech, captivate any audience, and leave a lasting impression that resonates.

I won't pretend that conquering your fear of public speaking is an overnight journey. However, armed with Aristotle's five secrets and a wealth of practical exercises, trust me - you will make steady, meaningful progress. The destination is a place of confidence and mastery - a place where you can speak your mind without hesitation and stand tall in any situation.

So, are you ready to take that leap? To transform from a hesitant speaker to a masterful orator? Well, swallow that lump in your throat one final time, and let's embark on the path to dynamic and confident public speaking. Your journey starts with the first step to mastery - right here, on the following pages.

Jared Johnson at Professional Skills Publishing

CHAPTER ONE

— • —

THE ART AND POWER OF PUBLIC SPEAKING

A s you delve into the world of public speaking, its significance becomes strikingly apparent. The art of addressing an audience is not confined to grand stages alone; it extends its influence into the fabric of our lives - whether it's within the confines of the workplace, the intimacy of our homes, or the camaraderie of friendships. On that note, our first chapter is dedicated to unraveling the enigma that is public speaking - why it wields such immense power and how it can shape our destinies, both positively and negatively. The journey ahead aims to dismantle the chains of fear that often bind us, preventing us from harnessing the potential this skill offers.

THE PHILOSOPHY OF PUBLIC SPEAKING

I want you to imagine the earliest days of public speaking, where one figure stood out with unparalleled power and charisma, leaving an indelible mark on history. Well, this figure was none other than the legendary Greek philosopher Aristotle. Moreover, his ideas continue to resonate throughout Western philosophy, science, rhetoric, and human ethics, shaping how we communicate and influence others.

Aristotle, a visionary thinker, believed in three fundamental factors that set the stage for becoming an influential thought leader. First and foremost, he emphasized that a successful speech should revolve entirely around the audience - not the speaker. This concept speaks to the importance of understanding your audience's needs, desires, and concerns to engage them effectively.

The second key factor Aristotle championed was addressing topics that bring "happiness" to the audience. Indeed, by tailoring your content to resonate with your listeners' interests and emotions, you create a powerful connection that keeps them engaged and receptive.

Thirdly, Aristotle advocated for speaking in the *language* of the audience. This means selectively using language, for one, but also using idioms and references that your listeners will easily understand and relate to. In doing so, you bridge the gap between yourself and your audience, fostering a deeper level of connection.

However, Aristotle's brilliance did not stop there. He introduced the powerful persuasion framework known as ethos, logos, and pathos. This framework forms the cornerstone of effective communication, allowing speakers to craft compelling arguments that resonate with their audience on multiple levels.

Rhetoric, the art of persuasion, is driven by Aristotle's insights. This framework continues to shape our daily communication in various contexts. Whether you are delivering a business presentation, a motivational speech, or even engaging in a casual conversation, the principles of rhetoric play a role in how you convey your ideas and influence others.

Now, let us uncover the five "secrets" of Aristotle's persuasion framework, known collectively as the five canons of rhetoric (Mind Tools, n.d.):

1. **Invention:** This refers to the process of gathering and developing ideas for your speech. It involves careful consideration of your audience's needs and interests, as well as selecting the most persuasive arguments.

2. **Arrangement:** Organizing your speech logically and engagingly is crucial. As such, Aristotle advised structuring your speech with a clear introduction, the main points, and a compelling conclusion.

3. **Style:** How you present your message matters. Using language that resonates with your audience, employing vivid imagery, and maintaining an appropriate tone all contribute to the effectiveness of your speech.

4. **Memory:** While this may seem antiquated in our digital age, memory was essential for ancient speakers. Memorizing key points allowed them

to engage the audience more effectively, enhancing the impact of their message.

5. **Delivery:** How you deliver your speech greatly influences its impact. Your tone, gestures, eye contact, and overall presence contribute to how your audience receives your message.

Aristotle's insights into public speaking and persuasion remain timeless, offering a treasure trove of wisdom for modern speakers. So, whether you are raising a toast at a celebration or delivering a pivotal speech that demands action, remember Aristotle's principles and the enduring power of effective communication.

SPEAKERS WHO CHANGED THE WORLD

Public speaking continues to be a vital skill in modern times, bridging the gap between the past and the present. Indeed, it has remained a potent tool for conveying ideas, motivating action, and shaping public opinion in many arenas of modern public life. The art of persuasive communication has been wielded by numerous famous speakers to influence and captivate audiences. Let us explore some examples of renowned figures who have utilized this skill effectively (Whitworth, 2023):

- **Ronald Reagan:** The 40th President of the United States, Ronald Reagan, was known for his eloquent speeches that resonated with numerous Americans. His communication style combined warmth, optimism, and a clear vision for the future. Reagan had the ability to make complex ideas accessible to a broad and diverse audience, fostering a sense of unity and shared purpose.

- **Barack Obama:** As the first African American President of the United States, Barack Obama was an engaging public speaker. In his "Yes We Can" victory speech, his use of anaphora in the phrase "Yes we can" created a chant-like momentum that transformed the speech into a collective call to action, embodying hope and change.

- **Martin Luther King Jr.:** A pivotal figure in the American Civil Rights Movement, Dr. Martin Luther King Jr. employed the power of words to inspire change and advocate for equality. His iconic "I Have a Dream" speech remains a prime example of how a well-crafted speech can ignite social transformation, leaving an undeniable mark on history.

- **JK Rowling:** In her 2008 Harvard Commencement Speech, the highly acclaimed author of the *Harry Potter* series captivated her audience with a masterful combination of humor, personal vulnerability, and insightful reflections. Rowling's ability to connect with her audience and convey her message in a relatable and engaging manner has made her one of the most influential and beloved writers of our time.

Today, public speaking goes beyond physical stages to encompass virtual platforms and digital media. Social media, podcasts, webinars, and online video platforms allow individuals to share their thoughts and ideas with a global audience.

Also, in today's world, public speaking involves not only delivering speeches to large audiences but also engaging with diverse communities on various topics. Whether delivering TED Talks, participating in panel discussions, or creating informative content online, influential public speakers can still sway opinions, raise awareness, and drive action.

Public speaking today requires adapting to new mediums. Furthermore, it also requires understanding the dynamics of virtual communication and tailoring messages for specific audiences. However, the ability to capture attention quickly, convey messages concisely, and evoke emotion remains essential. Moreover, in a world saturated with information, speakers who can deliver authentic, relatable, and impactful presentations are bound to stand out.

With all this being said, it's clear that today's successful public speakers have connected the art of rhetoric from the past with the technological advances of the here and now. While I am sure many of these speakers come to mind, it must be said that influential speakers like Reagan, Obama, Rowling, and King have left a critical legacy as we have entered our modern digital age, inspiring current and future generations to communicate effectively and make a meaningful impact on society.

WHY DEVELOP THE SKILL OF PUBLIC SPEAKING

In an era characterized by rapid technological advancements and ever-changing communication mediums, I cannot stress enough that the art of public speaking remains a cornerstone of success. On that note, let's explore how public speaking can empower individuals and transform lives:

- **Career advancement:** Public speaking skills are a coveted asset in the professional realm. The ability to confidently convey ideas, influence others, and lead discussions can set you apart and propel your career forward.

- **Idea sharing:** Public speaking provides a platform to share your thoughts, innovations, and ideas with a broader audience. As such, it is a catalyst for knowledge dissemination, sparking inspiration and driving positive change.

- **Boosting confidence:** Standing in front of an audience and delivering a compelling message boosts self- assurance and self-esteem. Overcoming the fear of public speaking can also translate into newfound confidence in various life situations.

- **Strengthening critical thinking:** Crafting and delivering speeches requires deep analysis and organization of your thoughts. Public speaking cultivates the art of structuring arguments and conveying complex ideas with clarity.

- **Exercising deductive reasoning:** Public speaking necessitates anticipating audience reactions and tailoring your message accordingly. This process hones your deductive reasoning skills and enhances your ability to connect with diverse audiences.

- **Expanding networks and enhancing leadership:** Engaging in public speaking exposes you to diverse individuals and opportunities. It cultivates leadership skills as you navigate conversations, inspire change, and influence groups.

- **Informing and persuading:** Effective speakers have the power to inform, educate, and even persuade audiences to adopt new viewpoints. This skill is crucial for driving social, political, and business changes.

- **Encouraging audience change:** Compelling speeches can inspire audiences to reconsider their beliefs and behaviors, fostering positive transformations on both personal and societal levels.

- **Driving personal development:** Public speaking challenges you to continuously refine your communication style, adapt to different audiences, and refine your message. This growth extends beyond the stage and ultimately enriches your personal journey.

- **Improving interpersonal communication:** The skills acquired through public speaking - such as active listening, empathy, and adaptability - greatly enhance your everyday conversations, leading to stronger relationships and better understanding.

- **Building connections:** Speaking engagements offer opportunities to connect with like-minded individuals, mentors, and collaborators. These connections can propel your career, creativity, and personal growth.

- **Creating lasting memories:** The moments when you deliver a captivating wedding toast, share an unforgettable idea at work, or spark thought-provoking discussions become memories that resonate with you and your audience.

In a world overflowing with information, public speaking remains a potent tool to captivate hearts, stimulate minds, and ignite change. As such, I encourage you to embrace the challenge with enthusiasm, as mastering this art can open doors to many opportunities, enrich your personal growth, and leave a deep impression on the hearts and minds of those fortunate enough to hear your words. So, step onto that stage with fervor, express your ideas with passion, and watch as the world trans- forms before your very eyes!

OVERCOMING GLOSSOPHOBIA

Glossophobia (glä-sō-ˈfō-bē-ə)– the fear of public speaking- is that elusive hurdle we must conquer to truly shine on stage or in front of an audience. So, let's break it down to get acquainted with it - and learn how to overcome it.

Glossophobia is more than just a tongue-twister to pronounce. It is a social phobia, one of the three primary types that can throw a wrench into our aspirations of becoming confident speakers. Typical glossophobia symptoms can range from sweaty palms and a racing heart to a shaky voice and that persistent feeling of "stage fright" that can put a damper on your presentation (Syed, n.d.).

What is behind this fear? Why does glossophobia rear its ugly head when we are faced with public speaking? Well, to put it bluntly, the causes can be diverse. Perhaps it's the fear of judgment or the worry that we will stumble over our words and look foolish in front of others. It could also stem from past negative experiences that have left a lingering scar on our confidence. The anticipation of potential embarrassment can be a powerful force, indeed.

And guess what? This fear is so deep-seated that it reveals itself in the very core of who we are when we are diagnosed. You can imagine it as a mirror reflecting your deepest fears and insecurities. But there is a way out of this daunting labyrinth!

Therapy is a lifeline for those who find themselves gripped by debilitating glossophobia. It is an option that should be seriously considered, and it complements the journey you are embarking on by picking up this book. However, exposure therapy is where the magic truly happens! You cannot conquer a fear if you are avoiding it like the plague. That is where the forthcoming chapters come into play.

So, get ready to embrace progress and push those fears aside because, from here on out, it is all about embracing stressful situations. That's right - we are going to chip away at that anxiety and break free from its hold. And what is this secret? Preparation and practice. These are your ultimate tools to conquer the stage and captivate your audience.

Why go through all this trouble? Because public speaking isn't just about address-ing a crowd - it is a gateway to thought leadership, professional growth, successful pitches, building your personal brand, and even delivering a heartwarming wed-ding toast. However, there is a caveat! You cannot tap into these exciting avenues until you have shattered the chains of social anxiety that are holding you back.

And here is an eye-opener: You cannot just "crush" glossophobia like any old phobia. Why? Because it is not a specific phobia - it is a social one. So, to conquer it, you must tackle the underlying beast of social anxiety head-on. Only then can you truly liberate your ability to speak confidently and engage your audience.

While the journey to overcoming your fears might seem like a steep mountain to climb, remember that the view from the top is worth every step. Embrace expo-sure, master preparation, and engage in a bit of practice, and you will transform into a charismatic speaker ready to conquer any stage in no time!

INTERACTIVE ELEMENT: EXPLORING YOUR FEARS WORKSHEET

Instructions

Take a moment to reflect on your fears and anxieties. Then, use this worksheet to identify and record what triggers your fears, how they make you feel, and where you feel discomfort in your body. This exercise can help you gain insight into your fears and take the first step toward disarming them.

Fear trigger: Write down a specific situation, event, or thought that triggers your fear or anxiety. It could be related to something you are pursuing or a challenge you are facing.

How it makes me feel: Describe the emotions and feelings that arise when you think about or encounter this fear trigger. Be honest and specific about your emotional response.

Physical discomfort: Indicate where in your body you feel discomfort or tension when faced with this fear trigger. It could be a tightness in your chest, a knot in your stomach, a racing heart, etc.

Possible root cause: Consider whether there is a deeper reason or past experience that might be contributing to this fear. Reflect on whether any past events or beliefs have shaped your current reaction. **Relevance to your goals:** Think about how this fear is connected to what you are seeking or pursuing, as mentioned in the book. Does this fear have any influence on your progress or actions?

Positive reframe: Challenge the fear by thinking of a positive or empowering perspective related to the fear trigger. How might you view this situation differently in a way that reduces anxiety?

Action steps: List one or more actionable steps you can take to confront or manage this fear. These could be small steps that gradually help you build confidence and overcome the fear.

Conclusion

By completing this worksheet, you have taken an essential step toward understanding and disarming your fears. Remember that recognizing and addressing your fears shows strength and growth. As such, you should use the insights you have gained to advance your journey of self-discovery and personal development.

Each thought, fear, and experience you have had has left an impression on your mind. However, the thing is, you will not have much success using Aristotle's framework or the inspiration from Martin Luther King Jr.'s powerful speeches if you cannot crush your fear first. So, let us focus on turning social anxiety into something you can work on in the later steps.

Chapter Two

—·—

Speak Up

Conquering Glossophobia

S tanding in front of an audience confidently and assuredly does not come naturally to many people. In fact, if you find yourself crushed under the weight of social anxiety and, as a result, are unable to speak publicly due to its harrowing clutches - let me assure you that you are certainly not alone. Nearly 90% of those who suffer from social anxiety also find the words becoming trapped in their throat when in front of an audience, as well as the bubble of panic rising in their stomach when tasked with a mere speech (31 Fear of Public Speaking Statistics (Prevalence), n.d.).

I won't lie; overcoming the fear of public speaking isn't easy. As we move into Chapter 2, you won't exactly be mastering the inherent genius of Aristotle just yet, but what you *will* do is learn some foundational secrets to crush your fear. Sound good?

SOCIAL ANXIETY

The nagging fear restraining you from delivering that perfect toast or speech and even simply sharing your ideas in a small working group is a fear shared among millions. What can be done to help you start overcoming this immense fear?

You might wonder whether you can erase your social phobia entirely, scrubbing its existence from the plane of your life. The unfortunate news is that no eraser will succinctly remove social phobia from your life. However, you can take steps to reduce that fear, transforming it from a massive beast to a minuscule bother.

"How can I do that?" I hear you asking.

Well, the first consideration that should linger in the forefront of your mind is that social phobia is not quite a *specific* fear. What do I mean by that? Simply put, I mean that social phobia is a broad form of anxiety rather than a fear of something specific itself. You don't necessarily fear the crowd or speaking; it's the concept of "speaking publicly" that causes the anxiety. With me so far?

To make this more straightforward, let's think of someone who *does* have a specific fear, such as arachnophobia. This is another pervasive fear within our society, and it typically involves a specific fear - *spiders*. So, someone with this phobia might be afraid of spider bites or the feeling of a spider crawling across their skin, for example. When it comes to public speaking, however, no specific fear is present - the simple concept of "public speaking" itself is an anxiety-inducing scenario.

With that in mind, how does this help us conquer the fear? In a sense, being able to view glossophobia and social phobia through this particular lens is helpful because it contributes some rational thinking to the mix. Anxiety is innately an irrational experience, but by recognizing it as such, the table is turned. Once you recognize this viewpoint of the fear of public speaking, you can begin to crush that fear once and for all.

Alright - now that we have that out of the way, I would like to take a moment to break down overcoming social phobia into steps that can make a difference. After all, it is only through organizing yourself, following a framework, and practicing your framework and outlines relentlessly that you can genuinely kiss this fear goodbye once and for all. Now, take a look at this more cohesive three-step process:

1. **Know what it is that you are speaking about.** Before you set out to embark upon public speaking, know what it is you are talking about. The more you care about a topic, the less likely you'll overthink or stumble.

2. **Formulate a framework for your speech.** You do not have to plan out your speech word for word meticulously; in fact, some of the best speeches rely heavily upon improvisation. However, it is essential to have a rough outline for your speech, one that follows a comfortable and cohesive order.

3. **Practice, practice, practice.** Once you know your topic and have a rough idea of what to say, practice that speech relentlessly. Practice in front of an imaginary audience and pour your heart and soul out as if you were giving the actual speech. Then, by the time the speech rolls around, you won't stumble.

Now, that might sound too good to be true, like you are staring at something so simple that it cannot possibly work. If this is how you feel right now, I encourage you to give these methods a chance and observe the results organically. Those three steps will, in time, become your most beloved companions in the realm of public speaking.

In the midst of your public speaking adventure, I know that the temptation to focus on the audience will overtake you. You cannot help but think about their eyes staring back at you, the perceptions racing through their heads, and worse, what happens if your speech is purely meaningless to the crowd? Overcoming this aspect of social phobia is as simple as training your mind to think of the speech and not the audience - at least at first.

Why exactly does this work? Well, think about the last time you witnessed an excellent speech. Think about how your brain latched onto the new information being thrown at you, leaving you mentally on the edge of your seat in anticipation. I will bet that you did not notice the words that the speaker stumbled on, nor did you notice them wipe their sweaty, shaking palms on the sides of their pants as they spoke. This is because the mind is trained to focus on new information.

While you are presenting to an audience, their minds will do the same thing. The new information becomes the focal point of the speech, not your nerves or anxious actions or even the presentation of said new information in some cases. So, while a gripping and compelling speech will captivate audiences more than a reel of information would, your nerves go largely unnoticed. This means that you genuinely don't have to worry about whether or not an audience can tell how anxious you are - they usually cannot.

Fear is the byproduct of a biochemical reaction. In cartoons and other TV shows, audiences always seem to be throwing rotten tomatoes at a speaker who dares to waste their time with something subpar. Obviously, this is not how it happens in real life; no tomatoes are being hurled, and hardly any judgment is being passed. So, where does this fear truly come from?

Fear, as it turns out, is a natural response within our brains that originates from a survival mechanism. We avoid ventures that scare us to prevent harm, and yet hardly anyone has been harmed due to simply giving a speech. Wading through your social phobia, you might ponder what the cause of this fear is and why you have it in the first place. The answer is simple: there likely *is not* a reason. Sometimes, social phobias are the result of fight-or-flight responses that make us feel anxious. As such, there is not always a clear-cut reason behind your phobia.

At the same time, you might have specific worries or doubts bounding around inside your head. Did you know you can challenge and conquer specific thoughts, fears, and scenarios that might scare you from making the perfect speech? Seriously - it is possible!

CHALLENGING NEGATIVE THOUGHTS AND WORRIES

For some people, social phobia takes the form of a racing heart, a thin sheen of sweat coating the forehead, and bubbling anxiety that has no correlating thoughts or worries. The anxiety simply... *exists*. But for others, their glossophobia manifests as a current of specific thoughts and worries - detailed considerations of "what if" or what could go wrong. This section offers tips for those struggling with excessive worries and thoughts to keep them at bay.

Now, there is a term for the type of thinking that leads to your worries. They are called "cognitive distortions." A cognitive distortion is an irrational thought or belief that centers around how you perceive the world or yourself. If you have ever thought that, for example, you were a failure because you did not meet a goal, then that is an example of an unproductive cognitive distortion that holds you back.

Cognitive distortions, believe it or not, tie directly into a fear of public speaking. Interlacing your thoughts are these distorted beliefs, doubts, and perceptions that negatively influence your ability to speak publicly. And beyond merely stopping you from making a wedding speech or pitching a new idea at work, cognitive distortions can be immensely detrimental when it comes to your mental and physical well-being. For example, those who suffer from cognitive distortions are more likely to experience isolation and low self-esteem, hindering socialization and provoking mental illness (Rice, 2021).

In the previous chapter, you got an intimate look at some of the thoughts and fears that hold you back. Now, it is time to become aware of such thoughts and fears. By understanding the cognitive distortions and generalized fears that provoke you to avoid sharing, speaking, and more, you will be able to overcome these distortions' effects.

Together, let's take a look at some of the most common distortions that ground people in negativity and ultimately stop them from reaching their goals:

- **Mental filter.** Imagine winning a million dollars, but there is a caveat - you have to wait a year to cash it in. In this instance, a mental filter would involve having such a narrow view of one isolated part of the situation that it becomes negative to you. So, rather than being elated over the million dollars, you come to have negative thoughts due to the year it will take to receive the money.

- **Magnification and minimization.** Consider how a magnifying glass makes small things much, much bigger; the eye of a needle can become a canyon. Well, this is how magnification works. If you magnify your thoughts, something that is not such a big deal can transform into a massive problem right before your eyes. Minimization, then, is the polar opposite - when you consider something that is a big deal (usually an accomplishment) to be irrelevant.

- **Discounting the positive.** Undoubtedly, positive occurrences exist within your life. However, for someone who regularly discounts the positives, these positives can become immensely difficult to see. Discounting the positives involves minimizing positive aspects in your life to focus on the negative instead. This can, of course, be incredibly harmful to your ability to be satisfied with life.

- **Emotional reasoning.** Emotional reasoning describes the fallacy many people fall into, wherein you assume that your feelings are equal to reality. For example, you may feel like your speech will crash and burn, and therefore, you assume that that is the reality of the situation. In reality, though? It's not!

- **Imperative statements.** Imperative statements include words like "should" and "must." This remains a common cognitive distortion because it serves to be a critical way that many people hold themselves back. They believe that if something does not go as it "should," then it is a complete failure. The reality is that there are degrees of success not accounted for by such imperative statements.

- **Personalization.** Sometimes, events and obstacles that have little or nothing to do with us personally can make us feel bad. Something falling over across the room can quickly spiral into a reflection of your failings if you are not in the right headspace. This is a typical example of personalization - a fallacy that involves attributing something unrelated to yourself or your worth.

What do all of these cognitive distortions have in common? Well, the answer is that all of these distortions have the villainous ability to tear you down, wrecking your chances of success as a speaker.

What this means is that overcoming the hurdles of cognitive distortions is your best chance at not only overcoming your social phobia but also becoming an assured speaker. Cognitive distortions are just that - distortions. They serve no positive purpose in our lives, and you can overcome them in part by challenging them as they appear. When you notice the creeping hands of distortion strangling your goals and aspirations, take a step back and think: *How can I prove this distortion false - and what purpose does it truly serve me?*

Concerning the thoughts hindering our progress toward overcoming glossophobia, the completing factor is *rumination*. Have you ever thought something over and over so often that it made you feel insane? And each time you thought about it, did the situation slowly worsen? That, in a nutshell, is rumination. Rumination is one of the most common ways that a simple worry can spiral into a whirlwind of anxiety.

In modern times, rumination has become so common that most people think nothing of it; however, if you genuinely aspire to trump your glossophobia once and for all, you must primarily become aware of *when* you are ruminating. Indeed, just noticing the rumination process in and of itself can be transformative. You can go from an anxious mess to a confident rockstar overnight if only you learn to spot rumination.

From there, you can effectively *stop* rumination by asking yourself a few questions, such as these:

- Is this thought helpful to me?

- Is this thought getting me closer to my goals?

- Does thinking it over help me to prepare, or is it just making me more nervous?

- Are these thoughts grounded in reality, or do they stem from a "what if" line of thinking?

- Does the thought I am having fall into a cognitive distortion?

Upon asking yourself some of these questions about your thinking, you might find that what you are doing is ruminating.

When you challenge the thought processes that hold you back- including cognitive distortions and rumination - you come one step closer to truly fighting an articulate battle, one where your glossophobia stands no chance in blocking you from your goals.

THE INTROVERSION BUBBLE

The road to overcoming the main obstacle of social anxiety does not end there. Something else that must be considered is something known as the "introvert bubble." For the vast majority of individuals who find the creeping clutches of glossophobia holding them back, it is also true that they consider themselves introverts. And while introversion itself is not bad, how we respond to introversion can make for a negative sting on one's life.

The notion of being an introvert is often misinterpreted. What most people likely don't know is that just because you are not fond of a roaring crowd does not mean you are an introvert - at least, not necessarily. Introversion has nothing to do with how much you love a crowd. In fact, a crowded party with dozens of guests can be your idea of a dream, yet you may be introverted simultaneously.

In all truth, an introvert derives energy or inspiration from solitude - not necessarily someone who *prefers* it. For many people who consider themselves introverted, this attribution is based on the fact that standing in front of a crowd and sharing ideas candidly can be a horrifying, nail-biting experience. Yet, if everyone who was weary of sharing their ideas publicly were indeed an introvert, then only a slim percentage of the population would be extroverted!

If you consider yourself an introvert, that also has no bearing on how "good" you are at public speaking; after all, an extrovert cannot assert that they are bad at being alone - that is not how it works. Introversion merely reflects what it means to recharge and, thus, is not where your skills lie.

So, what does this have to do with your overbearing fear? Well, as it turns out, someone who is trapped within the confines of the introversion bubble is unable to sustain personal growth. Yes, you heard me correctly. The introversion bubble hinders you from growing personally and overcoming obstacles.

If you consider yourself an introvert, you have probably waved a white flag regarding specific activities. Conceding that you will never be a partygoer or someone who flourishes in an intensely social setting, you have likely solidified the idea within yourself that various concepts are out of your reach. As such, this stunts your personal growth dramatically.

When you embody this personality trait, you tell yourself that you *cannot do something* - all because of a self-imposed label. In this way, the introversion bubble is like a sticky fly trap that withholds you from your dreams. The fact is that life is full of difficulties - for everyone! You cannot reasonably expect life to be simple at every turn. When you trap yourself inside the introversion bubble, the notion of challenge - the essence of what compels us to grow - is warded off in its entirety.

Fortunately, avoiding the introversion bubble is simpler than expected. All it involves is finding the strength to get out of your head and ditch those ruminating thoughts. For some, though, this may be easier said than done. I recommend revisiting the questions in the last section to defeat rumination and push yourself to do new things. Even if something seems "scary" or out of character for you, it's alright to do it - pushing yourself out of that introversion bubble is the only way to truly attain growth.

Another method for bursting out of that bubble is becoming more flexible. The walls of a bubble might seem malleable, giving pressure if you push on them, but that is just a mirage; those walls are inflexible, and they *will* crumble. The only real way to outlast this illusion is to become more flexible. Doing so involves allowing yourself to try new things, even if it feels like setting yourself up for failure. This also entails trying things that aren't "you," as this will allow you to grow outside the confines of the strict rules that the introversion bubble has imposed.

Furthermore, it might be time to shed the label altogether if you struggle to break free from the introversion bubble. I hear you gasping and clutching at your chest at the mere thought of this, but consider it for a second: Has labeling yourself as an introvert ever truly positively changed your life? If not, then it may be serving as an unnecessary constraint that prevents you from achieving what you aspire to do in life - specifically, preventing you from breaking down the barriers of glossophobia and the accompanying social anxiety.

Now, after hearing all of the information I shared with you throughout this chapter, you might be curious - what can be done to help you face your fears and challenge the thoughts that block you from greatness? Well, we are going to consider this next.

OVERCOMING SOCIAL ANXIETY

Look - facing your fears while challenging the thoughts that hold you back is, without a shadow of a doubt, one of the hardest things you can do. At the same time, though, it's also one of the bravest. When you find the inner strength to overcome these roadblocks, a world of opportunity opens up, including the world of public speaking. In order to overcome the social anxiety that provokes your glossophobia, you are going to need a few tactics.

"Flooding" is a dynamic tactic I espouse for those grappling with glossophobia. It operates on the fundamental psychological principle that fears are learned behaviors and, with the right strategy, can be unlearned. Consider the roots of your fear: is it the result of an innate discomfort or an unpleasant past event? Regardless of the origin, your fear has been ingrained through social conditioning. Flooding counters this by saturating your routine with public speaking tasks, challenging the validity of your fear by proving, time and again, that the dread is disproportionate to the reality of the situation. Yes, flooding is an upfront confrontation with your phobia. It might stir the pot of your deepest anxieties, but it also fast-tracks the realization that the fear, while emotionally tangible, is practically unfounded. The world, as you will find out, remains stead- fast as you speak.

You will notice a shift in your perception of public speaking by consistently placing yourself in the spotlight. The more you speak, the more the fear fades into the background, replaced by growing self-assurance and skill. Flooding not only diminishes the fear response but also sharpens your oratory capabilities through varied interactions and audience feedback. It's an open secret that the path to becoming a polished speaker is paved with the bricks of resilience and learning. Flooding, although intimidating at first glance, is a transformative journey that equips you with coping mechanisms for anxiety, such as strategic breathing and mental prep. While it's true that not every speech will echo with applause, each word you utter is a step away from fear and a step closer to becoming a confident, compelling public speaker. With professional guidance, flooding becomes not a trial by fire but a calculated ascent to eloquence and poise.

Furthermore, overcoming glossophobia can also be managed with these four tools:

1. **Preparing for difficult questions.** A major source behind the fear of speaking publicly for many is the question, "What if someone asks me a question and I do not know the answer?" Naturally, the solution for this is to prepare in advance for difficult questions. Research questions that may be asked in similar speeches and understand what a response would look like. Your preparation does not end there; rehearse your answers as if they were a part of your speech.

2. **Garner some perspective.** It may feel awkward initially, but try recording yourself as you rehearse your speech. In this way, you can play your recording back and understand whether any nervous habits appear, how

to improve your speech and any common pitfalls you are subject to. Overall, this will ensure that you are much more prepared.

3. **Visualize yourself succeeding.** Many people don't know this, but your brain often cannot distinguish between imagination and reality. Therefore, you can essentially "trick" your brain into calming down and envisioning success by genuinely putting yourself in a mental scenario wherein you have already accomplished your speech flawlessly.

4. **Accept your anxiety.** A small amount of anxiety is normal. When you try so hard to force "negative" feelings out of your life, it makes you even more anxious in the long run. As such, it is crucial to accept your anxiety rather than treat it like a force to cast out altogether.

By working with these skills, you can master your social anxiety fully and completely.

INTERACTIVE ELEMENT: IDENTIFYING RUMINATION

Instructions

As you endeavor to speak confidently, understanding how to identify your ruminating thoughts is vital. For this activity, you will grasp the identification of your ruminating thoughts in order to overcome them. Use this worksheet to guide you:

- **Feelings**: When it comes to public speaking, what do you feel emotionally and physically? Write these factors down.

- **Thoughts**: Are there any particular thoughts accompanying the feelings you just listed? Write those down as well.

- **Cognitive distortions**: Finally, try to analyze those thoughts that you just described. Decide whether they are based in reality or have evidence to support them and if those are helpful thoughts. See if you can name a specific cognitive distortion associated with your thoughts.

Conclusion

Friedrich Nietzsche said "invisible threads are the strongest ties." As you walk through Aristotle's five principle framework, your invisible threads hold your psyche together. It starts with reinventing yourself, overcoming self-doubt, and exuding confidence to challenge and reduce those fears from the first chapter and the ruminating thoughts from this one.

Chapter Three

— • —

The Building Blocks of Confident Communications

Invention

It is not uncommon to fear public speaking, and you are not alone in this. However, seeking help to overcome this fear is not very common. In fact, only a small percentage of individuals, only 8%, seek help to develop beyond this fear (31 Fear of Public Speaking Statistics (Prevalence), n.d.).

Feeling hopeless and helpless is a fate that troubles many people throughout their lives. When it comes down to it, it is something only you have the power to change.

Interestingly, studies find that one's comfort and confidence in speaking in front of others increases as one ages (31 Fear of Public Speaking Statistics (Prevalence), n.d.). Even still, that is a large portion of people who *never* become comfortable confronting their fears or standing in front of a crowd.

The point is that you do not have to fall victim to the same fate. Even if you don't necessarily seek professional help, know that the very act of reading this book is still an act of seeking and obtaining help in some form.

The beginning of genuinely overcoming your fear involves reinventing yourself through the development of confidence, practicing exercises that help you go into public feeling secure, and crushing the self-doubt that makes you victim to your fears. So, without further delay, let's get you inspired and confident enough to press forward!

INVENTION

In order to understand Aristotle's first secret to public speaking, we have to take a closer look. What is invention? What did Aristotle mean by using this seemingly simple term?

Well, the powerful secret of invention involves questioning whether something you say is factual. Invention in the context of public speaking involves using reliable resources to research your argument. In contrast, many people wrongly believe that invention involves pulling ideas out of thin air and fabricating the very contents of one's speech from start to finish. But make no mistake, this is not what invention is about.

At its core, invention invites quality; when you engage with invention, it is necessary to think about the *quality* of your belief in what you are saying. For example, what values influence your speech and its content? What informs it? Does what you say align with your personal views, the views of your company, or something else?

There are other factors to consider when it comes to Aristotle's first canon of rhetoric. First, start by asking questions to your- self such as:

- **What is the subject?** Considering the subject matter in detail is, believe it or not, an aspect of invention that's often overlooked. In order to make a great speech *and* feel confident about it, it is necessary to know what the topic of said speech is.

- **Can you define the topic and the elements that compose it?** This question involves understanding whether you genuinely know what you are talking about. If someone in the audience asks for clarification, you must know your subject and what it involves.

- **Have you selected an outlet for your message?** In other words, how will you convey the message to an audience? A speech is not always face-to-face; in modern technology, Zoom presentations or Instagram livestreams pose valuable options for conveying a message.

Additionally, invention necessitates that you know your audience. Suppose you step out onto a stage in front of an audience of first-time mothers. In that case, understanding their hesitations, anxieties, and concerns about parenthood will allow you to advertise this up-and-coming car seat company more aptly, for example. The point here is that when you know your audience, you can adequately speak to them in a way that leaves a lasting impression on their memory.

Understanding the basics of invention is a start, but how can you walk through its rhetorical steps? To do so, you must master self-confidence, release self-doubt, and be authentic in your connection to the audience, all of which we will delve into next.

RELEASING SELF-DOUBT

Mastering the art of invention begins with a journey of releasing self-doubt. As you set foot upon this seemingly treacherous path to releasing everything that makes you feel attuned to the words "I cannot," strive to bring those thoughts from the last two chapters - the fears and what made you *feel* those fears. This is vital, as releasing self-doubt begins on the back of self-awareness.

How you speak to yourself is referred to as "self-talk." For someone held back by the harness of self-doubt, it is crucial to analyze how you talk to yourself - out loud, in your head, or otherwise. Your doubts about your abilities stem from a place of negative self-talk, and defeating that habit is where self- awareness ties in.

So, what is it you need to do, exactly? To fend off these negative thoughts that drown you in doubt, you have to recognize that you are having negative thoughts in the first place. After all, you must be aware of the fire before you can put it out. There are a few steps to recognizing the sheer existence of your patterns of negative self-talk:

1. When you notice a negative or doubting thought enter your mind, stop. Just take note that a negative thought has occurred without trying to judge it.

2. Think about what you were doing, saying, or feeling before the negative self-talk occurred. This is going to be what *triggered* the negative

self-talk.

3. Repeat this process whenever you catch yourself thinking one of these thoughts.

The more you engage with these three simple steps, the more you will come to recognize patterns in what triggers a negative thought; you will understand, for example, whether a particular person, activity, or even song makes you feel doubtful about yourself.

After that, you have to charge forward and dispute the thought. At the moment, a negative thought can feel like the end of the world; your simple "I will never make a good speech" assertion can transform into a rigid rule that you have placed upon your- self right before your eyes. This is what we are going to change. Why? Because negative thoughts do not deserve such power over you.

When you feel the overbearing blanket of negativity, it can be hard to see through to the light of a situation - but you will have to force yourself to do it anyway. So, for starters, see if you can find any evidence to the contrary, as this will help disprove the negative thoughts bounding through your head.

For example, let us say the thought that "I will never make a good speech" is your negative thought. Has there ever been a time when someone commended you on a speech or even congratulated you? Or the opposite: Have you ever made a demonstrably bad and truly horrendous speech? Chances are, you haven't. Rationalizing your negative self-talk in this manner is the key to disputing such thoughts.

Furthermore, you can add two tools to your toolkit to over- come negative self-talk: the dynamic duo of "ability-talk" and "effort-talk." Ability-talk takes the lens that you are *already* good at something, even if you truly are not. Remember: the human mind cannot easily distinguish belief from reality, which means that telling yourself, "I am so good at public speaking," can convince your brain that this statement is entirely factual.

Effort-talk is similar. It involves speaking in a manner that conveys your willing-ness to put effort into a task. For example, telling yourself that "I will try my best" for a speech empowers you to put in the effort to do your best. Subliminally, this also assures you that you are good enough and do not have to stretch to meet the standards anyone else places upon you.

Releasing self-doubt also involves substituting any absolutes in your speech. Absolutes are phrases that indicate that something is always a shade of black or white when the reality is that several shades of gray come into play. The following are examples of absolute statements you might find yourself repeating:

- I will *never* make a good speech.

- I *always* mess up my public speaking.

- They are *always* judging me when I am speaking.

When you allow these absolutes to fester within your head, you lose the ability to release the self-doubt they facilitate. So, to put it simply, this means you have to move away from absolutes in your thinking. Take a look at these revised versions of the statements above:

- One day, I will make an *amazing* speech.

- I made a *few* mistakes, but I tried my best!

- My audience is *actually* cheering for me to succeed.

See how those absolutes became shades of gray that no longer confine you to a rule? By abandoning the rigidity of absolute statements, one can shed the coat of self-doubt and truly grow.

It is crucial to understand that self-doubt can be countered with an antidote. This remedy has the power to diminish even the most monstrous form of self-doubt, leaving it powerless. Self- love is the secret that nurtures the defeat of self-doubt.

It might sound like a joke, but honestly, we are conditioned by society to suppress the powers of self-love. However, self-love is the polar opposite of self-doubt, and so by inviting self-love into your life, you create an impenetrable shield between your- self and those negative thoughts. Finding the courage to fight doubt with compassion is one of the strongest, most positive changes you can make if you truly desire to free yourself from self-doubt.

REINVENT YOURSELF WITH GRATITUDE

As we inch closer to the line of invention, crushing self-doubt, and inspiring confidence, there is one unstoppable superhero we need to meet along the way: gratitude. Gratitude is so important because, without it, you cannot see your good qualities, nor can you truly crush self-doubt or inspire reinvention that dissolves your self-doubting tendencies.

One of the best parts of embracing an attitude of gratitude is that it allows you to mine for diamonds of positivity that can overshadow any spots of negativity in your life. You see, gratitude has the striking ability to boost our emotional well-being and happiness. With such a positive mindset, it can be hard to even think about the impact of negative self-talk or self-doubt.

You can also use gratitude as a means to silence self-doubt in action. When you have a thought that's less than appreciative of yourself or where you are in life, counteract it with gratitude for how far you have come and what you have accomplished. This kind of reframing can prevent self-doubt from negatively impacting your life.

Now, in order to make gratitude a regular practice in your life, try keeping a gratitude journal. A gratitude journal is one of the quickest ways to see a pile of wonder appear before your eyes. While most gratitude journals focus on being grateful for what you have or the world around you, let us give this one a little spin: Focus this gratitude journal on why you are grateful for *yourself*.

Journaling about your skills, abilities, and accomplishments allows you to appreciate your worth as a human being. You can even use prompts, such as the following, to inspire you as you journal:

- What are three things about myself that I appreciate the most? Why do these qualities or attributes make me proud?

- Reflect on a recent accomplishment or achievement, no matter how small. How did my efforts contribute to this success, and how can I celebrate it?

- Describe a challenging situation I have overcome. How did my resilience and determination play a role in my victory?

- List three aspects of my physical health that I am grateful for. How can I continue to care for and appreciate my body?

- Think about a mistake or setback from my past. How have I grown or learned from this experience, and how can I be grateful for the lessons it taught me?

- Who are the people in my life who support and love me unconditionally? How can I express gratitude for their presence and contributions to my well-being?

- What three things do I enjoy that bring me joy, peace, or a sense of accomplishment? How can I make time for these activities more regularly?

- Reflect on the personal growth and self-improvement I've experienced over the past year. How can I express gratitude for my journey of self-development?

- Write a letter to my future self, expressing gratitude for the person I am today and the progress I hope to make. What words of encouragement and appreciation can I offer my future self?

- What positive affirmations or self-love mantras resonate with me? Write them down and explain why they have significance in my life.

If you challenge yourself to journal for even 3 minutes a day about how grateful you are for yourself and your accomplishments, you will start to notice the demon of self-doubt shrinking further and further from your consciousness.

Okay, now let us return to the core idea of invention. How does reinventing yourself with gratitude for confidence tie in with invention?

First, the way that you speak to yourself matters. As I mentioned earlier, the self-talk you engage in plays a significant role in how you feel about yourself and your abilities. If you only ever fill your mind with negative self-talk, you will naturally not feel confident in your abilities; however, if neutral or positive self-talk becomes your new norm, you will be a powerhouse of confidence.

The fact of the matter is that if you have been invited to speak publicly or have the opportunity to do so, you probably have something of value that can be added to the pitch, conversation, or situation. Otherwise, someone else would have been asked or invited to speak.

In this instance, the best course of action is to try and place the information ahead of yourself. For this moment, consider the information you have to convey more important than your nerves, doubts, and anxiety - because, in many cases, this helps you avoid being held back by these things.

Being nervous, scared, or worried does not devalue the message you are trying to share. A stammering individual speaking compelling and useful words is much more worthy of an audience's attention than a confident person saying nothing of substance, after all. Keep this in mind: The people you are speaking to *want* to listen; if not, they would not be there. Remember that as you stand in front of the crowd, *they are all rooting for you.*

Mantra Rituals to Pump You Up

All of this talk is good, but you need something *great* to help you confidently walk on stage. That is where mantra rituals come into play. A mantra ritual uses repetition and self-talk to soothe you. If repetition, soothing language, and comforting words calm you, this is perfect.

Find a word or phrase, such as "I am calm and present," that connects to a positive, small goal for your speech. Then, look in the mirror and chant that mantra to yourself. It might feel silly at first, but you will find yourself more assured and comfort- able once you get into the habit of it.

AUTHENTICITY AND VULNERABILITY

Authenticity and vulnerability are like twins; together, they can also help you with the invention stage of unleashing your brilliance. Consider some of the best speeches and presentations that you have ever witnessed. I am willing to bet that the instances of that speech that spoke to you the most were those driven by authentic interaction and the willingness to be vulnerable. These are the skills we will help you hone to ramp up your performances.

If you have ever tried to imbue authenticity into a speech, you might have found yourself standing in front of a mirror, rehearsing a joke, blunder, or mistake that humanized you to the audience. While humanization is desirable, the mistake that you are making with this rehearsal is, well, rehearsing it at all! In other words, genuine authenticity does not come from practice.

Be yourself on stage. If you make a mistake in your speech, trip over your words, or crack a joke that does not land, the audience will find you endearing - someone authentic and vulnerable that they can trust, someone just like them. This leads to how you have to allow yourself to become vulnerable on stage.

Vulnerability does not come easy to everyone; it involves bearing your soul to a crowd of strangers, showing them a part of yourself that you might not even be familiar with fully. It can be frightening - something you fear adding to the already horrifying task of public speaking. Nevertheless, vulnerability can be the key to invention, helping your audience connect with you completely and honestly.

Now, you might be wondering how you can unlock authenticity and vulnerability on stage; after all, it is not like that is something you can narrow down to a four-step process, right?

It is! To unleash your authenticity and vulnerability for genuine crowd connection, follow these four steps:

1. **Play to your strengths.** The first step is playing to your strengths because using them makes it much easier to speak from an authentic place. For example, if you are a wonderful storyteller, include a gripping personal anecdote in your speech. Incorporate those strengths, and they will naturally form connections with the audience, promoting a more engaging speech.

2. **Find some balance.** Going into a speech full of rehearsed enthusiasm is just as likely to turn off a crowd from paying attention as complete disinterest can; you have to find a balance between your emotions and enthusiasm to captivate the crowd perfectly. Connect your verbal and nonverbal communication to what you are saying, and allow those facets to drive natural balance in your communication.

3. **Be purposeful.** Speak like you mean it, and ensure your personality shines through. At the same time, be careful to avoid over-manufacturing yourself for the crowd. They want someone honest and genuine to connect to, and that is only going to happen if you do not just sell your topic but yourself, too.

4. **Have passion.** Your passion for the topic is infectious; if the crowd sees your genuine passion and enthusiasm for what you are talking about, they will feel the same passion.

Your authenticity and vulnerability have to shine through in a speech for the audience to understand that they should be poised on the edge of their seat, ready for a thrilling presentation. With those four steps, you are well on your way to being the speaker they crave.

PRACTICING IN THE MIRROR

You do not want to go out to your speech's big day without rehearsing and re-rehearsing your speech. Whether practicing in front of a mirror or your family or even giving the speech to your beloved pet, you have to know what to practice for that time to be fruitful. So, what do you need to focus on for the perfect rehearsal?

It begins with taking measures to manage your nerves. Your nerves are no doubt one of the most debilitating aspects of the speech. By dusting off some methods for quelling your tense nerves, you can get off on the right foot:

- Learn about controlled breathing and how to do it, as this will help you feel more at peace as you stand behind the curtain, ready to present your speech. For example, you can practice square breathing, inhaling for four seconds, holding for four, then exhaling for four, holding for four, and repeating, a cycle that soothes the mind and steadies the nerves.

- Pick out some music to listen to on your way to the location of your speech. The right music can put you in a positive headspace, whether driving, taking a bus, or even boarding a plane.

- Select a mindfulness exercise or two you can engage with on your way there or as you prepare to walk out on stage. For example, you can practice a sensory engagement exercise where you identify five things you see, four you can touch, three you can hear, two you can smell, and one that you can taste to draw you to the present moment.

- Try not to consume too much caffeine - if any - before your speech. Caffeine is a stimulant, which can cause you to feel nervous - more nervous than you already feel. On top of that, caffeine is a diuretic, which can leave you with an overactive bladder to go with your nerves.

Also, remember that your audience does not know that you are nervous; unless sweat is pouring from your forehead and you are shakier than a bobblehead on the dashboard of a car, your nervousness will not be the first thing on the audience's mind. Before your speech and as you practice in the mirror or in front of someone else, try getting into the swing of soothing your nerves using the methods I just provided you.

Remembering to rehearse your posture is the next dynamic of an excellent speech. Posture, of course, refers to how you stand and even walk around up there on stage, and it matters greatly when it comes to what the audience takes away from your speech. Think about it: Someone hunched over a podium exudes far less confidence and trust than someone standing tall yet relaxed.

The fact is that bad posture acts like a barrier between you and the audience. On the other hand, when you have a clear and robust posture, your audience can be more receptive to what you are saying. Keep your arms uncrossed and relaxed by your side, your back straight, and your head up high as you speak to the audience; these, especially in combination, are the key to a confident and assertive posture. An open posture signals to your audience that you're comfortable, confident, and open to engagement.

For many people, standing upright with their arms uncrossed by their side, especially in front of a group, makes them feel very vulnerable. And it's true, in a certain sense - you are being *open*. Because it can feel uncomfortable, though, this way of standing is something worth practicing and getting comfort- able with. As you can imagine, it does not come naturally to many people.

Also, do not let something physically come between you and your audience. A podium, a laptop, or even a microphone stand can create dissonance between you and the audience. Instead of letting these items block you, step to the side and allow yourself and your audience to be face-to-face, with nothing between you but air and opportunity.

From there, it is time to focus on eye contact. Now, many people wrongly assume that because the audience is several feet away, they cannot see your eyes - this is typically untrue. Never doubt the power of your gaze. Therefore, you should allow yourself to make eye contact with the crowd and select members to lock eyes with. Do not stare them down, however!

And that is not all - think about infusing your speech with a touch of humor. If there is a prop you have dropped or if you trip over a microphone cord, make a joke about it and move on. By refusing to fixate upon mistakes and instead turning to humor, you can keep the audience's focus without drawing attention to minor mistakes. This is a perfect blend of vulnerability and authenticity for your speech.

INTERACTIVE ELEMENT: REFRAMING WORKSHEET

Instructions

Negative thoughts, as discussed throughout this chapter, can contribute to self-doubt and a lack of confidence in your speech. In order to overcome this, try filling out the following worksheet to reframe your thoughts. You can even give this a shot weekly:

- Is there significant evidence that proves my thought to be correct?

- Is there evidence that disputes my thought?

- Does my interpretation of this situation lack evidence?

- If I talked to my friends about this situation, what would they think?

- How is the situation different from a positive lens?

- Is this matter going to be important a year from now? Five years from now?

Conclusion

Roy T. Bennet said "if you can remove your self-doubt and believe in yourself, you can achieve what you never thought possible." And this is very true. So, on that note, start practicing your authentic self, confident mirror talks, and empowering reinvention. Then, you can move to the arrangement canon in Aristotle's framework to further your confidence and public speaking skills.

CHAPTER FOUR

— • —

CRAFTING THE ARCHITECTURE OF YOUR SPEECH

ARRANGEMENT

Preparation matters more than you might think when making a compelling speech that genuinely connects to an audience. Sure, it is possible to deliver a wildly successful impromptu speech. However, this possibility is likely pretty slim and, thus, something you should not rely on because success is not the typical outcome of an unprepared speech.

Indeed, a lack of preparation is responsible for the fact that 90% of people struggle to perform on stage, becoming anxious or failing at their speech altogether (31 Fear of Public Speaking Statistics (Prevalence), n.d.). This fact underscores the importance of preparation.

Another interesting consideration to note is that audience engagement skyrockets when you invite members to speak or interact with the speech in some way; at the same time, this is not something you can achieve without careful preparation.

This is one of the many reasons why careful planning is necessary to attain complete and succinct audience engagement.

Proper planning is crucial for delivering a good speech, and it all starts with preparing yourself for the presentation and effectively conveying your ideas. Even Aristotle emphasized the importance of planning in public speaking and acknowledged that every speech requires careful preparation.

I understand that preparing a speech can be nerve-wracking. That is why we have eight steps to help you get ready. While this will not be the outline you will use to form the final speech, it does break down key moments and steps you must prepare before you devise an outline.

UNLEASHING ARRANGEMENT

Aristotle's second canon of rhetoric is arrangement, which focuses on delivering influential and memorable speeches. The arrangement of your speech determines how you sell your idea, influence others, and prepare for debates that may arise. However, what makes a good preparation for speeches, whether at a wedding or to pitch an idea to a room full of investors (or even the boss who may promote you)?

Let's step through them now:

Step #1: Plan Your Speech Around the Occasion

It is essential to understand that certain occasions require an appropriate type of speech. For instance, you cannot attend a wedding and use a toast as an opportunity to pitch a business proposal. Similarly, you cannot use a wedding toast to request a promotion at work. Although this may seem obvious, understanding the occasion is one of the first considerations you need to arrange your speech. As Aristotle would advise, understanding an event's tone and point will guide you toward the speech you need to present.

So, in order to help you narrow down your occasion and what that means for your speech, there are a few questions that you can ask:

- Is this a formal event or one that's more casual?

- Will those in attendance be people whom I know or strangers?

- What is the purpose of the speech that I am making in the context of this event?

These questions are excellent for narrowing down the formality and connection that can be anticipated from a given occasion. In tailoring your speech to the occasion rather than hoping they match, you come to the table prepared and ready with something appropriate.

Step #2: Pick a Topic or Purpose

Now, no good speech is complete without a topic or a purpose. A topic may arise naturally when you think about the occasion you are presenting for. If not, ask yourself what the speech is about. Where are you and why are you there: at a conference, a school assembly, or your best friend's wedding? *That* would be your topic.

Once you have a topic narrowed down, you can begin to learn more about it. The best presenter is at least slightly more knowledgeable about the topic at hand than the audience. Beyond that, interest is of the essence - if you do not seem interested in the topic, your audience will not be either. Plain and simple.

Furthermore, think about *why* you are presenting your speech. "My boss made me" or "my cousin asked me to" are not answers that highlight the purpose. Are you trying to inform someone, persuade them, or even entertain them? Understanding the *why* helps plan a speech that is appropriate and interesting for your audience.

Step #3: Compiling Content

Of course, you cannot speak if you have nothing to say! Therefore, the next step of mastering arrangement involves gathering content that will be used in your speech. Sometimes, such as if your boss asks you to present data, you will already have that content ready. In other cases, the brunt of the research and consideration falls to you. This means you must dive headfirst into the world of research, untangling what you will say and its relevance.

An excellent tip for your compilation stage of arrangement involves gathering more information than you need. A speech should only contain the best of the best information; if you are presenting the benefits of a new product, irrelevant or uninteresting information will only distract your audience from the key message. If you gather together more information than you need, you can sift through what you have to pick only the best out of the collection.

Step #4: Organize the Contents of Your Speech

Chances are, you did not compile your information in the exact order that you will present it - actually, you probably *should not* present it in the order in which you compiled it. Careful planning also means that you have to intricately arrange the contents of the speech now that you know what the speech will contain.

For most speeches, there is a standard format you can follow. First, tell your audience what you are going to be talking about. Then, get into the heart of the speech, and lastly, finish off with a summary. This allows your audience to know what to expect, consume the content of your speech more readily, and then hear a snappy summary of it all again to keep it fresh in their minds.

Step #5: The Introduction

Your speech needs a compelling introduction that reels the audience in and keeps them captivated. Of course, you do not have to start with the most exotic or original line to keep your audience's ears and minds open; instead, all you need is to know your audience.

First off, in order to know your audience, consider their age. Does your audience come from a diverse age range, or are you presenting to a group from one particular age range? It will also serve you well to consider the culture, financial background, and family situations that your audience may fall into.

The point is that once you know your audience, you can hit them with a provocative question, a shocking statistic, a powerful quote, an amazing anecdote, or another introduction that truly knocks their socks off, keeping them enticed throughout your time on stage.

Remember, the introduction of your speech is your first chance to make an impression on your audience. A captivating opening can draw your audience in, setting the stage for a powerful and engaging speech. Whether you choose to open with a quote, a question, or a statistic, ensure that it aligns with your key message and resonates with your audience. After all, the best introductions are not just heard; they are felt. They don't just inform; they inspire. They set the stage for a speech that is not just listened to but remembered.

Weaving a captivating introduction is akin to carving the face of your sculpture. It's the first thing your audience sees. It reflects your speech's soul. It commands attention, incites curiosity, and builds anticipation. With a well-crafted introduction, you will not only capture your audience's attention but also their hearts and minds, paving the way for a speech that truly resonates.

Step #6: Visual Aids

Now, not every excellent speech needs a visual aid; you can certainly make a memorable one with nothing but yourself and some preparation. However, in situations where visual aids make sense, integrating them can help your audience envision your end goal. In other words, a few well-placed visual aids can compel your audience to understand your vision with total precision.

Think about a textbook you might see in a classroom. For a biology textbook mapping out a bodily structure, the textbook might bring up a chart or diagram next to the text that's relevant to the diagram. This reinforces the learning in the reader's mind while simultaneously clarifying the diagram and the text with one another. Then, during an exam, one can recall the material by drawing their mind back to the corresponding imagery. A visual aid in a speech serves a similar purpose.

Based on this, you should only present the visual aids in your speech as you talk about the relevant subject matter. For instance, a chart expressing a visual representation of a statistic should only be visible when mentioning the statistic; otherwise, the audience becomes mentally numb to that visual aid - and potentially any other visual aids throughout your speech.

A common mistake when presenting a visual aid is speaking "to" the visual aid. Many presenters make the mistake of facing the screen of their PowerPoint presentation rather than their audience, which creates a sense of dissonance. Now, it is okay to occasionally glance at the visual aid, even pointing if needed, but most of your focus should *always* be on the audience. This means you must have your visual aid memorized! And be able to speak to it and its details without reading from it.

Also, consider having hard copies of your material to distribute to your audience, especially if it's appropriate for your setting. Don't assume everyone can see your presentation on a screen. It can be helpful to visit the location beforehand to understand where the screens and stage are in relation to the audience. Additionally, providing physical copies of your material can help jog your audience's memory at the end of your talk.

Step #7: Phrasing

Alright, so the next step involves working with the phrasing of the speech. Now that we have the message, purpose, introduction, and various cues and aids ready, it is important to think about *what* you will say and *how* you will say it on the big day. This will make delivering or ending the speech much more natural and fluid.

One mistake that people commonly make is attempting to memorize the exact phrasing of a speech in order to recite it perfectly on the day of delivery. Trust me on this one - the audience can tell if you are providing a play-by-play of a pre- written speech. We intrinsically engage with particular intonations and vocal habits upon recital that make the speech seem mechanical and distant - and that is not what you want.

Instead of doing this, you will want to use something called "extemporaneous delivery." This means you walk into the speech well-prepared and versed in what you will say, but you do not have the exact phrasing memorized and ready to go. Instead, the wording is spontaneously created live and in the moment. This is the best way to deliver a natural-sounding and compelling speech from the bones of preparation.

Step #8: Rehearsal

The final step to mastering speech arrangement is rehearsal. This is where you rehearse your ode to the audience in the mirror, your family, or even your pet over dinner. Rehearsal is also the stage where you hammer out struggle points and prepare for mishaps, which we will focus on more in Chapter 5.

Altogether, these eight steps are the key to a successful arrangement. Indeed, this is the framework you need for any speech, whether a proposal to clients at work or a commencement address. With this compelling framework, you are sure to succeed. Even with these steps outlined, though, you may still have some questions - ones crucial to helping you improve upon applying these steps. Let us go ahead and address those now.

KNOWING YOUR AUDIENCE

By definition, the introduction to your speech is the first thing your audience hears. The first few seconds are a make-or-break part of your speech that can reel your crowd in or disinterest them entirely. In order to truly empower yourself through Aristotle's arrangement tactic, you have to make an introduction that paves the road to a truly great speech. The secret to doing so? You remember: *knowing your audience.*

The good news is that a few simple tricks can amplify your speech and awareness of your audience, minimizing the amount of research necessary to reach the same end goal. Let's consider what you need to know to make this your reality as you captivate the crowd.

The Three Keys

In order to know your audience *and* communicate with them in a meaningful way, you need to do three things:

1. Make sure your speech's topic, particularly your introduction, appeals to them.

2. Understand the approximate amount of knowledge your audience already has about the topic.

3. Use inclusive topics that can appeal to broad demographics, including being aware of when to include cultural considerations.

It really is that simple! In order to help you truly understand each of these three keys, I will expand on them further.

It all begins with ensuring the audience is interested in your speech. Sometimes, you can present a speech to someone who does not care about your topic and still make a bang if you go at it from the right angle; however, you will be far more successful if you present a topic your audience cares about.

And that's not all - you should also try to understand *why* they care about that topic. For example, let us say that you are pitching a new shoe company that prides itself on minimalism and nonslip bottoms. Now, are you pitching to nurses or fast food workers? There is a stark difference between the two, and by understanding the motivation, you can tug on their heart- strings a little more.

Of course, avoiding assuming the audience is just like you is also a good idea. The same reason that you care about a topic might not align with why they care about that topic, and that's fine - but you have to know *why* they feel differently and *how* they feel differently.

After that, you must aim to understand how much the audience already knows about the topic. And this is a fragile balance. If you talk to them as if they know nothing, but they are, in fact, professionals, then your approach may seem condescending. Conversely, if you talk to your audience like they are experts when they are inexperienced about the topic, they likely will not follow you too well, and from there, they will lose interest in what you are pitching.

This is one area where you might have to do some research or even ask someone who would be an ideal audience candidate what they already know. Doing so can give you a good lens regarding balancing technical terminology alongside examples and anecdotes.

Finally, consider the cultural differences your audience may have that make you an outsider. This does not just apply from country to country; someone in a different city can have an entirely different culture than you do. Leveraging that culture to understand norms and language can make your speech far more interesting to an audience.

Preparing for a Specific Audience

So, let us say you have a specific audience in mind - one that you know some basic details about and need to prepare for as you craft your speech. Now what?

First, do at least some research in advance if you can; try to contact the person organizing the event and see if they know anything about the audience or their expectations. This will provide you with a launchpad to begin your research. Furthermore, if you know you are presenting to a specific company or person, look them up beforehand.

If you cannot research the audience, it might be a good idea to greet them at the door if possible. In doing so, you can mingle and learn more about them - empowering you to use that information within your speech to make adjustments on the fly.

It might also benefit you to be familiar with the layout of the room in which you will be presenting. It might not seem important now, but see if you can look at the stage, meeting room, or other area ahead of time. By familiarizing yourself with the space, you can make sure of how best to lay out visual aids and engage with the audience, depending on the size of the space.

By including these methods in your speech arrangement process, you are on the right track for a compelling speech your audience can connect to.

CHOOSING A TOPIC

From the moment you begin arranging your speech, you will probably be wondering how exactly you are going to choose a topic around which to center it. At this stage, authenticity is the glimmering key that serves to unlock the doors to an amazing speech.

If you have complete freedom over the speech, authenticity will come from connecting the speech to something you feel confident about.

So, how can you truly ensure that the speech has some alignment with you while also speaking to your audience in a captivating manner? Believe it or not, it all starts with your core values. Before you select a topic, take some time to write down your core values - even if they do not seem relevant to the speech at all. Some tips to help you isolate your core values include the following:

- **Consider the people you admire.** Whether it be Abraham Lincoln or your mother, consider who you admire and why you feel that way about them.

- **Reflect upon your most meaningful experiences.** Evaluate which life experiences have left an indelible mark upon your memory and why you think that is.

- **Write down as many ideas, philosophies, or concepts as you find essential.** From there, you can consolidate them into groups or a central sentence expressing your values.

Once you have identified your core values and highlighted which ones are non-negotiable, there are three questions you should ask yourself before solidifying your topic.

1. **How much do I know about this topic?** In order to make an impactful speech, your audience has to consider you to be credible. Coming in with an armload of knowledge is the best way to assert credibility, and it helps if you have at least some preexisting knowledge on the subject.

2. **Is this a topic I am passionate about?** Someone passionate about a topic will deliver a more exciting speech nine times out of ten than someone who does not care about the topic. Passion influences all manner of your delivery, after all.

3. **Is this something that's going to interest the audience?** Remember that your speech is not for you - it is for the audience. If it is about a topic they have little interest in, they will likely tune you out early on.

Once you have everything in order, you can begin selecting and consolidating a purpose and topic for the speech. When we think about the purpose of a speech, the answer to the big "what's the point" question, you can give three short answers: to persuade, entertain, and inform. Every speech will fall into one of those three answers.

Your purpose, and isolating it early on, is instrumental to your speech and its quality. The purpose of a speech is not only to help you remain more organized but also to give you a central goal that you can aim to accomplish by the speech's conclusion. As a result, the audience can walk away and feel that they have either accomplished something or learned something valuable.

ORGANIZING YOUR TOPIC

After selecting your topic, it is time to lay out the main points of your speech. The perfect number of main points for a speech is not set in stone, although keeping the number low is a good idea. It can be tempting to lay out 15 main points for an audience, but then they may become overwhelmed, and the information will not stick. As such, an excellent format to follow is three main points, with evidence and a rebuttal for each - allowing you to address possible opposition before it happens.

At the same time, your main points must not appear disjointed; you have to find unity among them. Finding unity among the main points of your speech provides an unforgettable level of cohesion that the audience can continuously be drawn back to for the greatest impact.

A delicate relationship between separation and balance needs to be maintained simultaneously. While keeping your main points distinct, you should also balance each one and talk about them evenly. Some speakers get so caught up in their favorite point that they neglect the others, which can let the audience down.

Using parallel structure within your points for your speech is also wise. Parallel structure, or parallelism, is a powerful tool in speechwriting that enhances clarity and rhythm and can make your message more memorable. It involves using the same pattern of words to show that two or more ideas have the same level of importance. This can be achieved by starting each clause or sentence with the same part of speech, maintaining the same tense, or ensuring that nouns, verbs, and modifiers are used consistently.

For example, consider a speech on the benefits of environ- mental sustainability. To employ parallel structure effectively, you might structure your points like this:

"Environmental sustainability:

    1. Preserves our natural resources for future generations,

2. Promotes biodiversity and the abundance of wildlife, and

3. Encourages self-sufficiency and reduces reliance on non-renewable energy."

Each point begins with a verb in the present tense, creating a pleasing rhythm that reinforces the message's cohesion. When points in a speech mirror each other in this way, the repetition makes the content more engaging and more accessible for the audience to follow and recall.

In contrast, without parallel structure, the points may feel disjointed:

"Environmental sustainability is important because it:

1. Preserves our resources for future generations,

2. Keeping biodiversity in abundance is another reason, and

3. It also increases our self-sustainability."

The lack of consistency in the format can make the speech more complicated to follow and weaken the impact of your words. By aligning your sentence structure, you guide your audience through your points with a clear, strong drumbeat that drives home your message. Use parallel structure to give your speech a rhythm that resonates with your audience, making your message heard, felt, and remembered.

PERFECTING VISUAL AIDS

Earlier, I mentioned how helpful visual aids can entice an audience to focus on your speech. Now, I want to investigate this further and drive home some great ideas in this department.

Again, not every speech *needs* a visual aid, but a visual aid can be more than helpful for both you and the audience in following the *story* of your speech. Visual storytelling is a worthy skill for anyone looking to flourish at public speaking. However, what *is* visual storytelling exactly? As the name would suggest, visual storytelling involves using visual aids, cues, and gestures to transport the audience into a world of your own - one where you run the show.

You might think that visual aids only come in the form of boring flow charts and dull PowerPoint presentations, but that isn't the case at all. When you master the art of visual story- telling, you become aware that it is an entire world of opportunity just waiting for you to explore it. Indeed, visual storytelling is versatile and comes in many forms that can take your speech to the next level.

Visual storytelling transcends the boundaries of traditional narrative by incorporating visual elements that engage and captivate the audience. When delivering a speech, you must adapt these principles to the stage. This adaptation involves using gestures, props, or visual aids to create a sensory experience that complements the spoken word. By doing so, you craft a compelling narrative that paints a story vividly in the listener's imagination, fostering a memorable and impactful connection.

In addition, you should never forget the data - especially in presentations or pitches. Your audience will not want to hear every statistic about what you sell or offer. However, some compelling diagrams that make everything clear and visually based can leave a mark on your audience members. Nothing says "successful presentation" like an audience in awe from some mere data points.

Visual aids can also be perfected by focusing on showing rather than telling. Think about it: If a presenter tells you you are five times less likely to crash using their new car technology than a competitor's, that's good! But if they *show* you the evidence through charts or diagrams, including videos of the safety features, they have taken their speech from good to *great*. As such, adding a visual component to your speech - one that is logical and relevant - can make a difference in the quality of your presentation.

As you work on your arrangement, remember that visuals are far more than just what lingers on a screen. We live in a visual world and a world that is abundant in technology, meaning you have no excuse *not* to take advantage of it.

Many things can play a role in visual storytelling, from what you put on the screen to the handouts you give to the audience to how you dress. Never be afraid to use your resources - and do not hesitate to be creative! Your audience will appreciate it!

INTERACTIVE ELEMENT: DESIGNING VISUAL AIDS

Instructions

This activity focuses on helping you build a visual aid for an event like a wedding speech or toast. Feel free to follow along or reframe the activity to fit your needs for any given speech. The instructions are as follows:

1. Gather essential information about the wedding, couple, and venue before crafting your visual aid. This includes details about the couple's love story, the wedding theme, and any significant elements you want to highlight.

2. Select a pivotal moment or scene from the couple's love story to highlight in your visual aid. It could be their first meeting, a memorable date, or the proposal. Ensure this moment holds emotional significance.

3. Write a narrative that describes the chosen moment in vivid detail. Use descriptive language to create a mental image in the listener's mind. Include sensory details such as what the scene looked, smelled, and felt like. This narrative will be the heart of your visual aid.

4. Now, design the visual elements that will accompany your narrative. These could be photographs, illustrations, or a simple graphic representing the scene. Ensure these elements enhance the story and help your audience visualize the moment.

5. Choose fonts and colors that complement the wedding theme and the emotion you want to convey. Elegant script fonts and soft, pastel colors often work well for wedding-related visual aids.

6. Consider the layout of your visual aid. Arrange the narrative and visual elements in an aesthetically pleasing manner. You might want to use a digital design tool or create a physical collage, depending on your preference and skills.

7. Incorporate personalized messages and quotes that relate to the couple and the moment you are framing. These can be words of encourage-

ment, well-wishes, or famous love quotes that resonate with the scene.

8. Review your visual aid and narrative for clarity, grammar, and emotional impact. Make sure everything flows well and evokes the desired emotions.

9. Practice your wedding toast with the visual aid to ensure it fits seamlessly into your speech. Adjust your delivery as needed to synchronize with the visuals.

10. During the wedding toast, display your visual aid with confidence. As you reach the part of your speech related to the framed scene, engage the audience by referring to the visual aid. Speak from the heart and allow the narrative and visuals to enhance the emotional impact of your toast.

And voila! You have a compelling visual aid that can be used in your speech and a format to follow to create a visual aid for any event.

Conclusion

John Ford said, "you can speak well if your tongue can deliver the message of your heart." With those words in mind, find your values, align your speech's purpose, and inspire yourself to speak more confidently by preparing everything you can with the eight simple steps in this chapter - planning, picking a topic, compiling your content, organizing content, writing the introduction, planning your visual aids, working out phrasing, and then rehearsing. Some of those steps, of course, warrant some in-depth tips. So, with that said, let us see how you can create your Aristotle-style secret with communication and rehearsal.

CHAPTER FIVE

— • —

THE SYMPHONY OF SPEECH

STYLE

Picture yourself at a concert. The music starts, and the room fills with a diverse range of sounds from the orchestra. The booming drums, the soft whisper of the flute, and the rich melody of the violin - all blend to create a harmonious symphony. Now, let's transpose this orchestra to the public speaking stage, where your voice plays all the instruments. It can whisper, boom, and carry a melody - and learning to manipulate your vocal elements is like mastering the art of conducting a symphony.

Aristotle's third element involves mastering your voice and choosing to speak your style!

THE BASICS OF STYLE

Before choosing your style, we need to dig into the basics of style itself. Indeed, let us take a look at some of the background information you need to bear in mind.

Again, style is Aristotle's third canon of rhetoric. But what exactly is it? Simply put, style refers to how well you deliver your speech. It refers to what you say, how you say it, and its quality. For example, take a look at the two examples below, where each speaker uses their unique style:

- Speaker 1 comes onto the stage and greets the audience before launching into a technical analysis of some research. While the research is relevant to the topic, this speech is being given to a group of consumers - not professionals in the field. They walk away confused, even feeling stupid because of the speech's presumptions.

- Speaker 2 comes on stage and speaks to the same audience but emphasizes passion and conviction. This speaker's words seem to have personal importance, and any technical terms are defined. The speech follows a logical flow, only including technical terms or analysis when it naturally comes up.

If you saw those two speakers on stage and were a member of that audience, chances are you would trust Speaker 2. However, there are also instances where speaker one is preferred. This is why style is so important; your style helps the audience connect to you and can make or break their trust in you.

Why Your Style Matters

I honestly cannot overstate how much your style matters, but I am sure you are still wondering why that is the case. Well, beyond merely looking better in front of an audience, style matters for two key reasons:

1. Your style matters because miscommunication and conflict may occur if it contrasts heavily with the audience.

2. Your style matters because it informs the context of your visual aids and other factors discussed in Chapter 4.

If you don't spend time perfecting your style, you cannot make an awe-inspiring speech.

Different Styles to Explore

Before you endeavor to find or craft your style, you should take the time to explore some of the established styles and what they look like. This will allow you to consider which style fits best with your personality and your speech's purpose. Below are a few different styles, some of which you may want to consider emulating:

- **The teacher style.** When you embody a teaching style, you aim to instruct and explain. With outstanding content and the need to cram it into an allotment of time, you must balance your ability to connect with the crowd with your insightful information. Think of a teacher who can't keep their class captivated; this is a common struggle for teachers when it comes to style. In order to make a great teacher, one must focus on information *and* connection.

- **The motivator style.** Someone who embodies the motivator style has the goal of inspiring change. They primarily want those to whom they are speaking to take action. The motivator style, as the name suggests, is inherently motivating! However, those with this style often suffer from losing energy as the speech goes on. This is certainly something to be mindful of.

- **The storyteller style.** One of the most popular styles, storytellers, use emotion to connect with the crowd. This style is so popular because it's the voice of many great speakers throughout history, which is a testament to its effectiveness. Having a clear and focused point is the key to achieving success. Stay on track, and you'll shine like gold.

- **The visionary style.** Finally, we have the visionary style - someone who envisions a better world, along with the role that an audience can play in making that dream a reality. Visionaries compel audiences to see change that does not exist, thus facilitating actual change. The major drawback of this style is that many speakers are unclear on *how* to make that change - and the audience can tell.

These styles can be adapted to meet your needs and the particular point of a speech. You can even blend methods to meet specific goals.

Styles to Avoid

Despite all of those intriguing styles just mentioned, there are still a few that you should try to *avoid* at all costs - each in its unique way. For example, take a look at the following styles that you should avoid falling prey to:

- **The passive style.** If your speech style appears too passive, the audience may not take you seriously due to your lack of assertiveness.

- **The aggressive style.** If you head into the speech aggressively, it is likely to offend your audience.

- **The passive-aggressive style.** Mixing the passive and aggressive styles, this tone does not go over well with audiences - it seems noncommittal and dispassionate.

- **The overly assertive style.** As the name suggests, this style can come off as pushy and can thus discourage the audience.

Choose your style before focusing on anything else. Then, your context, visual aids, body language, and tone will follow from what you know the four styles offer.

BUILDING UP COMMUNICATION

Now that we have covered all the styles you can choose from (and the ones you should avoid at all costs), it is time to look at how you can build your communication skills using your selected style as a springboard.

First things first, and though I have mentioned this before, it is worth mentioning again: Do not memorize your speech word for word. Seriously. I can confidently say that walking into a speech with it fully memorized is one of the worst mistakes you can make. Rather than memorizing everything you want to say, come prepared with cue cards or a bare-bones script of your speech. This allows for a perfect blend of spontaneity and audience engagement.

In addition, don't rush your speech. One of the worst feelings in the world is getting through your speech and feeling confident, only to find that you still have 15 minutes left to fill. Solution? Make sure you take your time through the speech, fully enveloping your audience with your introduction before expanding on your main points. Between this and your practice rounds, you are bound to fill the time well.

Another vital communication skill is understanding when your audience's attention begins to slip away. If your audience begins to tire as you get into the heart of your speech, remember it may not be anything personal. The average attention span is growing shorter and shorter, which is why you need to come prepared with content to zest up the speech as you deliver it.

Communicating and following these tips can pave the way to an excellent ending by remaining confident and sticking to your main points. Sticking to the predetermined outline you have made will help your speech remain cohesive while being spontaneous and relaxed with your pace, which will further emphasize that you are a credible speaker in the eyes of your audience.

Furthermore, it would help if you made it a point to use *inclusive* language. While you might not identify with someone who needs or uses inclusive language every day, you never know who in your audience might appreciate some inclusive language on your part. By using inclusive language, you can further command the audience's respect. Some common ways to avoid unintentional exclusion include the following:

- **Using gender-neutral terms and pronouns where possible.** For example, supposing that only men will do a specific job or that women must fit into other roles can be offensive and upsetting to the audience. Be mindful of your terms and how gender roles can be negated.

- **Employing internationally and racially friendly terminology.** For example, referring to non-white individuals as "people of color" is more proper than other outdated terminology and will undoubtedly help the audience feel respected.

- **Avoid stereotyping the crowd.** Stereotyping can be based on race, age, gender, sexuality, or other identity- related bases, and it is never a good option.

Practice using inclusive language before you go on stage to ensure it flows naturally within your vocabulary - inclusive language should not be jarring!

BODY LANGUAGE

Make sure that you pay special attention to your body language as well. Your body language conveys messages beyond what your mouth says to the audience. Crossed arms and a podium blocking you the whole time make you appear closed off, whereas facing the audience with your arms naturally to your sides says, "I am confident and ready to chat with you," making communication a two-way street.

In order to help the proper body language come naturally to you, make sure that when you rehearse, you do so with the proper stances. Rehearse with a relaxed posture, which includes keeping your arms by your sides or gesturing appropriately. And speaking of, you can further emphasize your speech with subtle gestures. Indeed, touching your heart empathetically during touching moments, for example, can subtly influence the audience into believing your words.

Something that can help you with your body language is practicing the six basic body language movements for a speech, as follows:

1. **Posture.** Keep a neutral posture with your shoulders back and relaxed, your arms uncrossed and out of your pockets, and your body facing the audience. Your standing posture is like your silent introduction. It communicates volumes about your confidence, credibility, and openness.

   a. **Sitting Posture.** There may be situations where you must speak while seated, such as during a panel discussion or an interview. In such scenarios, maintaining a good sitting posture is crucial. Sit upright with your feet flat on the floor, your back against the chair, and your shoulders relaxed. Lean slightly forward when speaking to show engagement and interest. A good sitting posture can make you appear more professional, confident, and engaged, enhancing the effectiveness of your speech.

2. **Breathing**. It can be easy for your breathing to become labored on stage; use relaxed breathing to ensure you can project your voice and pause to emphasize significant points.

3. **Gestures**. Use hand gestures to emphasize and punctuate what you are saying, and use varied gestures to keep your audience's attention. Also, if you change a PowerPoint slide, look at it momentarily! This cues your audience to do the same.

4. **The Eyes.** The eyes are often referred to as the windows to the soul. In public speaking, eye contact can open a connection window between

you and your audience, making your speech more personal, engaging, and impactful. Let's delve deeper into the role of eye contact in effective communication.

a. **Eye Contact**. Make eye contact by looking from one face to the next and watching the crowd. It's a non-verbal greeting that says, "I see you, I acknowledge you, and I value your presence." It helps establish a personal connection with your audience, making them feel seen and engaged. Just as maintaining eye contact is important, knowing when to break eye contact is equally crucial. Constant, unbroken eye contact can feel intimidating or uncomfortable to your audience.

b. **Eye Contact with Large Audiences**. Making eye contact with a large audience can seem daunting. The key is to make each individual feel seen and included. Achieve this by dividing the audience into sections and alternating your gaze between these sections. Look at a person in one section, then shift your gaze to a person in another section. This creates a sense of inclusion and engagement across the entire audience, making your speech more impactful and engaging.

c. **Raising Eyebrows.** Imagine you're sharing an exciting piece of news with a friend, and their eyebrows shoot up in surprise. This slight movement can convey their surprise more effectively than words. Raising your eyebrows can express surprise, interest, or curiosity in your speaking.

d. **Eye Squinting.** Squinting is a facial expression often associated with skepticism, disbelief, or deep thought. In speeches, squinting at the right moment can convey to your audience that you're thinking deeply or questioning something.

5. **Movement**. Make sure to move around in the space you have for your presentation; when used effectively, movement can add dynamism to your speech. Walking across the stage can help you engage with different sections of your audience, while moving toward the audience can create a sense of intimacy and engagement. However, aimless pacing or fidgeting can be distracting and convey nervousness. If you choose to move, do so

with purpose and poise.

6. **Facial expression.** Make sure to smile! Think of a time when you were greeted with a warm, genuine smile. You likely felt a sense of warmth and positivity. A smile is a universal sign of happiness and friendliness. In public speaking, smiling can make you appear more approachable, confident, and enthusiastic.

  a. **Frowning.** A frown can express a range of emotions, from worry and confusion to disagreement and displeasure. In public speaking, frowning can signal to your audience that something is serious, concerning, or deserving of their attention.

When you take the time and patience to build up your communication skills for a speech, you will notice marked improvements in your confidence and your audience's engagement.

ENHANCING YOUR VOICE

In the grand symphony of public speaking, your voice is your most powerful instrument. It can whisper like the breeze, roar like the ocean, or resonate like a drum. Each element plays a unique role in shaping your speech's melody. By understanding and manipulating these elements, you can conduct your symphony with skill and finesse, captivating your audience and making your speech a performance to remember.

Start by focusing on your speed. Chances are, you are more likely to speak far too fast than too slow - which many nervous people suffer from. One way to find a good pace for yourself is to find an excerpt of text of about 150 words. Make sure that it takes you over a minute to recite that passage; this is the speed at which most people can comfortably listen to and retain information.

In addition, the speed at which you speak can influence how your message is received. Speaking quickly can convey excitement, urgency, or passion. Speaking slowly can emphasize important points, create suspense, or give your audience time to absorb complex information. By controlling your speaking speed, you can guide your audience's attention, enhance comprehension, and control the rhythm of your speech.

Next, make sure that your pronunciation is clear as well. Everyone has an accent of some shape or form, and some people mumble when speaking faster or more nervously. As you speak while rehearsing, note any words you tend to smash together or stumble over or where a regional accent takes hold. Then, if you plan to use these words, practice enunciating them more clearly. Furthermore, ensure you can pronounce any technical terms clearly and correctly for the audience.

Now, imagine you're at a coffee shop, overhearing two conversations. At one table, a woman's voice drips with sarcasm as she says, "Nice job, really." At another, a man's voice brims with genuine enthusiasm as he exclaims, "Nice job, really!" The same words but completely different meanings are conveyed through tone.

In public speaking, your tone is the emotional undertone that shapes the meaning of your words. It's the difference between "I'm fine," said with a cheerful tone, and "I'm fine," said with a resigned tone. Your tone can express a range of emotions - from excitement and enthusiasm to seriousness and sorrow. By varying your tone to match your message, you can make your speech more engaging and emotionally resonant.

This leads us to pitch. Have you ever heard the screech of a car's brakes or the deep rumble of thunder? The high pitch of the screech and the low pitch of the thunder are hard to ignore. Pitch, the highness or lowness of a sound, plays a crucial role in public speaking.

A high pitch can convey excitement, urgency, or enthusiasm, while a low pitch can suggest authority, calmness, or serious- ness. By varying your pitch, you can emphasize key points, express different emotions, and keep your audience's attention. Just like a song that uses a variety of pitches to create a melody, a speech that uses a variety of pitches can be more engaging and impactful.

Finally, chunking and pausing are some other skills to be mindful of. Remember how I mentioned earlier that you can use timed pauses to emphasize what you are saying? That is true, but it helps a ton if you take the time to chunk what you are saying into logical clusters and *then* pause, emphasizing a group of matching information. Pausing after iterating a point or making a shocking statement works better than in the middle of an explanation.

Using strategic pauses is like using punctuation in writing. Just as a period signals the end of a sentence and prepares the reader for the next one, a pause signals the completion of a thought and prepares your audience for the next one. By mastering the art of strategic pauses, you can enhance your speech's clarity, emphasis, and rhythm.

Try recording yourself as you rehearse to help you understand where there might be room for improvement within your speech. It might feel awkward at first, but by listening to the recording you made, you can find areas of the speech that might be confusing, clunky, or able to be improved upon as you give the speech for real.

Voice modulation is like the paintbrush in the hand of an artist. It allows you to add color, depth, and texture to the canvas of your speech. With the proper techniques, you can train your voice to be more flexible, expressive, and impactful. Let's explore some techniques to help you fine-tune your voice modulation skills and ways to warm up before you go out on stage.

You can do this by practicing a few vocal exercises and running your speech one final time before you go on. If you are interested in vocal exercises to try, consider the following:

- **The nonsense exercise.** For about one minute, pretend you are giving your speech, but speak complete gibberish. Rather than focusing on content, spend this time paying attention to tone, speed, pitch, and other facets of your voice.

- **Singing Exercises.** Singing is a natural way to improve your voice modulation. It helps enhance your vocal range, tone control, and rhythm while warming up your voice. Sing along to a song you like, paying attention to how you modulate your voice to match the melody. Practice different types of songs to challenge your vocal range and control.

- **Tongue Twisters**. Tongue twisters are the verbal equivalent of an obstacle course. They challenge your articulation, speed, and pronunciation, making them an excellent tool for improving your voice modulation. Practice saying tongue twisters slowly at first, focusing on clear articulation. Then, gradually increase your speed while maintaining clarity. This exercise can help improve your pronunciation, speed control, and vocal agility, as well as warm up your voice just before a speech.

- **Read Aloud.** Reading aloud is like a workout for your voice. Choose a piece of text - it could be a book, a newspaper article, or a script - and read it aloud. Pay attention to how you use your voice to convey the meaning of the text.

Focusing on your voice gives you that special something to truly optimize your speech. Dedicate time to these exercises, and watch as your voice transforms from a mere sound into a symphony that captivates your audience and resonates long after the final word has been spoken.

INTERACTIVE ELEMENT: FILLER FREE SPEECH

Instructions

Fillers are the worst nightmare of an audience who came for an eloquent speech. Use the following exercise to help you break free from the clutches of filler words and phrases in just 60 seconds:

1. Choose a simple topic you can speak about for one solid minute. It could be a personal anecdote, a brief hobby description, or a favorite book or movie review.

2. Use a timer or stopwatch to limit yourself to 60 seconds. This constraint will encourage you to be concise.

3. Stand in front of a mirror, maintaining good posture and making eye contact with yourself.

4. Begin talking about your chosen topic. Focus on delivering a clear, coherent message without using any fillers. Speak at a steady pace.

5. Instead of using fillers, practice inserting brief pauses when collecting

your thoughts. Pauses are much more effective at maintaining your flow than fillers.

6. As you speak, pay attention to your reflection in the mirror. If you catch yourself using a filler, start the timer over and continue from where you left off.

Perform this exercise multiple times with different topics to build your confidence and improve your ability to speak

without fillers. It is also a good idea to record yourself as you do this exercise, as this can allow you to reflect on what the camera sees, not just what you remember. After each practice session, reflect on your progress and identify areas where you tend to use fillers. Focus on improving those areas during your next practice.

Conclusion

Oprah Winfrey said, "great communication begins with connection." How you communicate with your audience is everything and will help you become more confident and deliver memorable speeches. Speaking of memory, it's time to see how you can engage a room, keep them engaged, and leave a memorable impression.

CHAPTER SIX

— · —

THE BLUEPRINT FOR AN ENGAGED AUDIENCE

MEMORY

Did you know that the average attention span of an audience is only six to eight minutes (31 Fear of Public Speaking Statistics (Prevalence), n.d.)? Capturing an audience's attention can be challenging, whether it's your family, friends, investors, or employer. You need skills to capture and maintain their attention to make an impressionable speech. Therefore, this chapter will help you find your captivating skills, even if you're a nervous speaker.

ELEMENTS OF KEEPING AN AUDIENCE ENGAGED

It's not enough to know how to speak to an audience, you also need to know how to keep them captivated. Therefore, before you can truly master the art of engaging an audience and ensuring your speech remains fresh, let's learn some crucial facts about audience engagement.

Aristotle knew he had to engage an audience to trigger their memory and keep them captivated. This was an idea as plain as day to him - an audience who was not engaged would be unable to pay close attention to the speech, forgetting words as fast as he spoke them. With this comes the knowledge that rehearsal is one of the keys; it prevents you from stumbling as much, making you a more compelling speaker. However, the magic behind captivation does not stop there.

The bottom line is that you cannot keep an audience engaged without first capturing the heart of their attention. How are you meant to do that? Through your introduction, of course! Contrary to popular belief, you can think about your speech's introduction as the *central* part of the speech. During your introduction, you have the floor and the ability to captivate or alienate the audience. It is, therefore, vital to start with some- thing that instantly captures their attention.

Momentum is your best friend for keeping an audience on the edge of their seats. Momentum keeps your speech flowing, allowing your audience's interest to ebb and flow naturally; just when they think you are done, you hit them with another point of interest and begin the process all over. There are many different ways to employ momentum in your speech, but one of the best ways to do so involves humor!

So, to sum up the elements of keeping an audience engaged, you need three key components: capturing their attention, building momentum, and rehearsing. Combined, these three elements show that you are confident and help you engage the audience and maintain their attention. Now that you know what is required, let us see how you can work on developing those skills.

HOW TO KEEP AN AUDIENCE ENGAGED

An unengaged audience is the worst nightmare for a speaker - even the greatest ones. Speaking to an audience who is disinterested, heads lolling back into a light sleep even, can be disheartening. You spent all this time preparing only for the audience to pass out halfway through! How mortifying. Well, let's see how you can keep that audience perfectly engaged so that you don't fall victim to this nightmare coming true.

I have mentioned it before, but your audience will not care about a speech on a topic they are not interested in. Plain and simple. If you have the choice as to what your speech is about, you absolutely cannot skip tailoring it to the audience. Indeed, you have to keep in mind your audience's interests, expertise, and knowledge as you prepare for the speech. Even when you *cannot* pick the speech's topic, you can still tailor it!

Tailoring your speech to the audience does not have to feel like an uphill battle. Just a few ways that you can do so include the following:

- **Define terms.** Provide a definition if there is a term you think the audience might be unfamiliar with, especially if it is technical or scientific. At the same time, do not define basic terms your audience is likely already well-versed in; doing so can seem condescending!

- **Use anecdotes.** Anecdotes are stories that you can pepper throughout your speech. Try infusing your speech with relatable stories and characters that speak to the audience, allowing them to identify with your words.

- **Make statistics matter.** To you, the statistic might make perfect sense in the context of what you are saying. The thing is, your audience may not feel the same. So, use statistics in context, even drawing comparisons between ideas to make those statistics meaningful.

In addition, you can help build engagement and interest in a speech by interacting before the speech starts. Mingle with the audience and initiate small conversations with those in the crowd. Then, when you step out onto the stage, audience members will be drawn to you - saying things like, "Wow, I spoke to that person earlier! Let's see what they have to say!"

Another tip for keeping the audience engaged is using humor. Be yourself when using humor. Even dry humor can work when delivered authentically. Not only does laughter reduce stress, but a joke that lands nicely can captivate the audience and help them relate to you more. At the same time, balance humor with earnest speaking and steer clear of offensive or questionable words or phrases. Again, offending the crowd is *never* the way to go.

You can also make use of shocking or interesting facts in order to get the audience to listen. Within the particular field you are presenting for, whether it's a toast or a product launch, there are bound to be striking facts or news articles you can share. Not only does this direct the audience's attention to you from the first moment, but it can also help contextualize your speech a bit more for the audience.

Moreover, it would be best if you made it a point to include interaction in your speech. Audiences cannot ignore your words if they genuinely feel part of the speech. Mention that a Q&A session will be included, and try to include unique points of audience participation within your speech to make it more exciting for everyone involved.

As much as you can add to a speech to keep the audience engaged, there are also modes of speech that can dissuade an otherwise engaged audience from listening. One of the major culprits of disinterest for an audience is the use of filler words. If you have ever listened to a speaker whose speech was rife with words like "like," "um," "uh," or "you know," then you understand how vital dismantling filler words can be. They don't add anything, and regardless of why you use them, they can sound uneducated, too. So, try to prune these filler words from your speech as much as possible, revisiting Chapter 5's activity to help.

Lastly, try to add key takeaways to your speech before moving into the momentous parts of it. This is especially helpful if you use the teacher approach mentioned earlier. Including key take- aways keeps the content fresh in the minds of the audience members.

BUILDING THE PERFECT MOMENTUM

Now that you have some advice for keeping the audience engaged, you must look at building the perfect momentum. Snowballing the speech from the ground up is the best way to keep it enticing and to build anticipation and excitement for the speech as you go. How exactly can you work to build flawless momentum?

In order to build momentum for your speech, you have first to understand what exactly momentum *is*. Building momentum means using visual or verbal cues to continue guiding your audience throughout your speech. Think about building a snowman; you roll the snow up into a ball, and that ball gets bigger and bigger until boom - you have a finished snowman. A speech is just like that; momentum helps you transition the audience from one topic to another. In essence, momentum is significant because it boosts the speech and supports its transitions.

On that note, your transitions matter significantly. They have to be smooth but noticeable. Transitions should be catchy yet indicate that the topic is gliding elsewhere and should also be used to bridge the content as well. Examples of transitions include:

- **Use visual aids.** For example, do not just rely on a PowerPoint; include charts, physical items, and more. This keeps the audience enticed and helps them understand the flow of the speech far better.

- **Encourage chatter.** Instead of making the audience listen to you the entire time, encourage them to talk with one another and then share ideas. This allows for a break from listening and for more engagement.

- **Use videos.** A short video can break up bigger chunks of your speech and make it more palatable, as well as the inclusion of visual displays of data or actions you describe in your speech.

You can make a stellar speech that snowballs momentum and engagement by rehearsing for proper transitions.

Speaking of snowballs, just like how they build up from small to large, so should your speech. Start with the most minor jokes and topics before steadily building up to more intricate topics and jokes. This gives your audience time to acclimate to the topic and helps them build anticipation as you speak.

If you have not noticed by now, anticipation is vital to building momentum. You can also build anticipation by pausing between transitions and topics. Pausing during a speech is a great way to punctuate statements - *literally*. A pause serves as a vocal punctuation mark to help your listeners complete a thought, meaning pausing between transitions can be great for building momentum to the next central point.

Being yourself is, believe it or not, another spectacular way to build momentum in a speech. No one wants to listen to a speaker who is clearly being inauthentic or pretending to be someone they are not. Because of this, it's essential to be yourself. Think of yourself as a character because, to your audience, you are. So, how would you build your character arc naturally while using the speech as a catalyst?

In order to keep your momentum going and allow the audience to follow along with the brilliant cadences of your speech, you should not fear going off-script. You may plan, rehearse, and re-plan your speech countless times over, but it may surprise you that the off-script moments are what truly catapult your speech into greatness. As such, you should allow yourself to be natural and *improvise* if your speech calls for it in the name of momentum.

As you progress and hope to build up true momentous power throughout your speech, do not forget the power of story- telling. Use storytelling to create an air of personality, as it can infuse your personality as you present your information to the crowd. For example, you could use one narrative that links throughout all your points, ultimately reaching a stunning conclusion. This is just one technique that employs storytelling for momentum success, and I highly advise it.

It also helps keep your speech going if you ask the listeners questions. Your audience might not know what to ask, and they might not know where the speech is headed either. But if you start asking questions, it leaves them in anticipation of an answer. Good questions to include are ones that ask about a solution to a problem, how we know what we know, or the effects that one thing can have on another.

These methods are beautiful ways to build momentum, but what if you want something more subtle? One of the most valuable tactics you can learn is "idea building," where you allow a point, idea, or concept to start small and then build throughout the speech. This is a good momentum tactic because it tricks the audience into feeling like they have played an active part in the development of the speech.

Now, at the end of your speech, what you do with all the momentum you have built up is vital. You cannot just build the audience up only to disappoint them at your conclusion. So, how do you use the momentum wisely? There are a couple of ways in which you can go about this. One of the best ways is with a *call to action*.

A call to action is a statement, often at the end of a work, speech, or persuasive document, that encourages the attendee to take action aligned with the contents of the speech. For example, a call to action about the launch of a new car seat might sound like "the options are clear; there is one brand that will truly harness your baby's safety and comfort for the optimal car ride. Do not let this opportunity pass you by."

However, your call to action does not have to convince someone to buy or do anything. You can encourage them to ask questions, carry a message with them, or otherwise feel compelled by your words. Indeed, a call to action does not have to seem demanding. Whatever you choose to end your speech with, it should be powerful and capitalize on the momentum you built up.

HANDLING CHALLENGES MID-SPEECH

As much as we would like our speeches to go well, with no challenges, that is obviously not always what happens. Sometimes, you will be asked challenging questions that are a trap or that you could not have prepared for; other times, you will walk on stage to a reactive audience - and there's nothing you can do to change that.

When this happens, you might feel discouraged and frankly afraid as you stand in a vulnerable position before an audience. What are you to do in a situation like this? The good news is that there are solutions and ways to navigate this, and I will share those with you now.

Before you launch your speech, ensure the audience knows that questions are welcome. Make them feel comfortable asking you anything, and do so with confidence *and* humility. You might think it is a bad idea to welcome questions right from the start, but you accomplish a few things in doing so. In fact, you:

- Dissuade people from trying to catch you off guard intentionally - because sometimes those rude individuals exist.

- Disarm a reactive audience from thinking you are some overconfident, money-grubbing individual by showing them that you are open and there for *their* benefit.

- Imply that while your speech does its best, nothing is perfect. This keeps audiences light on you while demonstrating that you anticipate questions, thus making you a more credible speaker.

So, despite what you might have thought beforehand, inviting questions at the start of a speech is a good practice.

Naturally, because you are inviting the audience to ask questions about the contents of your speech, you should also anticipate those questions. Consider the audience and their background as you review your main points, visual aids, and other components of your speech. If you were sitting in that crowd and came from the same background, what questions might you ask a speaker? Anticipating these questions and preplanning your answers is one magnificent way to avoid stumbling on stage.

It is also a good idea to try to view incoming questions positively. When someone asks you a question, it provides ways to improve your speech moving forward. If you have to repeat the speech later on, you can include those answers in your speech; if not, you know what kinds of questions to anticipate being asked in the future.

Of course, the most concerning parts of your speech - the ones that genuinely unnerve you or trip you up - may not even come from questions. Maybe they come from the audience instead; after all, we are not always fortunate enough to have a respectful and receptive audience. When you have an audience that is aggravated, unnerving, unwilling to listen, or just plain reactive to everything that seems to come out of your mouth, a few tactics can make the speech easier for you.

For example, it's a good idea to make sure that you maintain eye contact with the audience. I have mentioned it before, but it is imperative to maintain eye contact with a resistant crowd-think high school assemblies! It is not about eye contact itself; instead, these types of audiences focus on your *lack* of eye contact, as not making eye contact can expose you as a feeble speaker.

It is also wise to, if your audience asks a question, truly ensure that you understand their question or point. Remember: *You* can ask questions even though you are the speaker! Before launching into a passionate answer, ensure you know what needs to be answered; otherwise, you risk making a fool of yourself in front of a potentially unforgiving audience.

Furthermore, if your audience asks you something or interjects, take the time to validate what they have said. Many speakers can seem dismissive when they answer questions or reply to comments; avoid doing this to extend respect to the audience and heighten your credibility.

I want to ensure you are more prepared than ever when handling these mid-speech challenges, showing the audience and yourself that you mean business. In addition to the above, do your best to remain calm. The audience can tell if you are becoming riled up; if they are there to taunt or aggravate you, they will use that to their advantage.

Moreover, keep in mind that you can be *honest*. If you aren't sure of an answer, strive to be honest with your audience. Let them know you are unsure of the answer but will undoubtedly put in time to expand your knowledge. And, of course, make sure that they know you genuinely appreciate the question. This prevents hostility while showing that it is okay for you not to know everything and prevents the spread of misinformation.

Now, whatever you do, avoid making attacks, whether directly or passively, on the audience. Even if you have the rudest audience in the world, responding with rudeness wipes your credibility as a speaker away. Beyond that, it turns any neutral or positive parties against you and may even prevent you from being asked to speak again.

I also recommend checking in with the audience throughout the speech. An audience is more likely to become volatile if they remain confused for large portions of the speech. As such, instead of allowing this confusion to fester, ask the audience if they have any questions throughout the speech - and again, be receptive to those questions as well.

Lastly, try your best to end the speech positively, even if the course of the speech was not the best. More so, this means that you should not end on a negative note. The last few moments of your speech are what is going to stick in the mind of the audience. Ending on a positive note proves that you are a good speaker; on the other hand, letting yourself become pessimistic toward the end invites them to negate everything you said!

INTERACTIVE ELEMENT: 10-MINUTE MOMENTUM BUILDER

Instructions

In just ten minutes a week, you can master the process of building momentum into a speech. Here is how:

1. Find a quiet and comfortable space where you will not be interrupted and clear your mind. Set a timer for ten minutes before you begin. You will mock-draft a speech, helping you build confidence in your momentum mastery.

2. Pick a topic that interests you and fits the context of a short speech. This can be anything from a hobby to a topic you are learning about.

3. In one minute, write down the opening of your speech. This should be an attention-grabbing statement or a thought-provoking question related to your topic.

4. In the following minute, write a brief introduction that provides context for your topic. Explain why it is relevant or important.

5. In the minute after that, list the main points or key ideas you want to cover in your speech. These are the building blocks of your speech.

6. In the next two minutes, jot down a sentence or two for each main point, briefly explaining or expanding on them. Write a transition sentence that connects your introduction to your first main point smoothly.

7. Finish by writing a concluding sentence that connects your main points and leaves a memorable impression.

8. With five minutes remaining, start speaking your speech out loud. Focus on articulation, clarity, and maintaining a steady pace.

9. Within the speech, practice building momentum. Focus on transitioning from your first main point to the second, starting from the introduction and building momentum as you go, culminating with your conclusion.

10. After the timer goes off, take a moment to reflect on your practice. What went well, and what could be improved?

If it takes more than ten minutes your first time around, don't sweat it; keep practicing until you master this skill!

Conclusion

Leslie Stephen said, "the only way in which one human being can properly attempt to influence another is by encouraging him to think for himself; instead of endeavoring to instill ready-made opinions into his head."

You cannot maintain your audience's attention entirely without getting them involved, building momentum, and captivating them with incredible stories, facts, or visual aids. Try practicing the methods you discovered in this chapter, and once you're feeling confident, it will be time to move on to the final stage before everything comes together: delivery.

Chapter Seven

— • —

The Art of Mastering Persuasion with NLP

Delivery

D iscover the secrets to engaging your audience, influencing their thoughts and actions, and delivering a speech that leaves a lasting impact. In this chapter, you will learn how to connect with your audience by addressing their fears and using simple tactics to persuade them. And that's not all – you will also master Aristotle's final framework element: delivery. With powerful diction, psychology, and clever tricks, you will learn how to deliver your speech with confidence, even if you start off feeling nervous. Let's take your public speaking skills to the next level.

ALL ABOUT DICTION

Even the most captivating speech can sound monotonous if delivered without passion. Why is that? It is because of *diction* - the words you say and *how* you say them. Make no mistake, these play a huge role in what your audience takes away from your speech. It is like cooking - if you set the finest ingredients in front of someone who could burn water, they will not become a master chef, will they?

Because of this, looking at how you deliver a speech with confidence is vital. Aristotle devised that delivery was the final canon of rhetoric in making a speech go from okay to extraordinary, and now we will explore just that. You will find influence and persuasion over your audience through these methods that allow you to command your diction like an expert.

Now, it seems simple enough, but what does delivery really entail? At a glance, your delivery of a speech is going to involve body language, tone, and diction.

This means that what you say and how you say it matters equally as much as how you command your body. In previous chapters, you mastered tone and body language; now, it is time to take a look at that skill of diction for flawless delivery.

You might recognize the word "diction" from your high school English classes back in the day, but if not, that is okay! Defined, diction refers to the choices you make in a speech to convey something. For example, you can say, "The plane flew over the school," but that exact phrase with better diction would be something like, "A mammoth of a plane soared unforgivingly above the school." In the latter phrasing, so many implications about size, shape, and even pilot skill are added - all thanks to diction.

This leads us to how diction can help your speech. Beyond providing a more vivid picture for the audience, what are the benefits of speaking with good diction? Well, some of those benefits include the following:

- **A tone that supports your purpose.** Diction contributes massively to the tone of a speech. Using diction alone, you can transfer the context of a speech from a casual conversation to a scientific report. Thus, diction is also crucial because it helps ensure that your speech is appropriate to the context.

- **Support of the setting.** Diction benefits the storytelling of your speech, helps you foster credibility, and more "setting"-based influences as well. When you make strong diction choices, you do not have to worry about whether the audience has enough context.

- **Establishment of a narrative voice.** Diction helps you establish a central voice for the story you are telling across the narrative arc of your speech. This helps the audience view you consistently, positively, and credible as you present.

As you can see, diction is an invaluable tool to take a speech to the next level, commanding persuasion and confidence.

Something that many people are unaware of is that there are actually *eight* different types of diction. This means you have eight different diction types to choose from when considering how you elevate your speech. Those eight types of diction are as follows:

1. **Formal diction.** Formal diction involves the use of elevated or sophisticated language. You will not speak with slang riddling your language if you need to use formal diction. Furthermore, syntax - the structure in which your sentences take shape - tends to be far more complicated in formal diction contexts. Formal diction is usually best suited for professional or legal matters.

2. **Informal diction.** Informal diction often takes a more conversational shape. It's the language used in fiction stories or general communication which boils down to the fact that we typically use informal diction within everyday life. Informal diction is often prized for its ability to offer a heightened level of freedom for writers and speakers alike, which means that your wedding toasts or casual speeches might benefit from a more informal air.

3. **Pedantic diction.** Pedantic diction involves being highly academic or detailed within your language choices. Usually, someone who uses pedantic diction explicitly picks most words by hand, carefully crafting each word to hold ample meaning for the work. Naturally, this style lends itself best to more formal writing and speeches.

4. **Colloquial diction.** Colloquial diction employs colloquialisms like regional slang and diction to add vibrancy and dimension to a work. It adds culture in certain respects, but do not force colloquial diction into your speech if it does not flow naturally.

5. **Slang diction.** As the name would suggest, slang diction employs slang terms within it. This is usually done to loosen formalities if it fits naturally into your authentic voice and you are trying to connect with the audience.

6. **Abstract diction.** Abstract diction occurs when you use more abstract phrases to describe a point. It is not the same as a colorful metaphor; abstract diction is vaguer and not necessarily as logical. Abstract diction can be used effectively in certain types of speeches.

7. **Concrete diction.** Concrete diction uses words in their most literal sense and often uses language that appeals to the five senses. This can help speeches be interpreted more literally and without open interpretation due to the detailed yet specific nature of the word choice.

8. **Poetic diction.** Poetic diction involves lyrical words that reflect a central theme, and although this form of diction is commonly used in poetry or literature alone, you can find specific spaces for it in a speech.

The diction that you will want to use for your speech depends on the purpose, audience, and context. You can even blend different forms of diction for a perfect, idiosyncratic tone for your speech.

Introducing... Neurolinguistic Programming!

Now, it is time to discuss something called neurolinguistic programming. Also referred to as NLP, neurolinguistic programming can be a valuable tool and skill in the context of a speech. You are probably wondering what neurolinguistic programming is and how it can relate to diction, so allow me to clarify that now.

Neurolinguistic programming is a pseudoscientific approach to communication, personal development, and psychotherapy. The theory of NLP is that there is a connection between neuro- logical processes, language, and behavioral patterns learned through experience, which can be changed to achieve specific goals in life.

Neurolinguistic Programming can enhance communication and engagement in your speeches. Let's review how NLP principles apply to public speaking:

1. **Rapport Building:** NLP emphasizes the importance of connecting with the audience. You can use techniques such as mirroring body language, tone, and tempo to create a sense of empathy and connection with the audience.

2. **Sensory Acuity:** You should be acutely aware of your audience's reactions to your speech. By paying close attention to non-verbal cues such as facial expressions, gestures, and postures, you can gauge your audience's engagement levels and then adjust your speech, speed, volume, tone, or even style to keep the audience engaged.

3. **Representational Systems:** Individuals perceive the world using their primary sensory systems- Visual, Auditory, Kinesthetic, Olfactory, and Gustatory (VAKOG). Your speeches should incorporate language that appeals to all these senses to make them more vivid and memorable. For instance, you can use visual language to create an image, auditory language to evoke sounds, and kinesthetic language to express emotions.

4. **Anchoring:** This NLP technique creates a stimulus- response pattern that can be triggered at will. For example, you might use a specific gesture, a physical location on the stage, or a phrase to anchor certain emotions in the audience, such as enthusiasm or calmness, to support your message.

5. **Meta-Model:** NLP's meta-model is a tool for understanding and clarifying language. You should use it to craft clear, concise, and specific messages, reducing ambiguity and increasing the impact of your speech. For example, let's imagine you have received a question from the audience. The meta-model involves asking targeted questions to uncover specifics hidden by deletions (missing information), generalizations (broad, sweeping statements), and distortions (assumptions presented as facts); it encourages precise speech. For instance, if someone says, "I'm stuck," asking, "How exactly are you stuck?" can lead to a more productive conversation.

6. **Milton Model:** Unlike the Meta-Model, the Milton Model uses deliberately vague and metaphorical language to allow listeners to fill in the gaps with their own experiences and interpretations, making the speech more relatable and persuasive. You can use this in your speeches to weave stories and suggest ideas that resonate on a personal level with your audience, allowing for a more inclusive and engaging experience.

7. **Reframing:** This is about changing the frame of reference for a particular situation or statement to give it a different meaning. In your speech, this can be useful in overcoming objections, presenting alternative perspectives, or turning challenges into opportunities by simply reframing them into something positive or neutral.

8. **Pattern Interrupt:** This technique breaks the audience's expectation pattern, regains their attention, or changes the interaction's direction. To use this technique, you might use humor, silence, or a thought-provoking statement as a pattern interrupt. Alternatively, if you see your audience drifting, pause and clap your hands really loud. All eyes will be back on you!

9. **Embedded Commands:** These are indirect commands placed within a longer sentence, designed to bypass the conscious mind and speak directly to the subconscious. They can subtly direct the audience toward a desired action or response. For example, "As you begin to relax, notice how you can 'let go' of tension" embeds the command "let go" within a soothing message. When giving speeches, using embedded commands can subtly direct the audience towards desired actions or emotions. It's effective for speakers to highlight their key points by using a distinct tone, pause, or gesture, thereby signaling the subconscious to pay attention to specific phrases without making the command overt.

10. **Storytelling:** Stories can be a powerful way to convey a message. Stories structured with the techniques above can be used to resonate with the audience's values and beliefs, making your points more persuasive.

There are enough nuances, details, and sub-topics that entire books are written on NLP. Here, I wanted to introduce the topic and highlight key concepts you can start bringing into your speeches today. Some people believe that NLP as a method is quite manipulative. The tool of NLP itself is not a manipulation tactic. When it comes down to it, the intended use determines if it is manipulation.

When you employ neurolinguistic programming in your speech, be sure of your intention. While it can certainly be a powerful tool, in the wrong hands, NLP can be a very negative thing. With this book, I aim to focus on the positive usage of such a tool.

THE POWER OF NEUROLINGUISTIC PROGRAMMING

With those basics of NLP established, it is time to explore how to use NLP to build connection and confidence.

Mirroring

One of the most popular and effective neurolinguistic programming tactics is "mirroring." Mirroring is a powerful tool to help you build rapport with your audience. This skill primarily applies to body language, so it is particularly effective for speeches in front of smaller or more intimate crowds. Still, let's go over how you can employ mirroring, and then you can decide whether it fits within the context of your speech or not.

Fortunately, the mirroring technique is among the easiest to master. It is said that the vast majority of communication is relayed through body language, which means that it is undoubtedly a good thing that such an easy technique stems from body language. With this technique, you will mirror your body language to meet that of the audience.

Of course, it's not easy to mirror an entire crowd simultaneously, which is why I said this works best for more intimate groups. However, you might mirror a few key individuals' body language, which can work. For instance, you could mirror your boss or a particularly influential audience member. Some ideas for speaking with mirroring include the following:

- If they lean in, you lean in too.

- Match what they are doing with their arms or legs.

- If they nod their head, follow that movement and nod with them.

If an audience member or two gets the chance to speak to you during your speech, you can also mirror how they speak; following their speech with a parallel structure is an excellent way to go.

In public speaking, mirroring shows that you are in sync with the audience and understand and empathize with their reactions. However, taken to the extreme, it can be overdone. So, balance it with your natural body movements.

Modeling

Modeling is another successful NLP technique that you can employ to your benefit. It is one of the most successful NLP methods for entrepreneurs and others to gain success and confidence.

Modeling in neurolinguistic programming is the process of replicating the skills of exceptional speakers. It involves observing and mapping the successful behaviors, thought patterns, and beliefs of those who excel in a particular field or activity to learn how they achieve their results. The goal is to create a "model" that you can use to accomplish similar outcomes.

So, to properly engage with modeling, I recommend finding speakers - either in-person or online - whose style of speaking you love. Study their style, including verbal and nonverbal communication. Study how they move and how they stand. Their body language. Their speech patterns and choice of words. And note anything else you would like to emulate. Then, bring your notes into your practice. As you focus on improvement, you will attract that improvement to yourself thanks to modeling your work after what you thought was successful in others.

Modeling is one of the foundational techniques of NLP because it is based on the premise that if one person can do something well, you can, too, through effective modeling.

Imagery Training

Imagery training is another skill that coincides with neurolinguistic programming. This is more of a rehearsal technique than a technique you will use with a crowd, but what you practice during rehearsal certainly shows during your speech in front of a crowd. Also called "mental rehearsal," imagery training posits itself as one of the most essential NLP skills because of how effective it is.

As we briefly considered earlier in the book, the brain struggles to distinguish a strong visualization from reality. Because imagery training relies on visualization, you effectively train your brain to experience reality in a new light. It sounds far-fetched, but it is relatively simple.

You will visualize yourself on stage giving your speech, and that visualization will radiate perfect success. This is going to convince you and your mind that you *are* a successful speaker, already embodying everything it takes to be that vision of success. Moreover, during this visualization, you will want to envision your body language - language that communicates confidence and assuredness.

From there, you will also want to envision clear communication and receptiveness of the crowd. Even running the speech through your head is an excellent idea, which can further enhance the visualization. The more you practice this, the more your confidence will rise.

Neurolinguistic Programming Incantations

The next skill I have to share with you comes in the form of NLP incantations - which, contrary to their name, have nothing to do with magic (although this method works *like* magic!). Incantations were born from affirmations - positive statements that encourage assurance and confidence in various areas of our lives.

Incantations take affirmations to the next level, working to change both your mind and your body to enable a sense of confidence. You must embody what you are trying to say with your whole self, reprogramming your mind for powerful beliefs. This involves combining affirmation-like thoughts with putting yourself in an aligned position, such as affirming success during rehearsal.

More on this in the interactive element at the end of the chapter!

NLP and Thought Leadership

Neurolinguistic programming is believed to enhance one's confidence by improving their "thought leadership" abilities. Thought leadership involves expressing ideas that show your credibility within a given field. This is something that many academics, entrepreneurs, and science-based employees prize themselves on and strive for, and naturally, thought leadership can build your credibility in a speech setting.

The idea of thought leadership is that you are a leader in *thinking* about a particular subject. Who is to say, then, that you cannot be a thought leader in the particular field in which you are presenting? No one! You can become a thought leader and exude credibility by embodying your confidence through NLP methods.

At the same time, trying to use thought leadership means focusing on your experience. Seriously - thought leadership relies heavily on building trust and rapport with an audience, which means you must draw on experience. You *cannot* be a leader in an area where you are inexperienced. That said, drawing on thought leadership ideas is perfect if you present in an area where you have personal, professional, or academic experience.

All in all, these NLP techniques will make you a more compelling speaker. From the words you say to how you pose your body, the audience will pick up on even the most subtle cues you emit. This means that you can intentionally set yourself up for success through the use of NLP tactics. Now, let's move on to where NLP and diction intersect, as this is where you can make even more successful strides!

USING NLP FOR PERSUASION

Okay, first off, let us draw our focus back to the connection between neurolinguistic programming and diction for a minute. The words you pick and how you employ them can coincide significantly with the NLP tactics you learned in the last section. So now, we must focus on how you can use them to entice your audience to listen to you as you speak.

One method you can use is to appeal to all five senses in the speech. By this, I mean you can use language that indicates or influences the senses. So, rather than describing the aroma of a candle as "pumpkin"-scented, for instance, you can bump up the imagery and describe it as a "light but creamy pumpkin scent with notes of cinnamon and vanilla intertwined." The latter paints a more resilient picture of how the candle smells while appealing to other senses.

It's also a good idea to use words that evoke strong emotional responses to employ NLP strategies alongside diction further. For example, keeping with the candle, we can add on by saying that the scent is "dreamy and ideal for cherishing the fall season," which paints the picture of fall as something joyous and even adds hints of family involvement (something many people cherish, of course). You can do the same as you describe various concepts in your speech.

In order to pick persuasive words that hit the mark for strong diction, you must first know how to identify a strong word. You can generally tell when a word is strong by how unique it is, how descriptive it is in nature, how action-oriented, or even how surprising it is. These strong words are the opportunity to shock your audience into paying attention, no matter their attention span. Moreover, it's important to note that words elicit particular emotions; use them to build a connection with your audience.

Diction also involves using powerful words and phrases to introduce your topics. Even if your topics are full of stellar word choices, it can kill the flow of your speech if those transitions or introductory phrases are dull or aimless. Some good ways to introduce a topic include a rhetorical question or outstanding statement, for instance. Now, good rhetorical questions are going to be ones that propose a benefit at the same time, like "Are you ready to unleash a new life empowered by self-care?"

You must also walk into your speech armed with powerful words and phrases that help you make a *point*. Sure, your speech and its various points should be strong enough to stand alone, but even the strongest speech must fight against the eight-minute attention span. The words and phrases you unleash into your speech make a difference in how easy it is for your audience to pay attention. Good ways to model that you are reiterating, expounding upon, or hammering in a point include words like "therefore" or "in other words."

At the same time, the words you use to support your points must also be strong. It is not enough to introduce the speech strongly and passionately; that passion has to extend throughout other parts of the speech, too. In order to manage this, you should infuse your vocabulary with phrases like "for example" or "it is evident that." Also, you should not recycle the exact two or three phrases over again. After being used once or twice, a phrase lulls into the back of the audience's mind; therefore, you should come to bat with a handful of phrases you like.

Carefully choose your "unique transition phrases." For example:

- "With this in mind..."

- "Let's pivot to the idea that..."

- "Now, consider the flip side..."

- "As a result..."

- "To illustrate..."

Powerful terms and words must entangle themselves throughout the speech, so it's crucial to have powerful words to end your speech. We will dive into more detail surrounding the conclusion of your speech in Chapter 8, but for now, let's focus on those terms. You should try to spice up your ending phrases a bit. "In conclusion" works, but you can also try things like "If you want to see similar results, then you have to try it yourself." This also doubles as a call to action to inspire the audience.

When all's said and done, it's essential to make sure that you combine neurolinguistic programming alongside strong diction in order to make a lasting impact on the crowd. Remember that your diction should fit your purpose and intent, and simultaneously, it should be appropriate for the context in which you are speaking.

INTERACTIVE ELEMENT: USING NLP

Instructions

Now that you have learned the ins and outs of neurolinguistic programming, let us take a look at a simple activity that can help you master those skills:

1. Locate a quiet space where you can stand in front of a full-length mirror. This exercise is most effective when you can see your entire body.

2. Close your eyes for a moment and visualize yourself speaking confidently in front of an engaged and supportive audience. Imagine yourself standing tall, speaking clearly, and radiating confidence. This sets a positive mental framework.

3. Open your eyes and stand in a "power stance." This involves standing up straight with your shoulders back, feet shoulder-width apart, and your hands on your hips. This posture not only conveys confidence but also boosts it.

4. While maintaining the power stance, look at yourself in the mirror and repeat positive affirmations about your speaking skills. For example, say, "I am a confident speaker who commands the stage. I connect with my audience, and I deliver speeches everyone remembers." Repeat these affirmations several times.

5. Continue to stand in your power stance and practice deep breathing. Inhale deeply through your nose, expand your diaphragm, and exhale slowly through your mouth. This calms your nerves and improves vocal control.

6. Close your eyes briefly and visualize a supportive and engaged audience. See their smiling faces and feel the positive energy in the room. This creates a mental image of a receptive audience.

7. Open your eyes and, while maintaining the power stance, practice the opening lines of a speech or presentation you would like to improve. Enunciate clearly and confidently.

8. Close your eyes and visualize receiving positive feedback from your audience. Imagine hearing their applause and cheers, seeing them nodding in agreement, and feeling their handshakes as they congratulate you with praise. This reinforces positive outcomes in your mind.

9. Open your eyes, return to a neutral stance, and take a moment to reflect on the confidence you have cultivated in this exercise. Let the confidence soak into you.

10. Close the exercise by affirming that you are better prepared to speak confidently. Believe in the positive changes you have created through this practice.

11. Repeat often!

Conclusion

Benjamin Franklin said, "if you would persuade, you must appeal to interest rather than intellect." Interests and building connections will help you persuade people better than trying to force your expertise or opinions on others who have their own. Once you know how to use the techniques in this chapter, you can move on to the final stage: outlining a speech, which finally shows you how to end one properly!

Chapter Eight

— • —

Bringing it All Together

Aristotle's Steps to Speech Mastery

This final chapter outlines how to tactically create your speech by walking through Aristotle's wisdom and bringing full circle the eight steps in Chapter 4, which will now include the ending of your speech. In this chapter, I have provided an outline that aims to inspire you to plan every part of your speech by following the necessary steps and considering the advice, rehearsals, and exercises you learned from each of Aristotle's main secrets.

STEP #1: WHO IS YOUR AUDIENCE

Let us revisit and add to some of what you mastered earlier in the book. As you embark upon this first step in outlining your speech, the brunt of your focus needs to be on the audience and what they need at that particular occasion. You don't want to walk on stage with a toast when you are supposed to be presenting your quarterly findings for a company, after all.

As mentioned earlier, you need to truly take the time to analyze your audience. Understanding their background and needs - among other things - will allow you to perfectly refine your speech toward what they need from you, making for a perfect speech that easily captivates everyone.

At the same time, there will be some expectations that you need to check throughout the speech planning period. Ensure you aren't starting with unreasonable expectations for your audience. Things you should consider while planning your speech include:

- Who is your audience, and why are they here?

- How much does your particular audience know about the topic?

- Whether any relevant social or cultural backgrounds play a role in the audience's reception.

- How would that audience usually respond to a similar topic?

- What would be inappropriate in this particular context?

Ensuring that you keep the audience and their needs in mind from the very inception of your speech is the best way to go.

STEP #2: SELECT YOUR TOPIC OR PURPOSE

You will not always be told what you have to present on specifically; sometimes, you are only told that you have to make a speech. The responsibility then falls to you to pick a relevant topic or purpose that the audience will enjoy and remain enthralled by. A general rule is that you should be able to condense your topic into one sentence - usually called a "topic sentence."

In forming your topic or purpose for the speech, you should also try to form a thesis statement. A thesis statement generally follows the format of "[topic statement] is true because of A, B, and C." This aligns perfectly with what we discussed earlier, with a good speech typically having around three main points. You don't have to explicitly state your thesis statement while on stage, but having one ready keeps your thoughts and plan for the speech nice and organized.

Remember, avoid opting for a speech on a topic you aren't familiar with. Even if you do the research, lacking personal experience is something that the audience will be able to pick up on. Therefore, try to pick a good topic that you know well.

You should also ensure that you find the topic at least *somewhat* interesting. While it is of utmost importance that your audience enjoys the topic, it can be a harrowing experience to present on a subject in which you have zero interest. Trust me, you can only fake it for so long! So, ensure you care about the topic at least a little.

STEP #3: GATHER YOUR SPEECH CONTENT (RE-SEARCH)

The next step involves gathering the contents of your speech. This mainly refers to the body of your speech - the three or so main components you must expand upon between the windows of the introduction and conclusion. Generally, you are going to want your speech to follow an outline such as this:

- Introduction

- Main point 1

  - Evidence 1, 2, 3

  - Addressing potential counterarguments

- Main point 2

  - Evidence 1, 2, 3

  - Addressing potential counterarguments

- Main point 3

  - Evidence 1, 2, 3

  - Addressing potential counterarguments

- Conclusion

Your speech outline can be as long or as brief as you would like, but it should not contain everything you want to say. I recommend always writing your speech in bullet points and avoiding complete sentences. You can confine yourself to six or seven words per bullet or two sentences per main point to help you out with the length of the outline.

This is also the point in your planning process where you should find room for audience engagement - if you plan to have any, that is. You don't want to overload your audience with transitions and engagement, so plan wisely and determine where each engagement instance would occur.

STEP #4: ORGANIZE YOUR SPEECH

Okay, so you might wonder how this differs from Step 3. While step 3 focused on gathering the content, akin to pouring a puzzle out on the table before putting it together, this step involves putting it together! Organizing your speech is what really gives it that extra kick, enabling you to be perfectly prepared along the way.

Now, during your organizational period, it's a good idea to pick a few transitional segues that you can use in your speech. You don't have to memorize them word for word, but you can outline whether you want to use a joke, anecdote, visual aid, or something else to guide the speech along to the next point. This saves you time and stress later, so you don't have to worry about transitions at the drop of a hat.

You can use a few different organizational techniques to better structure not just the overall flow of the speech but the structure of each point as well. Consider those below, for example:

- **Cause and effect.** You can structure it logically by explaining how one cause leads to an effect that's relevant to the point of the speech.

- **Problem and solution.** Another format for your speech points is presenting a problem and then providing its solution.

- **Time.** If you find that you can logically plan your speech in order of time, that can be another excellent option for organizing!

- **Pros and cons.** Ensure that you include pros and cons, which can become the entire layout of your speech - if it makes sense to do so.

- **Steps.** Simply put, you can also use a step-by-step format to organize your speech.

Beyond that, make sure that you have subpoints for each of your main points. You can go on all day about the speech's main points, but without subpoints to truly flesh out the contents, your audience will get bored fast.

STEP #5: OUTLINE THE INTRODUCTION

No, the steps are not in the wrong order - you should *really* outline the introduction *after* you outline the body of your speech! When you work on the introduction later, you have the foresight of having planned the body of your speech in mind. This helps you flawlessly fine-tune the contents of your speech.

Much like the body of a speech, there is an outline you can (and should try to) follow for the introduction of your speech. This is as follows:

- **An attention-getter.** This should be the very first thing that you say - something so compelling that the audience cannot help but listen.

- **A hook.** This is where you introduce yourself and your topic in a smooth and catchy manner. You could use a powerful quote; quotes are like concentrated drops of wisdom. They can express profound truths, evoke deep emotions, and provoke thought. Alternatively, start with a provocative question; questions stimulate curiosity. They engage the mind, making us think and wonder. Opening your speech with a provocative question lets you instantly engage your audience's attention and pique their curiosity. Otherwise, start with a shocking statistic; when used effectively, statistics can be eye-opening. They provide concrete, quantifiable information that can surprise, alarm, or intrigue your audience. Opening your speech with a shocking statistic can grab your audience's attention and highlight the significance of your topic.

- **Your purpose.** Whether subtly or explicitly, you should make a statement that outlines the central point of the speech. What is the purpose of you being here today?

- **Main points.** Make sure to provide a brief outline of your main points!

- **Transition.** Then, you get to transition into the heart of your speech.

It might seem like a lot, but this all happens quickly when you are on stage, getting underway with your speech. You can get as creative as you would like, but the point is that these are, without a doubt, the essential points of any captivating and functional introduction.

STEP #6: PLAN YOUR VISUAL AIDS

The next step that you have to take is planning your visual aids. This is one of the last steps in the process because, ultimately, your visual aids support the rest of your speech. Once you have everything planned up until the end, you can more sufficiently decide what visual aids to use and *where* they should be used throughout the speech.

Refer back to the interactive element at the end of chapter #4 to build an engaging visual!

STEP #7: PLAN PHRASING, TONE, AND BODY LANGUAGE

Next up, you are going to plan the phrasing, tone, and body language of your speech. This naturally comes quite near the end of the process because you have to build your tone and body language around the contents of your speech. You do not want to plan out every little gesture, of course, but taking the time to make plans for major points of your language will certainly be helpful. With your style chosen, it's time to start bringing in the different elements of NLP. Which ones fit the type of speech you are delivering? Which ones will help you engage and connect with the audience?

STEP #8: THE CONCLUSION

Now is when you need to plan the conclusion of your speech for a memorable and impressionable finale, tying everything together succinctly. A great conclusion comes along with four key steps:

1. **A summary.** In order to keep your points fresh in the audience's minds, your conclusion should contain a brief summary of each of the key points of your speech. The human brain is wired to remember the first and last things it encounters; psychologists call this the serial position effect. As your speech draws to a close, your audience is likely to re-member your final words. Therefore, it's crucial to summarize your key points.

2. **A thesis.** You should also make it a point to restate the thesis or central idea of your speech. When your audience members leave and get asked what they heard about, they will have your memorable thesis ready to recite!

3. **Benefits.** Mention again how what you have covered benefits the audience, further incentivizing their remembrance.

4. **A clincher or call to action.** Finish with a bang - a call to action is a powerful conclusion tool. It's an invitation to your audience to take a specific action based on your speech. It could be to adopt a new perspective, make a change in their lives, or even ponder a thought. The call to action serves two purposes. First, it gives your audience a tangible way to respond to your speech. Second, it extends the impact of your speech beyond the event!

Your conclusion cannot be an afterthought or something you create quickly at the very end. Your conclusion is the last thing your audience will hear from you. It must be powerful and leave an impression if your goal is to deliver a speech everyone remembers.

STEP #9: REHEARSE, REHEARSE, REHEARSE!

The last critical step to delivering a great speech, which is mentioned the most in this book, is to rehearse that speech *tirelessly*. And then, just when you think you have rehearsed the speech enough, rehearse it *once more*. Indeed, a good speech is built on the foundation of dedicated rehearsal, which is why this is the final and perhaps most crucial step of the process. Make use of the activities and advice throughout the book to help you get the most from that rehearsal time!

Finally, know there is no shame in keeping some note cards on hand to keep you on track. While burying your head in note cards throughout the entire speech should be avoided, having cue cards to hold onto gives you something to anchor yourself with so that you don't fall too far off course as you improvise on stage.

Conclusion

Colin Powel said, "there are no secrets to success. It is the result of preparation, hard work, and learning from failure." Preparation and hard work always pay off in speaking. Work through these nine steps. Do not rush. Work through each step and review the concepts presented in this book. As General Powel said, your success will result from your preparation and hard work!

SHARE THE MESSAGE

My dream is for you to close this book and immediately plan all the elements of your next public speech. It inspires me to imagine you organizing your talk, working on style and delivery, and crafting a story that will keep your audience curious, engaged, and open to your message.

I hope you can share your own enthusiasm with other readers, by letting them know that this book can help them become the kind of communicators that audiences look forward to listening to.

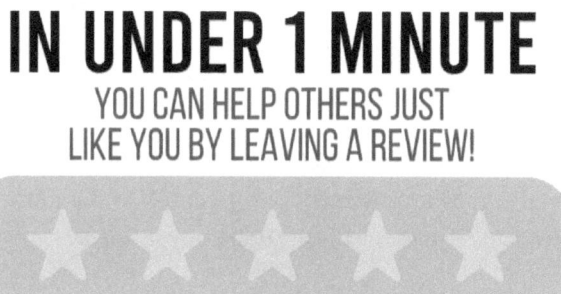

IN UNDER 1 MINUTE
YOU CAN HELP OTHERS JUST
LIKE YOU BY LEAVING A REVIEW!

Thank you for being part of a community that values the power of connection.

Here's to many public speaking adventures and to the sharing of vital information that can make so many lives better!

Simply leave a review where you found this book! Thank you!

Jared

— • —

Conclusion

Reflecting on the key lessons and strategies we have explored is important as we navigate to the end of our shared journey. We have delved into the nuances of public speaking, from over- coming fear and embracing self-belief to fine-tuning your delivery and connecting with your audience. Each chapter has armed you with practical strategies to mold you into a confident and effective speaker.

Remember, the journey of mastering public speaking doesn't end here. Mastering it demands continuous improvement and practice. It is a journey that evolves with every speech you deliver and each audience you engage.

The tools and strategies in this book are stepping stones on your path to becoming a compelling speaker. Throughout this guide, we touched on:

- How public speaking sets impressions - the basics of public speaking and why public speaking serves such a pivotal role within our society.

- How to crush social anxiety - tangible methods to fight off the social anxiety roadblock that prevents so many from making compelling speeches.

- Mastering self-confidence - everything you need to unleash radiant self-confidence to overcome doubt and hesitation at any stage.

- The ins and outs of arrangement - how to prepare the speech of your dreams with luxury and ease, concluding in a step-by-step guide.

- Your personal style - making your mark on the audience by embodying your speech methods.

- The essentials of memory - what you need to do to make your audience remember what you said and the key points of your speech.

- Delivering your speech like a pro - thanks to the power of Aristotle's final canon of rhetoric!

But now, the future is in your hands. I wish you the best on your journey forward. I am confident that you have everything you need to succeed. Just use these tools and keep practicing on your public speaking journey, and soon you will have mastered these powerful strategies and be...

... commanding the stage, speaking confidently, and delivering the speech EVERYONE remembers!

Then reach out and tell me your story!

Jared@ProfessionalSkillsPublishing.com

REFERENCES

Bernard, M. (2023, July 25). *Speaking clearly for presentations*. Students. https:// students.unimelb.edu.au/academic-skills/resources/speaking-and-present ing/speaking-clearly-for-presentations#:

Blanda, S. (2013, April 23). *The introversion bubble*. I. M. H. O. https://medium. com/i-m-h-o/the-introversion-bubble-7d9a96581949#:

Calm Public Speaking Nerves: Let's talk about self-talk. (n.d.). Buckley School of Public Speaking. Retrieved October 11, 2023, from https://w ww.buck leyschool.com/magazine/articles/calm-public-speaking-nerves-lets-tal k- about-self-talk/#:

College, A., & News, R. L. (n.d.). Preparing great speeches: A 10-step approach | Sullivan | College & Research Libraries News. *Crln.acrl.org*. Retrieved October 12, 2023, from https://crln.acrl.org/index.php/crlnews/article/view/19102/22119#:

8 strategies to engage your audience & keep them interested. (n.d.). Www.knowled gehut.com. https:// 8-strategies-to-engage-your-audience-keep-them-interested

Engaging and energizing audiences through purposeful play: An Interactive Exercises Model And Method. (n.d.). MentalHelp.net. Retrieved October 21, 2023, from https:// through-purposeful-play-an-interactive-exercises-model-and-method/#:%20Empathic%20Icebreaker

5 (NLP) Neurolinguistic programming techniques. (n.d.). Retrieved October 21, 2023, from https:// niques/#:

Guarino, Joseph. "Top 20 Public Speaking Quotes." Institute of Public Speaking. Accessed November 16, 2023. https:// top-20-public-speaking-quotes/

How thoughts drive fear. (n.d.). Explorable.com. Retrieved September 26, 2023, from https://explorable.com/e/how-thoughts-drive-fear#:

How to speak with confidence in public. (n.d.). Virtualspeech.com. Retrieved October 12, 2023, from https://virtualspeech.com/blog/speak-with-co nfi dence-in-public#:

Nieuwhof, C. (2019, November 20). *The 4 different communication styles and how each can improve.* CareyNieuwhof.com. https://careynieuwhof.com/the-4-different-communication-styles-and-how-each-can-improve/#:

Rice, A. (2021, September 13). *Challenging negative thoughts: Helpful tips.* Psych Central. https://psychcentral.com/lib/challenging-negative-self-talk#ho w- to-stop

Speech topics: Guide to choosing a successful topic. (n.d.). Virtualspeech.com. Retrieved October 18, 2023, from https://virtualspeech.com/blog/guide- choos-ing-successful-speech-topic#:

10.4: Organizing Your Speech | Introduction to public communication. (n.d.). Retrieved October 18, 2023, from intro/chapter/ 10-4-organizing-your-speech/#:

31 fear of public speaking statistics (Prevalence). (n.d.). Www.crossrivertherapy.c om. Retrieved September 26, 2023, from https:// public-speaking-statistics#:

Tips & guides - Engaging your audience. (n.d.). Hamilton College. Retrieved October 20, 2023, from https:// communication/guides/how-to-engage-your-au-dience-and-keep-them- with-you#:

What is natural language processing (NLP) & how does it work? (n.d.). Levit y.ai. Retrieved October 21, 2023, from https://levity.ai/blog/how-natural- lan-guage-processing-works#: